Sugar Words

Sugar Words

Musings from an old Vermonter

Burr Morse

Morse Farm Maple Sugarworks
Montpelier, Vermont

Published by

Burr Morse

Morse Farm Maple Sugarworks

1168 County Road, Montpelier, VT 05602

and

PrintTech, Inc.

128 Commerce Street, Williston, VT 05495

ISBN: 978-0-9835308-3-1

Edited by Steffen Parker

Cover design by Elizabeth Tomsuden

Cover artwork by Steven Welch

Back cover photograph by Burr Morse:

"When I go into the woods with my chainsaw, I'm always on the lookout for interesting shapes in trees. I get especially excited when I find "letters" so I set out many years ago to spell a word. I found both a "T" and a "U" easily, two letters that trees do quite naturally. After many years, one day an "N" emerged from a soft maple tree. My word finally "spoke" to me when at age fifty-four an "S" came to me from an aged cherry tree...Ahhh, sweet rewards, I had my word... "N U T S"... and the way I figure it, you gotta be NUTS to require fifty-four years to spell one four-letter word!"

Printed in the United States of America

3rd Printing, August 2013

www.morsefarm.com

Contents

Acknowledgements

This, my third book, finds me for the third time writing an acknowledgement... who helped most? Who invested heart and soul? Who dare I not forget? After deep thought, I've come to a conclusion...just copy the other two but make it a bit longer! Yup, it's these folks who really "wrote" all three books through their friendship, dedication, love...I just punched the keyboard.

First of all, Betsy, Robby, and Tommy, the three people who can both find me the biggest pain in the butt and love me unconditionally. Elliott, Tick, and Susie, my sibs. Harry and Dot Morse, cheering from above. Steffen Parker, my editor, (has a knack for literary correctness, trombone playing, and maple sugarin'). Steve and Martha Welch, and Lyz Tomsuden for creating the sweetest book cover ever. Martha Holden for the prayers. Morse Farm staff. All my music and maple friends. Tourist friends. Times Argus friends.

Finally, eight generations of Vermont living and all the ideas that go with it.

Blessings,

- *Burr*

Forward

When my husband Burr's editor asked me to write the forward to Burr's third book, I thought long and hard. I finally realized that what's in my heart had already been written:

"It's not often that someone comes along who is both a friend and a good writer." E.B. White

- Betsy Parker Morse

This book is being dedicated to the millions of sap drops in my sixty-four springs. Without them, my life would not be nearly as sweet.

Prologue

As a sixty-four year old, I've seen a lot of change. In my lifetime man first walked on the moon, Elm trees went away, and computers took over the world. Every generation has its claims so I know I have no corner on that. I do regret, however, not "living" a few of the changes on my parents' watch like the transformation of horses and buggies to automobiles and that magical new thing called electricity, the light bulb... the radio! No, I didn't "live" those transitions but, fortunately, I had good accounts from the folks who did.

For my e-newsletter, I recently wrote a story on the "metamorphosis" of dentistry during my tenure as a patient and, no thank you, I have no desire to "turn the hands back" on that clock! My good friend George Voland eloquently responded to my words:

"Great piece, Burr. I'm sure many of your readers will connect with their own childhood dental experiences, thanks to the great specifics you included in this piece. I don't know about you, but, god, I ate SO much candy as a kid. Who knew any better? As a result, man, did I have cavities. When Rob and Caryn reached the appropriate age, our dentist, the wonderful Dr. Viskup in Vergennes, applied a sealant over a couple of year's six-month cleanings. As a result of that sealant, neither of them has EVER had a cavity! That's the good news. The bad news? They won't have any engaging dentist stories like yours to share!".

"Indeed!" I say...George left us with a good question: do life's little "advances" somehow gyp modern folks out of something important? Should we feel pain?Does "stength come from adversity?". My readers seem to think so... tales of milkin' cows the hard way, gatherin' sap from a bucket, or "snow drifts deep like the old days" always create "warm and fuzzy" feelings for folks.

I'm an old guy now and full of stories, gnarly ones that create "warm and fuzzy"feelings. No, Rob and Caryn will never have stories like mine but they'll have stories of their own. Do I think they've been gyped...yes I do. You see, we all think our generation suffered the most, "dove the deepest and came up dryest" and I'm no exception. Reality suggests though, that there will always be stories to tell and someday it'll be Rob's and Caryn's turn to tell 'em and for them, there'll be rewards in them-thar stories. I'll be dead and gone by then but my stories, well...they'll still be "the best ever" but just a little deeper in the book.

- Burr

SUGARING

Three Evaporator Life • Crunch Time Crunch • The Maple Gene • Bulk Syrup and Booze Bottles • Rich for a Season • A Sugarmaker's Thank You • The Last Day

One day during sugar season, Gerald, Chris and I were in one of the sugarwoods. The snow was still deep and I think the wind had just come up. We were tired and it was close to the end of the day. We had just a few buckets to empty before getting back on the tractor and heading to the sugarhouse. I was near the tractor, just having emptied my 5 gallon buckets of sap and Gerald was sitting in the drivers seat of the tractor. Chris was still gathering sap. Chris yelled over to Gerald, asking: "Gerald did you get that tree?", as he pointed to one off in the distance. "Nope" Gerald replied. So, Chris, none too happy about having to trudge over to the tree in his snowshoes, began the slow walk over... When he was almost at the tree, Gerald yelled; "But I got the sap!" Gerald almost fell out of the tractor laughing so hard. I caught the laughing bug as well, and we were hard to stop. Chris on the other hand did not find it at all amusing. I don't think he talked to us for the rest of the afternoon. In fact, I don't think Chris spoke to Gerald for several days after that! Gerald was happy as a clam that day.

- Kathi Squires, VT

Three Evaporator Life

How many ways are there to measure a lifetime? Let's see, there are the traditional years (I have over sixty so far) and milestones like key trips, presidential elections and, these days, numbers of spouses. Thank God I can claim only one spouse (Betsy's a keeper) and, yes, I've had a few key trips and lived through a few elections but right now I'm thinking of something a bit sweeter...evaporators; I've had a "three evaporator" life so far. That's right, we're just yanking out the evaporator from our sugarhouse that my dad and I bought when I was in my 20s and will soon replace it with a brand new one that my son, Tommy, and I are buying.

Evaporators are big, heavy things; you don't treat their passing lightly. The other day we had to organize a small army to lift off the evaporator's piggyback pan which stood at eight feet high and weighed in at 600 pounds. We got it off at considerable effort and the next day organized an even bigger army for the even bigger flue pan. In a way, it'll be sad to see it gone; that evaporator watched our farm's transition from the end of dairy farming to full-swing tourism. If it could talk, it would report lots of queries from thousands of tourists, inquisitive visits from sugarmakers past (we're convinced my father's spirit still dwells in the Morse Farm Sugarhouse), and hours and hours just sitting idle waiting for the next short sugar season.

Thinking back over their tenures, I recall a couple of interesting stories in honor of the two past evaporators. Our first evaporator stood right where our second one did but lacked the "bells and whistles" of pre-heaters and piggybacks. It just had an open front pan where syrup was finished and a flue pan where sap first entered and did the heavy boiling. Back then we had no retail store; we were dairy farmers and the few sugar-on-snow parties that we threw in those days took place right in the sugarhouse. One time my father had a group of bankers in for sugar-on-snow. My mother had prepared the sugar-on-snow and was serving it, along with homemade raised donuts she had just fried in deep fat. The old evaporator was stoked up with wood and boiling "to beat the band". Dad suspected the bankers were a bit "stoked" up as well, possibly from a bottle they had stashed out back in a snowdrift!

Our sugarhouse was quite small in those days and there was just enough room for a makeshift table beside the old evaporator. The bankers, although crowded in there, were having a great time but my father was suddenly perplexed...he couldn't make the sap boil. "That fire was 'hottern' hell'" he said, "but the sap just sat there simmerin'!" In all the years Dad had sugared, he'd never encountered this problem before. He was just about to give up when he looked toward the back of the sixteen foot long evaporator and saw a hand reach down inside the flue pan; instantly Harry Morse knew what was wrong...those bankers were all dunking their donuts in the boiling sap. Adding grease to boiling sap triggers a scientific process called "breaking the surface tension" and suppresses boiling like adding water to fire. For years my father told the story of those tipsy bankers stopping his "cash-flow" with their greasy donuts!

My second evaporator also experienced a sudden "interruption of cash flow"...we were in the midst of a huge sap run and I had to boil into the middle of the night. Mother Nature had blessed us with a sweeter sap that year and I was "cranking out" batches of fancy maple syrup (the type of syrup a seventh generation sugarmaker protects with his life!) quicker than ever. It was a clear and crisp night, the kind of night where the draft works best and fires burn hotter. All of a sudden I looked up and saw flames lapping around the collar ties at the peak of the roof...seems my fire had gotten a little too hot! I knew that I needed to use the liquid closest to me, the boiling sap just inches away, to throw on the flames...but I hesitated, held in utter limbo for fear of wasting a drop of that precious liquid! I stood motionless for a few seconds watching the flames grow stronger until I was finally able to pick up several scoops full of sap and fling them toward the flames. As it turned out, my little "diversion" with a burning sugarhouse was short-lived...the sap worked as well as water to extinguish the fire and I went on to boil the rest of the night in seventh-generation maple bliss.

Our new evaporator is smaller and will have more "bells and whistles" than ever...modern technology, like sugarmakers, works overtime. I'm excited to see it go in and, no, I don't expect to see it come out; the law of averages indicates that it will, indeed, outlive me. I'm sure it will make a lot of maple syrup in its time and Tommy, the eighth generation, will someday tell its stories. In the meantime, I'll enjoy the rest of my years as they go by, my time made sweeter by the maple in my veins and richer by the memories of a "three evaporator life". 🍁

Crunch Time Crunch

I started tapping my trees last Sunday; let's just say I attended the Good Church of the Sweet Maple. It was one of those moody mid-February days with a "fancy grade" sky and a "grade B" chill—cold! I'm a seventh generation Vermonter and spend eleven months pining for my one month of sweet ecstasy, sugaring time. Because of several winter thaws and a dry January, the snow was only ankle-deep. My snowshoes still hung on the barn wall back home, unneeded. I labored, comfortably, in my quilted Dickies that bulged with tools of my trade. A few thousand maples stood before me, looking drowsy from their long winter's rest, willing subjects for my sharp tapping bit.

Ours is a different sort of sugarbush. Besides the usual sights and sounds of a maple forest, ski trails surround our maple acres. That Sunday there were lots of skiers dressed brightly in streamlined clothing. They glided gracefully past where I worked, acknowledging my presence with a fleeting "hey". I mused about our difference in attire and purpose but also considered our similarities: We all thoroughly loved what we were doing and moved at a fast pace, as though we had a deadline. The skiers had waited painfully long for snow this year and needed to maximize their time before winter's mood changed. It was sort of a Nordic crunch time. Although the weather was cold that Sunday, our early February had presented us with a few days of freezing nights and thawing days, "sap weather" to a Vermont sugarmaker. Sap weather makes us prick up our ears like dogs and follow our noses to the woods. We used to have a handshake deal with tradition and wait till after the first Tuesday in March, Town Meeting Day, to start tapping. This year, however, Mother Climate breached that contract. Some bold sugarmakers began tapping early in February, beating slackers like me to the punch. That made me anxious and boiled down to one thing—crunch time for sugarmakers.

"Crunch time"—reminds me of an old hired man we had once, named Jim. Jim was a loyal worker and, like most Vermont farmers, lived for sugaring. He was on of those guys who looked like he was either born with a pipe in his mouth or picked up the habit shortly thereafter. He had a slight problem with stuttering and it got worse when he was excited; sugaring peaked Jim's stuttering like a ride on a run-a-way sap tank. One time we were talking about our favorite part of sugaring. He removed the pipe before he spoke:

"I l-l-love sh-shiggerin' and my f-f-favorite part is the c-c-cr-u-nch!"

I would have accepted his comment had his choice been something more pertinent, but crunch? On questioning, however, I quickly understood Jim's point: Sugaring happens at the time when terra firma can't quite make up its mind. By day, because of the thawing, the ground is either muddy or slushy. By night, when the temperature dips, it firms up to a unique crispness. When we walk home at night the crunch we make speaks with a language only a sugarmaker can understand, the language of freezing and thawing. That wonderful crunch means the cold is doing its job to charge the maple trees up for another day's run! Jim has since gone on to the great sugarhouse in the sky, but I'll always remember him and his favorite crunch.

Our tapping is almost done. Winter has returned for a while and the skiers ski while the sugarmakers wait. We wait for our buckets and tanks to fill with spring's goodness, but we can't be impatient; we are Vermonters and understand the rules. Our trees will wait for the language of the freezing and thawing—crunch time for sugarmakers. ❧

The Maple Gene

Last spring I was going to write about some special maple sugarmaker friends but I ran out of time. You see, sugarin' ended suddenly and writing about sugarmakers when they're not practicing their art is like, well, gatherin' all the sap and never boilin' it...the fun's in the boilin'; the cracklin' fire, the beaming faces, the tiny batches of syrup blessed by huge amounts of pride. These friends are all small-time, "put-your-feet-up-by-the-evaporator-and-have-a-beer" type sugarmakers...the kind I envy. They're not all Vermonters but contrary to common thought, the "maple gene" can show up anywhere and even though Vermont syrup is the best, the maple gene is the maple gene.

Todd and Thomas Parker are both Vermonters but when Thomas "puts-his-feet-up", it better be sans the beer...he's only nine. Thomas got the maple gene the natural way, from his dad, Todd, who lives, breathes, and dreams maple. I knew Todd as a small boy and every spring, a few special trees around his parents' house over on Vincent Flats would blossom with a rag-tag collection of milk jugs, lard buckets or anything else that would hold water. That "blossoming" was a rite of spring and the whole neighborhood knew that little Todd was sugarin'. Todd went on to become a heating expert and, through his job, has inherited a rather unique way of boiling sap. For every oil burner he services, there is a small amount of disposable fuel oil that drains from the old filters. He takes that home and pours it in a barrel. Over the course of a year, that barrel fills with enough free oil to replace an otherwise, sizeable woodpile... "Not romantic like a crackling fire", you say?... "Maybe not", I say... "but it's sure being smart, like a Yankee trader!"

Last year I went over to visit the Parker boys in their sugarhouse one night after I had shut my own evaporator down. I drove east, through the mud-season ruts of East Montpelier's Barnes and Dodge Roads, to the same place on Vincent Flats where Todd grew up. As I drove into the yard, I noted the absence of a traditional, pitched roof sugarhouse. Upon opening my car door, however, my olfactory senses directed me to the end of a long tool shed, where the heavenly fragrance of boiling sap spewed from a makeshift cupola. Inside, Todd Parker stood (no feet up this time) at his "Papa-sized" evaporator beaming at Thomas nearby at his own "Baby Bear" evaporator... both rigs were oil fired and boiling to beat the band. Before I left that night, I asked young Thomas if he truly loved sugarin' or if he was just doing it to please his dad...I knew he couldn't fool me. His smile radiated sweetness and his eyes crinkled with a seasonal glow. I knew that I had just received an "affirmative" from Young Parker, master sugarmaker and holder of the maple gene.

The other special sugarmaker is a gal named Patty Hebert, admitted Boston-born flatlander. I first met Patty a few years ago when she and her family came into our store. I've witnessed thousands of folks entering that same door but will always remember Patty in particular because she had that "maple" look about her...yes, there's such a thing as "the maple look". The maple look takes many forms but, and I swear on a stack of evaporator catalogues, when Patty Hebert from Framingham, Massachusetts came in, a "medium amber halo" hovered inches above her head! When she opened up about her short-lived but no less sweet maple experiences, I knew she had the maple gene.

Patty claims her maple gene got jump-started six years ago on a trip to Vermont. While she and her husband, Chris (who is a Vermonter), were up here, they visited the Maple Museum down in Pittsford. There she bought seven taps and the book, "Backyard Sugaring" and went home. Patty said the minute she put the book down from reading it cover to cover, she went right out and tapped those seven trees. She only had plastic milk jugs to hang on the spouts and a turkey fryer to boil her sap on but when you have the maple gene, "country crude" is fine because you're livin' on love...the love of maple.

I emailed Patty last spring to ask her if she had any funny stories to tell about steaming off the wall paper or burning a pan. It was her reply that absolutely proved her maple legitimacy to me: "THANK GOD! And I mean it, THANK GOD, I've never burned a pan. A sugarmaker's pans are sacred!". That's what convinced me...you see, only a maple sugarmaker can lie like that...we've all burned a pan or two but for a sugarmaker, burning a pan is a shame equal to sampling Aunt Jemima once years ago and saying "it's not that bad"! We always lie about that time we turned our back on a boilin' batch and scorched the pan to the point of meltdown...nice job, Patty...sweet lie...you got it down! 🍁

Bulk Syrup and Booze Bottles

Since it's sugarin' time, I'd be remiss to not write about a couple of my more memorable sugarhouse visitors this year. The first billowing steam always draws 'em in, novice flatlanders and seasoned sugarers alike. The other day a man came in who might as well of had "Vermontah" branded onto his forehead. Mr. Frank Barnett grew up over in Peacham where maple history's as colorful as all those Peacham pictures you see on postcards and placemats. He recalled days of sap gathering with teams of horses and men working through deep snow...snow like we "used ta" get. It was a story he told, however, about the finished product, drums of bulk maple syrup, that really perked my interest.

In mid-season, speculation about the bulk price of maple syrup starts spewing from Vermont sugarhouses right along with the steam. The annual frenzy between maple maker and maple buyer, although a bit sweeter, is kin to horse trading. Mr. Barnett talked about a sugarmaker over Peacham way who was called Pump Handle Donaldson. It was looking like a good season and Pump Handle needed desperately to sell some of the barrels of syrup that stood wall to wall in his sugarhouse. One day he got a call from a syrup buyer named Palmer who, as the grapevine rumored, was paying top prices for syrup. Palmer, however, made a fatal, though innocent, mistake right off the bat; he called Mr. Donaldson by the only name he knew of, "Pump Handle".

Quicker'n a sugarhouse-a-fire, Mr. Donaldson shouted into the phone, "Thou has cast stones at my house...you'll get no syrup!". With that, he hung up, leaving Palmer totally at a loss as to what he had done wrong. You see, Pump Handle had inherited his nickname back in his youth when a group of friends saw him drawing water from a well for a girl who he was trying to impress. Typical of small towns, that "handle" stuck like spilled syrup to pant legs but was hated by the man who carried it for life, Pump Handle Donaldson.

Two other visitors of note were Charlie Taplin and his wife Theresa, who hang their hats down in Brookfield. The Taplins, both native Vermonters with sugarin' in their blood, came in one day when I was boiling hot and heavy. They still live on the farm where she grew up but, depending on the cache of sweet in their larder, depth of the snow, or whether or not the spirit moves, only tap their trees on certain years. On the "off" years, they seek out another sugarhouse to hang out in, soaking up their quota of steam for the year; this year, it was my turn.

The flow of sugarhouse traffic was heavy that day, like the flow of sap; it was Vermont's Maple Open House Weekend and, for once, both nature and the economy gave us a "thumbs up". Most of the visitors stayed long enough for a couple deep "whiffs" and the same number of questions but Charlie and Theresa hung around most of the morning. They talked with sweet reverence about Theresa's father, Gaylen Brown, who was a great old sugarmaker and now resides in a nursing home. Gaylen's sugarhouse was within eyesight of a main highway and Charlie told a story about a sugarhouse visitor his father-in-law had once.

Mr. Brown and another man were busy boilin' mid-season syrup when a car stopped up at the highway. A person got out...they knew it was a city-slicker by the looks of the car...and started sprinting toward the sugarhouse. The person made a circuitous route around patches of snow that still clung to the pasture and hurdled the brick wall that interrupted his path. As he approached, they could see it was a man dressed in a business suit. He rushed in through the wide opening that led to the woodshed.

"Can I buy some of that syrup?" he asked, out of breath.

"Got no containers", Gaylen said.

With that, the city-slicker about faced, sprinted the same route, over the stone wall and around the snow patches, back to his car and returned with a half-full liquor bottle. He unscrewed the cap and offered it to Mr. Brown and his helper who both shook their heads sideways, the language of teetotalers. "That city fella looked at Gaylen and his helper like they were from Mars" Charlie said, "downed the whole thing and handed it over to be filled with maple syrup!" He paid Gaylen Brown for the syrup and ran that course once more, this time meandering a little more exaggeratedly!

Yup, we get sugarhouse visitors of "all stripes" this time of year. All types come for the atmosphere and for the syrup, but there is that select few who visit because they have to; they're drawn by instinct, like honey bees to flowers. I enjoy them all but especially the ones who give me a story, and thanks to Frank Barnett and the Taplins, my larder's a bit sweeter. 🍁

Rich for a Season

I'm rich...I'm RICH! Yup, my view of the valley this morning brings bright sunshine, springtime snow now appearing in patchwork, and the pledge of another sap run. And for a Vermont maple sugarmaker I say, what more can you ask than that? Money, you say? I say "money t'hell!". No, I've never had much use for big salaries or to put it in native Vermonter lingo... "ain't no p'centage in that". In fact, I was approached back in January by that supplement to the Sunday paper, "Parade Magazine" to be one of those folks who gets their picture published along with their salary. I thought about it (lot's of p'centage in free national mention!) but decided to pass it up...again in Vermont lingo: "ain't nobody's business how little I make!".

No, I don't make much but I am truly rich. The other day a couple, Seth Frisbie and Erika Mitchell from the wilds of Adamant, walked into the sugarhouse. They are an interesting couple, not native Vermonters but I didn't hold that against them. He holds a doctorate and is a professor of chemistry at a local university. She is a great photographer and was snapping sugarhouse shots that day "t'beat the boilin'". They asked the usual questions about the evaporator and how our season was going but soon we were on the subject of growing our own food. Seth allowed that they have a huge garden every summer, raise a pig or two but specialize in chickens. They process so many chickens, in fact, they still have a freezer full here at the end of winter. As Seth related this, his eyes narrowed... "Please don't think I'm rich but I do have a 'Featherman Pro' automatic poultry plucker with 114 rubber fingers.". My reaction was instantaneous, and in retrospect, rude...I laughed, rather, cackled, like an old mother hen... "Hahwp, hahwp, hahwppppck...that's funny" I said just before I realized that Seth was serious; this hard working college professor with a doctorate actually thinks someone will consider him rich because he owns a 'Featherman Pro' automatic poultry plucker with 114 rubber fingers!

"I'm s-s-sorry" I stammered, laboring for composure, "but you gotta realize how funny that sounds." Seth wasn't upset and even cracked a smile. He went on to describe the contraption with "finger-lickin'" enthusiasm: "It'll undress a full-grown turkey in 30 seconds...Gosh there're times I've even considered throwing my wife in!". At that, Erika lowered the camera and glowered at him. Suddenly the humor came on with a whoosh, right along with the steam.

"I betcha Bill Gates doesn't own a chicken plucker." Erika said.

"For that matter, probably doesn't even make his own syrup!" Seth chimed in.

And I provided the punctuation, "Hell, ol' Bill ain't rich at all compared to us!".

I love that ancient sugarhouse for many reasons; the top-notch syrup we've been making lately and the connections to my past it provides, but one of my most favorite reasons is because of the folks who come in. Yup, we've had some great ones down through the ages and Seth and Erika rate right up there with the best of 'em! Erika "Facebooked" me some of the best pictures of the old place that I've ever seen. Seth provided me with plenty of "meat" for a story and I, well I ended up getting the best sap run in years and made lots of fancy syrup...fancy syrup, more new friends, an old sugarhouse to work in with the heavenly fragrance of fresh syrup boiling and steam against my face...yup, I'm rich all right. Eat your heart out Bill Gates! 🍁

A Sugarmaker's Thank You

Recently a friend from Texas sent me a cartoon from a vintage magazine. It shows two codgers sitting on the porch of a cabin in the middle of the woods. Surrounding the cabin, hundreds of bucket-clad maple trees stretch as far as the eye can see. One codger turns to the other and says "It ain't the boredom that gits me, Jake. It's that constant drip, drip, drip." For a maple sugarmaker, the dripping means lots of sap rather than anything resembling boredom so let's just assume those codgers aren't sugarmakers! These days, thanks to modern agriculture and the demands of the economy, we don't get to hear that sweet "drip, drip, drip". In fact, a current take on the same cartoon might find those codgers surrounded like flies in an endless cobweb of plastic tubing. The logical caption: "I've heard of Spiderman, Jake, but this is ridiculous!"

Oh I know, you all pine for a return of the "drip, drip, drip" and buckets full of lost romance. For a hardened sugarmaker like me, though, I say ENOUGH! Those of us "in the trenches" all these generations, forever ache for ways to make sugarmaking easier and plastic tubing to us is like a rocket to an astronaut. In that vein, our "Robert Goddard" is a man by the name of Nelson Griggs, born in 1914 right here in Montpelier, Vermont. Nobody knows how he acquired the "sugarin' bug", for he was a city boy, but he had it in spades, right down to a lifelong quest to make the process easier.

Nelson was a born inventor. He left Vermont for a time and worked for the Walter Kidde Company and for Eastman Kodak. According to his daughters, Jackie and Sandy... "Our dad obtained patents in 56 countries. He primarily worked on valves for military tanks and fire extinguishers, but also did work on color photography. The only two designs he developed and patented outside of work were the inset ski edge and the closed sap collection system." They said his ski edge was part of one world record in downhill racing but was discontinued because it could not be mass-produced. On the other hand, world records for maple production pile up these days like tall stacks of pancakes thanks to tubing systems that started with Nelson Griggs.

I was a small boy when he did some research on our farm. He'd always show up with a station wagon full of tubing supplies and a head full of passion for his project. Our place not only provided a research site close to his home in Montpelier but a maple savvy brain to pick in the person of my father, Harry Morse. My father's knowledge of "hands on" sugaring was the perfect complement to Nelson's technical know-how and many times the two of them would pour over maple manuals and speculate about the project right in our living room. He had become almost another member of our family when suddenly a long remission he had enjoyed from multiple sclerosis ended. His research stopped prematurely and Nelson Griggs passed away before the sap gathering system that had been his passion was fully completed.

My brother, Elliott, was old enough to have worked "in the field" with Nelson and recalls a funny story about his research here at Morse Farm. Elliott said a clump of maples over on the hillside west of our place resembled more the wooded workshop of a scientist than a maple sugarbush. Certain trees had been fitted with pressure gauges and workstations stood randomly under temporary roofs. At the lowest point of the woods, tubing culminated in a small collection tank. Elliott said one morning, the day after a huge sap run, Nelson arrived early to measure the volume in the tank but, alas, there was nary a drop. He appeared back at the Morse dairy barn just as the men were finishing their milking to report the drought. "We all finished what we were doin' and went over there." Elliott said. "We walked up into the sugarbush and found Nelson's tubes were all re-routed...followed 'em back and, by God, all of a sudden realized they'd been pulled down a woodchuck hole!". Elliott said Nelson had a good laugh with the rest of 'em about how a family of woodchucks outsmarted the scientist.

I've been communicating with his daughters lately. They recalled trips to the farm with their dad when they were young but I was struck by the memory that stood foremost on both their minds. Being children, scientific research was not their "cup of tea" but instead, they remembered things like the wood fired evaporator and the heavenly fragrance of the steam. Top on their list of sugarhouse nostalgia, though...Dot Morse's raised donuts! Yup, raised donuts are, indeed, a piece of Vermont maple romance that will never die. In order to maintain these few cherished traditions, though, we must keep the maple industry alive; it's efficiency or bust. For that, we need folks like Nelson Griggs, inventor and visionary...a man "driven" to make the sugarmaker's job easier. 🍁

The Last Day

Sugarin' for this year is over and a great one it was! Nature cooperated by giving us nice cool "sap weather" and son Tommy gave nature a good sized nudge with his savvy use of all things vacuum and tubing (sugarin's a little sweeter these days with a gentle blend of young blood and technology). Our main storage tank out back of the sugarhouse was full all season long and we even had to bring in three other tanks for reinforcements! It was a season to behold...hectic and extremely tiring but satisfying...well, all except the last day. In spite of the "ooohs and awhs" we hear from sugarhouse passersby on that day, I'll be honest: to a Vermont sugarmaker, the last syrup boiled is the dregs. Yup, 'bout the time old "Jack Frost" forsakes the North Country and maple buds start to swell, the personality of sap changes. Instead of appearing crystal-clear, it takes on a milky sheen and boils down to buddy, bitter, putrid syrup (never fear that this stuff might end up from our store to your pantry...it always gets sold to a "bulk" market and no-doubt ends up in that nationally branded so-called pancake syrup). A wise sugarmaker would dump the stuff down the brook but being Yankees, most of us will hold our noses and hang in there for the last day of boilin'.

One time up on the ancestral farm in Maple Corner, my father coupled his distaste for that day with the calendar date, April first. He had already smelled "bud" in the boiling sap and wanted no more of the stuff; all of a sudden a creative April fool's joke came to mind: Dad whittled a wooden plug which he used to plug the pipe that carried sap from the distant dumping station into the sugarhouse storage tank. He knew the gatherers were due with a load of sap and, sure enough, soon heard the "clucking and cursing" of men driving horses. He looked out to see the gruff Chester Haggett manipulating the sap sled into place at the dumping station. Normally the sap flowed quickly down the run of pipe. That day, however, the combination of blockage and "head" caused a spectacular fountain. Sure enough, Chet's reaction was instantaneous and booming: "What the &**@# hell's goin' on!". From the old sugarhouse, Dad witnessed several rag-tag sap gatherers pirouetting away from the deluge. He said they kept diving back in futile attempts to fix the problem and were all thoroughly soaked when he finally ambled up to let them know they had been duped! "Just my way o' tellin' you I'm all done boilin' that putrid stuff", Dad said to an already conniving Chester Haggett.

Chet knew it was Dad's turn to do the barn chores the next day and he turned a creative mind toward chore time's final task...wheeling the collected cow manure across a plank "cat-walk" to dump on top of winter's mountainous accumulation. After he dried off, he went to the barn to begin "staging" his caper. Taking a handsaw out to the "cat-walk" Chet carefully sawed two-thirds through the plank that traversed the highest point above the pile. He then turned the plank over so that it looked as strong as ever and stood back, swiping his palms together in satisfaction.

The next morning my father finished up the milking and released the cows into an outdoor exercise corral so that he could clean the gutters. He filled a wheelbarrow up with the first load of very "loose" cow manure and headed out toward the pile. The plank broke when he was just half way across and Dad landed with a huge KERPLOP, "ass over tea kettle" six feet below in deep, brown slime. Chet and his crew materialized from all corners of the barn beaming with satisfaction as they peered down. "Guess I asked for that one", Harry Morse sputtered. Although he was "frosted" from head to toe, they knew there was a grin on his face, this time a pinched crap eatin' grin!

The words "it's all in fun" come to mind. Yes, we Vermont sugarmakers do have fun during our season and why not...it's pure and invigorating and sweet and fleeting; yup but when it's over, it's over and it usually ends "long 'bout April Fool's Day". ✿

AN OLD VERMONTER

OK for a Spell • Springtime Pros and Cons • Veggie Adventure • A Good Sport • Weird New Seasons • Diggin' In • Our Newest Cow • Sweet Tooth Tyranny • Dog Days of Baseball • Horn of Therapy • Dreams of Motoring and Music • Friend Wayne • Awkward Ag • Clip-Clop with a Volt • All Puffed Up • Dairy Dilemma • Furnace Figurin' • More "Wisemen" Needed • Shine On • Only in Vermont • Contrasting Comforts • Russian Rides

I really don't know if Burr Morse exists or not...could be a copywriter with the gift of Vermont colloquial gab and a flair for writing in dialect. I will tell y'all that as a Texan...it's great to revisit the area through his stories. We traveled through Vermont about 3 years ago...in the summer...and visited Morse Farm. Burr brings back a wonderful memory of that trip every time I read his email. Keep up the good work...and the writing, as well.

- Judy Killion, TX

OK for a Spell

"Can't see the forest for the trees."...we've all heard that expression more times than you could throw a birch stick and I'm still not sure what the heck it means. All I know is that I'm going to that place often with a chainsaw these days tackling its inhabitants one tree at a time. Yup, the economy has 'stimulated' my need to create the biggest possible woodpile in the shortest amount of time to feed the 'hungry' wood boiler we're about to install down at our store.

I prefer to call the forest by its more colloquial name, " the woods". You go to the 'forest' to spread out a cloth and picnic with wine and crustless sandwiches. The forest is where field trips are held to study Fagus sylvatica and the common polypody. Bears don't poop in the forest...they poop in the woods. In the woods, you can pass gas as loud as you want, scratch yourself wherever you please, and swear at the chainsaw. Your purpose in the woods is singular and in my case, selfish; I love to cut wood. Plotting where each tree will fall, 'felling' them and then bucking off chunks brings a real feeling of accomplishment. I especially love the cracking and popping sounds the chunks make on my splitter and knowing that, like snowflakes, there are no two split pieces alike.

Although I've spent little time in the forest, the woods have claimed huge amounts of my existence. Recently in fact, I've found things out there that 'spell' real definition to my life. As I wrote in my book, "Sweet Days and Beyond", every time I went to the woods for my first 55 years, I watched for letters of the alphabet that grew naturally in trees. My quest was to spell a word before I died and that happened when I spelled 'NUTS' at age 55. The word, 'NUTS', quite appropriately represents the middle portion of my life because it suggests a carefree, "sky is the limit" feeling and that describes me to a T at that point. A second word was never in the picture but, low and behold, it happened last week when I was helping my son cut a large ash tree. Ash trees often offer artistic things because the limbs start from nodes at right angles to each other and then curve into all sorts of shapes.

That ash had started to die at the top and was obviously at the end of its life. Its trunk curved radically, making it unsatisfactory for the pretty, wide-grained lumber that ash makes; it begged 'woodpile'. The minute it fell, I had a strange feeling about its offerings and kept my eye out for anything artistic as I bucked off 18 inch chunks. Although I had never planned on spelling another word, I never precluded it...a friend once gave me a very unique H that resulted from the limb of one Balsam fir growing into another, so I had words with H tucked in the back of my mind. The letter L is easy to find in trees so I didn't think much of it when an L appeared up toward the top. When my buzzing chainsaw exposed a perfect, cursive E on the next cut, however, I felt a shock like being struck by a springing tree limb...the thought that another L would give me the word 'HELL' was even more shocking! "If the final message these trees leave me is 'HELL', that's not good", I thought. Then it occurred to me that I had once found a Q in a Scotch pine and I went to the barn where I had tucked it away long ago. Remarkably, it was still there and when I picked it up, I found that cutting off the Q's tail would make a perfect O...whew...I had the word 'HELLO' within arm's length!

Most folks would probably think nothing of these experiences but, being a deeply spiritual person, I place great meaning in them; trees are 'spelling' out my life starting with 'HELLO' for the beginning and 'NUTS' for the middle (admittedly the chronology is confused but confusion is quite normal for me!). Holding that thought, I fear that all that remains for me is to spell the word, 'BYE', and then I'll pass away but, you see, I'm not ready...think I'll stay away from ash trees...better yet, I'll go for 'DENOUEMENT'...on second thought, think I'll look for a whole sentence... "I BID YOU A HARDY AND VOCIFEROUS FAREWELL, MY DEAR FRIENDS AND COMPATRIOTS." That ought to keep me in the woods for a while yet!

Springtime Pros and Cons

Spring sure keeps us on our toes...it not only provides us with new maple syrup, cheery bird songs and black dogs lying in the warm sun but also a few eyesores when winter's white blanket peels away. You see, our winter is so long and our snow is so deep that when the curtain opens on spring, there are always surprises, both good and bad. As my friend, Dan Darling recently said in a sugarhouse conversation: "I like it here in the spring when there's no leaves on the trees...you can see what's in those woods". He stressed the "in" and winked his eye which translated to "junk cars, discarded manure spreaders, ragged pieces of plastic tarp, and muddy messes". Dan's an ex-bus driver from Illinois so he used to visit when things were neatly tucked into the colorfully clothed woods. I'm not suggesting that Vermonters are messier than other folks but that there's a special "psychology" here in the north country...spring's quick transition from pure white snow to bare ground "brings out" our litter like no other season.

It's human nature to horde but here in America, our habit is magnified by a thing I call the "Wal*Mart mentality"; yup, we'll buy anything if we think it's cheap enough. Reminds me of a story I heard once about a great aunt of mine: Aunt Ilda was a prim and proper woman. She was a regular churchgoer and never publicly uttered anything stronger than "my goodness!", that is 'til one day she was over at the Worcester Village Store with her young twins, Tony and Ferdy. It was back in the early 50s when general stores were transitioning from pickle barrels and pie safes to modern brightly colored "packaging". Aunt Ilda had her "hands full", literally, with the collection of staples she carried and those begging twins who were magnetized to packages of every shape, size and color of the rainbow. It had been just another peaceful day at the village store full of quietly browsing shoppers until suddenly from somewhere in its bowels, the shrieking began... "You kids would buy sh-- if they put it in a brightly colored package!". Aunt Ilda, the "prim and proper" gentlewoman, had reached her boiling point with modern merchandizing and active children!

Earlier I mentioned "black dogs lying in the sun" because we have two of them right here at Morse Farm, Averill and Ferny. I love to see them stretched out on springtime's bare spots sopping up the rays. I wonder if dogs are wise to the change of seasons or if they worry about why the snow went away? One thing I know is that dogs are wise with their hording. Except for green tennis balls and plastic dog toys that foolish folks buy in places like Wal*Mart, dogs choose their possessions very carefully. Our house is littered with small sticks from the woods and marrow bones that butchers just about give away, all stuff that blends naturally into the springtime countryside. Dogs are also more giving than humans with their processions. When I get home, I'm always greeted by friendly barking and a scurrying to fetch some gift for me. "Thank you" I say, "but you can have that stick...that can be your stick". The other day when I came home, it was almost like Averill and Ferny had rehearsed a skit. When I opened the door, two black labs greeted me with big fat carrots teetering from the ends of their mouths, pleased as pups with their imitation of Groucho Marx!

As the new week starts, we three creatures will proceed with our life routines; I to my business and the two labs to a beaver dam in the valley south of here. I will spend my day cleaning up after sugarin' and pondering the economics of it all. The labs will go for a swim, scout out the countryside and probably each select a new stick for their collection back home...the rhetorical question looms as natural as spring itself: who is living life right, man or man's best friend? 🍂

Veggie Adventure

We used to make the biggest chunk of our living growing vegetables on this place after Dad got fed up with milkin' cows. He built a small roadside stand and sent me off the horticulture school thinkin' I'd come back some kind of 'Jack of all beanstalks'. I lacked a certain passion for things the University of Vermont's Plant and Soil Science Department had to offer, though. "It's all just weeds and seeds to me with a little dirt thrown in", I used to say but I persisted out of respect for the land and came home with that 'piece of paper' in 1971. Back then as soon as we cleaned up from sugarin', we'd get out there and prepare the fields for whatever would grow in this region's fleeting growing season. I remember it being a mad rush to get everything in on time and sometimes we might as well have thrown the seeds to the wind for what we ever got out of 'em...we were 'troubled' by a couple of our own personality quirks.

You see, my father was a superfluous sower of seeds because of a life-long bout with optimism and a love affair with those better-than-life pictures in the seed catalogues. "Time'll fetch it!" he'd always say with a twinkle in his eye, like the seeds would somehow miraculously sprout fruit sans the hard labor. I was a willing accomplice for another reason...I loved to plow. Plowing soil was like a sickness to me. I craved hearing the hummm of the tractor and seeing the fertile, worm-filled furrows torn from the ground and flopped upside down. Because of my 'sickness', I always plowed more land than we could take care of and because my father had usually bought too many seeds, we sowed them in that extraneous plowed ground. Most years, they were swallowed up by the weeds that never got pulled. One time though, we planted acres of beets that grew to healthy plants and produced like zucchinis. Come harvest time, our farm was red with huge beets plucked from the ground and plunked into assorted containers, including all our sap tanks. Come sugaring time, we needed our tanks for sap so the still unsold beets had to be picked out and hauled through the deep snow to be composted in the 'back forty'.

We've since gone on to other endeavors at our farm and haven't grown that voluminous array of veggies for 15 years now. I must admit that lately I've felt a slight hankering to have a garden and I mentioned it to Miriam Bernardo, my son Rob's girlfriend, who lives over at our farmhouse. Miriam is a gardener from her light coffee-colored skin right down to her green-lovin' heart and soul. Mention of my hankering one day called Miriam to action faster than a rabbit in a lettuce patch. "Why don't you come down and garden with me?" she asked. She grows her veggies out back in the old barnyard where the loam is as fertile as the Garden of Eden.

To accommodate one extra grower some additional ground had to be prepared, a perfect cue for me to 'dust off' my trusty two-bottom plow, hook it on my tractor and head for Miriam's garden plot. First we peeled back her Gestapo-height deer fence and then I backed up to where she beckoned me, lowered the hydraulics and crept ahead. Instantly it was like I had never stopped plowing; the earth's fresh aroma mixed with diesel fumes from my steel beast. I watched, head turned backward, as the plow pulled each furrow up and over. When I had reached the end of the school bus length plot and made a second swipe, Miriam made a motion for me to stop. I shut off the engine... "That's all...three minutes of plowin's all I get?" I shouted. "Yes! Enough!" this granddaughter of Cuban refugees shouted back. Miriam, no doubt, has the ability to work small plots of land built into her genes. I started the tractor and drove away feeling droopy like a 'punkin' on December 1st.

When I returned, Miriam was flinging the moist soil one way and then another like a gopher-gone-berserk. "Where's your rototiller" I joked. "Don't need no stinkin' rototiller" she groused in a fake Latin accent. By that time my wife, Betsy and a couple others had appeared and we spent the rest of the day putting the fence back up and fine tuning what is sure to be a luscious work of art under Miriam's tutelage. My father has now gone on to sow seeds in the sky but I'm sure he's smiling down on the friendly, Cuban girl worthy of another of his eye twinkling remarks, "She ain't bad to look at either!". Yes, Harry Morse approves but I'm sure he's hopin' we'll sow a little extra next year. ❧

A Good Sport

As I remember it, the dialogue went something like this:

Jeff Bean: "It'll be football."

Burr Morse: "Baseball."

Jeff Bean: "I SAID FOOTBALL!"

Burr Morse: "OK…football."

Jeff had my shoulders pinned firmly to the grassy playground of the Four Corners School. I knew he could lick me with one hand behind his back so why keep arguing? He was the strongest kid in school: we called him "The Persuader". It was 1961 and we'd just talked Mrs. Kreis into another extended recess. We could talk her into anything, especially on an Indian summer day in mid-September. We'd been back to school only about a week and were already sick to death of those four walls. I'd reached the closet first and grabbed an armful of baseball paraphernalia when Jeff took over with the "persuasion factor".

You see I was a farm boy and farmers, especially "Morse" farmers, had no time for sports. In fact we were downright righteous with our scorn—"Gahl-ramned mindless interruption to work," by grandfather called it. Being fall, it was the beginning of football season ("fu'bahl" to my seventh grade class-mates), and I knew better than to push for baseball. To me fu'bahl was just a, well—gahl-ramned mindless interruption. It started with a bunch of shoving, ended with a sissy-like tag (or a hard tackle when the teacher wasn't looking) and had no rhyme or reason in between. The few times I got the ball I had no clue which way to run.

I was equally confused about baseball and never good at it, but it was the one sport I loved—how could you not love something next of kin to hotdogs and apple pie? I used to watch my buddies, Billy and Bobby Brown play Little League down at the Montpelier Rec Field. I had a special place, out beyond the centerfield fence where the woods began. From there I saw the whole game, not just the players. Players are only half of the game; the other half is the fans who provide the heart and soul. I recently attended a Vermont Mountaineers game down by that same Little League field. We're proud of our Mountaineers and their manager, John Russo, for making it to the top this year. They were playing the Newport Rhode Island Gulls that night in a "best two of three" fight for the championship of the Northeast Collegiate League. They needed an extra dose of heart and soul because the Gulls were the favored team—enter Greg Hudson, a lanky Montpelier teenager with a heart of gold and the spirit of a trooper. Greg was born three months early and has lived with a mild case of cerebral palsy ever since, but it doesn't stop him from being the undisputed head coach of some four thousand regular Mountaineer fans.

I recently called Greg to talk about his roll. He was a bit guarded at first but brightened when I mentioned the Mountaineers. Suddenly words like "Like wow!" and "That's cool!" shot like line drives from the phone. He said he rides the team bus to every away game and all the guys give him their cell phone numbers. I learned that the letters 'VT' and '15' (for first baseman Chris Joachim) were recently shaved on each side of his head and that Greg Hudson thoroughly knows his baseball…and his fans.

I watched the last half of that championship game from just outside the centerfield fence that night. The field stood under eight tall light towers, well groomed and neat. A sliver of a moon hovered overhead, tipped up as if pouring out good will. At the bottom of the ninth inning the Gull center fielder waited a few feet from where I sat, in anticipation of the Mountaineers' final out. By that time I knew it would end in favor of the Gulls. In the distance a huge, noisy bank of Mountaineer fans churned and cheered. I sat on the dampening grass, remembering that time long ago on the grass at the Four Corners School. "Baseball—it's BASEBALL!" I yelled. From across the field, one voice rose above the din—the only one who yelled louder than me was Coach Greg Hudson, coach of the heart and soul. 🍁

Weird New Season

In another story, I wrote about "Blossom Season" which was my father's special term for the time of year between sugarin' and hayin'...Harry Morse loved God's sweet flora enough to honor it with a season of its own. I'm an equally passionate person but my passions, alas, go in much less glamorous directions; I'm thinking of the picnics, cookouts, ball games and holidays that come with early summer, so here goes...I hereby designate that time of year "Hot Dog Season". Yup, we've known for a long time that the American favorite "path of least resistance" is the stomach and sometimes the stomach is not all that discretionary.

The highly seasoned, cigar-shaped, easy to prepare hot dog... "often made from meat slurry", according to Wikipedia, might well be something we shouldn't eat at all. They're chocked-full-a nitrites, fats, salts, dyes...but then I digress...the fact is, dammit, I like a good hot dog once in a while! Betsy recently bought a package labeled "Hebrew National"...she'd heard there were fewer preservatives in the "Hebrew" brand. I just went to the fridge, grabbed the package and brought it back to the computer for research...let's see...big, friendly letters boast "reduced fat, no by-products, no artificial flavors, no artificial colors". Then there's a "foot-long" list of ingredients in tiny print at the bottom but I'll just trust that things like "sodium diacetate", "sodium nitrite" and "potassium phosphate" are all okay. I was about to return the package to the fridge when a line stamped at one end caught my eye, "sell by Aug 15, 2010"...yikes, they seem to suggest that meat'll stay fresh for the next two months!...but then again I digress...dammit, I like a good hot dog once in a while.

I recently had a revelation about how hot dogs got their name. It came to me in a flash, sort of a "hot dog epiphany", because at the time it seemed I was the only person in the world who had figured it out. A few weeks ago Betsy and I were in England taking a tour through Anne Hathaway's cottage. Anne, of course, was the wife of William Shakespeare and mother of his two girls. We learned lots of interesting things there about life back in the late 1500s, like how they used to catch the oldest chicken, tie its legs with a rope and force it down the chimney...there's nothing like flapping wings of a frightened chicken to clean th' old flues, you know. And then, you guessed it, they'd have chicken soup for supper on chimney cleaning days! The fireplace was the "heart and soul" of an English home in those times. It took up one whole wall of the room we were in and was used right around the clock for cooking, bread making, and heating. Of course, women and children played the major role in those projects but our female guide pointed out that, like chicken power for chimney cleaning, animals were used whenever possible.

She described a sort of "pre-Rube Goldberg" contraption that employed dog power to turn meat on a spit. The "spit dog" was a special small breed, long and lean, much like a dachshund, that was placed in a "squirrel cage" drum hooked up by linkage to the spit. To keep "Poochie" on task, they had purposely mounted his cage very close to the fire. Not surprisingly, a group gasp punctuated our guide's description of that poor little dog and then my revelation hit...I blurted out "hotdog!...that's where the term, 'hotdog' came from", to our group of twenty. Our guide allowed that no one had ever put that together before and that "maybe I had a point". I left Anne Hathaway's cottage that day fully aware that our generation has no corner on cruelty, and also a bit smug about my "hot dog epiphany".

Nature is great at providing us with scads of fresh, wholesome foods and then man steps in and tweaks them for the purpose of packaging, preservation, and marketing. Even though, dammit, I still like a good hot dog every once in a while, I'm well aware their history is a bit "shady" right down to the possible way they were named. And speaking of nature, I'm not sure my term, "Hot Dog Season" will ever sprout legs. Harry Morse's "Blossom Season" rings much more pure but the fact is, maybe we humans should leave the terminology of seasons up to nature...she's so good at it, right along with those "expiration dates". ❦

Diggin' In

Folks have been calling native Vermonters "woodchucks" for quite a while now. I can't say I'm wild about that after of all the years I spent sharing the vegetables we grew on this place with those low-lived cusses. I gave up growing their favorites years ago; put up the white flag, I did... "Alright you" I said. "When it comes to survival of the fittest in the world of cabbage seedlings, Romaine Lettuce, and tender peas, it's your world, not mine.

My son's girlfriend, Miriam, recently tried it again over by the foundation of our old barn. Woodchucks love to dig in around rock piles, ledges and old barn foundations. It's not just because these places are more bullet proof than wide open fields but they've figured out our attack strategies; they know we may resort to gas or smoke bombs, and that the seams and fissures found around rock piles, ledges and old barn foundations can't be sealed up...wicked smart they are! Miriam planted a veritable woodchuck smorgasbord not once, not twice, but three times! After her third failure, I found her flailing her head against the old barn's side and bawling, "I give up...I can't take this anymore!"

I approached her, trying to ease her pain with some of my "old Vermonter knows better" advice: "Now, now, don't worry. I'll get my gun and kill the thing" I lied, remembering the thousands of times the devils had dodged my bullets and outsmarted me. "Oh no, don't do that" she said, between sobs... "guess it was just his turn this time."

There was something about her pacifist attitude, or whatever it was, that penetrated my thick armor. A "light bulb" moment, if you will, or even maybe a minor epiphany that included rodents, came over me. Suddenly I wanted to learn everything there is to know about the woodchuck, groundhog, whistle pig, or in terms of my new enlightenment, another of God's creatures.

Google immediately led me to the "New World Encyclopedia" which presented the basics, like Latin name (Marmota monax), size, and gestation period, but as I delved beyond the basics, that "light bulb" reappeared. I began seeing a parallel between this creature and that other of God's creatures otherwise known as the Native Vermonter. The encyclopedia said "Like other sciurids, groundhogs have exceptionally dense cerebral bones, allowing them to survive direct blows to the head that would cripple other mammals of the same body mass.". I thought to myself "Hmmm...hard heads....native Vermonters".

It went on to describe many other traits of the Marmota monax that rang a "next of kin" bell to this native Vermont Homo sapien: when preparing their burrows, they move 700 pounds of dirt. Thoughts of my own house building 35 years ago surfaced; I moved hundreds of yards of dirt with a round shovel and a wheelbarrow. It said they are "asocial" except when breeding. Wow... fits Vermonters to a tee; a native Vermonter really has no use for odd folks around unless they're absolutely necessary. It also said woodchucks'll "retreat to their burrows when threatened; if the burrow is invaded, the groundhog tenaciously defends itself with its two large incisors and front claws". Similarly, native Vermonter's will "turn the other cheek" to a point and retreat but in the end, they will exercise their "right to bear arms" and use 'em!

The thing that really sold me, however, was when Google led me to a piece called "The Truth about Woodchucks" by a Sy Montgomery. Mr. Montgomery's treatise largely echoed the encyclopedia but for a couple things at the very end: "Fastidious housekeepers, they renovate burrow entrances several times a week." That one sentence suddenly brought total closure to any of my reservations; "My God" I thought, "he's saying that Betsy's more of a woodchuck than I am!"

I'll end with one last thing from "The Truth about Woodchucks": Sy Montgomery said "Naturalist Meade Cadot thinks it's time to rehabilitate the woodchuck's reputation. First, he'd just stop calling the critter a woodchuck... or even its other name, groundhog, of February fame. 'Really, it's a marmot' says the Antioch New England Graduate School professor. 'And marmots aren't vermin', he says."

Well I say "excuuuuuse me" to Mr. Meade Cadot but I am not a "marmot"! I am a woodchuck, along with my wife and my kids, and I'm damned proud of it! And, as far as my needs for cabbage, Romaine Lettuce, and tender peas go...I'm glad to buy mine at the supermarket from now on, thank you very much! 🍂

Our Newest Cow

We have a VIC here at Morse Farm...that's "Very Important Cow". Her name is Ilene and she has some great history behind her. First, however, I've got to tell you about another very important lady in our lives. Her name is Dorothy Walka and she used to sell crafts and nick-nacks at our place of business. I'm not good with crafts...can't tell a dried flower wreath from a Yankee Candle, so I usually keep those sales reps at arms' length but Dorothy was always different...she'd purposely seek me out when she was up here. It didn't take me long to figure out Dorothy was a "pistol"...she'd speak her mind, loved a good joke, and, strangely, had an interest in everything "farm". In fact she told me once that she herself had farmed, for a while.

Fast forward to December, 2009: I was running errands in downtown Montpelier when my cellphone rang. It was Mike Doyle, classmate from Montpelier High School, good friend, and owner of Doyle Guest House. Mike started the conversation with the words "Burr...I'm calling about a Christmas present you're gonna love" and then went on to say the woman who lived across the street from him was in the hospital and not expected to live. "She farmed for ten years until the 'economy' forced her out." he said. It seems those ten years were the best years of her life and when she quit, she had her favorite cow, Ilene, sculpted in granite and set up at her house down on School Street in Montpelier. Mike said the woman was fretting about what would become of Ilene after her death and asked him for advice. I felt honored when he told me he had recommended our place...I was floored when he told me that the woman was Dorothy Walka!

It was ironic that I had never seen or heard about Ilene, and also that I was almost within a "stone's throw" of her when Mike called. I headed right over there, pulled up in front of the Baptist Church at the corner of School and St. Paul Streets and there, on a tiny patch of urban dooryard, stood the monument I had come to see. Mike was there and we shook hands... "Let me introduce you to Ilene" he said, beaming about the "deal" he had just put together. As we approached her, I noted that the sculptor had captured perfectly the "gentle curiosity" of a cow. She stood on a granite pedestal which bore the inscription "For Vermont Family Farms" and I instantly accepted her as the world's prettiest sculpture. Mike said that when he had mentioned Morse Farm to Dorothy, she recalled the conversations she and I had had and instantly agreed to the plan. All I had to do was write a letter saying I would accept Ilene and she would be ours!

They brought her up yesterday in a bit "unorthodox" way for cows being delivered to Morse Farm...she arrived atop a platform crane truck instead of a messy cattle trailer. The truck backed up beside a concrete base that we had previously prepared in a special place by our sugarhouse. One of the "attendants" was a young man whose interest went way beyond a simple delivery... Gampo Wickenheiser, Ilene's sculptor, later told us that he had promised Dorothy Walka he would preside over Ilene's relocation...he proceeded with the care of a seasoned herdsman as they lowered her onto the base. Gampo belies the traditional "Barre granite sculptor" with his youth and lack of Italian heritage. I marveled that he had created this world-class work of art that would adorn our patch of ground in perpetuity, a promise that I had made to Dorothy Walka in my letter to her.

One of the first people to see Ilene in her new setting was a farmer friend of mine from the neighborhood. "Good t'see th'old que (the way a real Vermonter pronounces "cow") up here in th'country where she belongs...always looked kinda outa place down there in th'city", he said. I agreed with him to a point...yes, Ilene looks peaceful and very appropriate up here in the country but she was totally "at home" down there on School Street in Montpelier, Vermont...she memorialized one woman's dream and such memorials belong everywhere. Dorothy Walka learned the hard way that farms come and go, driven by things like economy and short human lifetimes, but the land is here forever and waiting around for the next family farm...Ilene'll see to that. 🍁

Sweet Tooth Tyranny

I normally keep my stories non-political but something has come up that I can't ignore: there's a Vermont state senator who's proposing a tax on sugar. Sugar! Sugar's one of our unalienable rights even though the writers of the Declaration of Independence forgot to put it on their list; blasphemous over-sight, I say! You see, 12 years before the Declaration, King George the 2nd tried to mess with sugar and that caused some hard feelings. Then George the 3rd picked on tea and things went to hell-in-a-hand basket. Well, there was a war—you know how it goes—and we were finally in charge of our own dietary essentials, along with a little "Life, Liberty and Pursuit of Happiness." Next we added a few freedoms, Speech, Press, Religion, etc. but, by gosh, they forgot to add Sugar to that list, too! Somehow we've kept our undocu-mented Sugar Right intact all these years in spite of a few "King George" types of our own—until now, that is.

This senator wants to tax sugar and says she's serious. Here's her tragic ra-tionale: "My favorite tax to pay for health care has always been the junk food tax. I have refined that idea and I would like to place a tax on all foods that have some kind of sugar listed on the first four ingredients on the label. I don't think there are many folks who will argue that all the sugar we con-sume is good for us. "I beg to differ, Senator, for one thing sugar is not "junk food!" It's our Right. I hereby call on all loyal chocoholics, Ben and Jerry-o-philes, and, especially, lovers of Maple, the Holiest of Sugars. Will we stand for this—I SAY NO!!! Rise up, my fellow Vermonters, put down this tyranny ONCE AND FOR ALL!!!

I'm sorry, slap, slap…I got carried away…but, really, the senator is flawed in her thinking. Sure, there are some abuses of sugar. I mean, if you drink a case of Pepsi each week, or eat the equivalent in Twinkies, you're abusing sugar (when you go to feed the cows, do you feed 'em the whole barn full?). I say sugar's good if you work it off, but folks these days are leaving out the "work" part. We used to have hayin' to do, cows to milk, and wood to split—wood to split—reminds me of my friend, Mac, who is a real Vermonter. He's a healthy, retired IBMer who's got more projects than you could shake a splitting maul at. His neat ranch house sits at the edge of a wooded lot over in Richmond, Vermont and a handsome woodpile stands in his back-yard. I asked him once why he had a woodpile, since he spends every winter in Florida. "You know, Burr," he said, oozing wisdom, "It just don't seem American to not have a woodpile." Wow…such profound words, no doubt sweetened with plenty of sugar. You see, Mac works it off. He accepts his Sugar Right with discipline and that's what we all need to understand: if we're more moderately taxed and more generously encouraged to do the right thing, we'll stay healthier. We all need a "woodpile of our own," built with hard work and a good attitude.

I've considered organizing a protest over at Burlington Harbor. We'd dump tons of sugar into the harbor and probably write some history, you know, the famous Burlington Sugar Party, but I'm sick of harsh protests like that. Let's just have a good old-fashioned pancake breakfast. I'll invite the senator and we'll talk it over. We'll have coffee (I take mine with two teaspoons of sugar, thank you), buttermilk and honey (that's h-o-n-e-y) pancakes. We'll top the pancakes with real butter and, of course, cascades of Vermont maple syrup. After breakfast we'll all split and stack wood for an hour. I think the senator will see the light—sugar's our Right, plus it sure helps with the Pursuit of Happiness. ✤

Dog Days of Baseball

I woke up one morning a few years back feeling the affects of an epiphany. Yup, after I shook off the sleep seeds and downed some strong coffee, I knew my life had changed forever...you see, I had turned into an avid Red Sox fan sometime in the night. It's a function of things like geography, heredity, drinking water...a real Vermonter simply has to be a Red Sox fan whether he wants to be or not (and I did not as I had always hated sports). Since that fateful morning, I have religiously watched or listened to my team and when they win, the high I get rivals my first draw-off of fancy maple syrup. A loss, on the other hand, is awful. Take the other night, for instance, when Marco Scutaro had both a sharp broken bat and a lightening-fast grounder coming at him...he let the grounder escape to save his life and I was pissed! That's when I made my decision... "gotta quit...This is gettin' outa control!".

Realizing the "cold turkey" approach might not work, I searched for a viable substitute and all of a sudden, the two Black Labs Averill and Fern came to mind... "They both need exercise and are up for outdoor activity." I thought "Maybe I can satisfy my addiction vicariously through those two guys.". All it ever takes with them are three words "wanna play ball?" and they're on their feet quicker'n a packed stadium after a grand slam. Betsy has a mesh bag full of new tennis balls hanging up in our foyer but there are lots of abandoned ones out and around. Just like the big leagues, Averill and Fern expend a huge number of balls for every single game. When I say "Where is it?", they both hot-foot it to the bushes and one of them always quickly emerges with a ball.

I get control of it and the three of us head for the parking area where our driveway goes downhill. My two friends reach peak excitement on the way out but the first pitch is important to me. I keep the ball until we get there. I throw like "a girl" these days but despite the source, gravity makes my first throw fast. Averill, the "Dustin Pedroia" in our family, is after it like greased lightning. Fern's more like Big Papi, huge, gangly and almost aloof. She knows, however, that it's important to both Averill and me so she'll always "play along".

The game is much simpler with the dogs than the Red Sox...I throw, they catch...I throw, they catch. For the sake of my "therapy" though, I have to figure out small ways their game compares to the real thing. For instance, they do "talk strategy" similar to the way catchers and pitchers do; you see, Averill has a problem giving up the ball once she's got it. She'll catch it and bring it back but to pry it from her bear trap jaws is impossible. She's obviously embarrassed about this but she can't help herself (it's a "dog" thing). Fern, on the other hand, will dutifully drop it right at my feet every time. A while ago they got together on this problem; Averill catches the ball because she's the better player but after a quick conference, she hands it off to Fern who gives it to me!

Recently Betsy injected her own strategy to our game. She's a "healthy dog" person who believes in walking them for miles every morning. She loves it when I, a "lazy dog" person, take them to play ball but her ulterior motive always includes a little doggie hygiene... "work 'em till they, you know, go to the bathroom" she says. Lately I've been kind of "keeping score" every time one of them heads into the tall grass for a little "personal time". When our game ends and the three of us head back to the house, I'm always quick to announce the score... "We had one pooper" or, the grand slam of doggie baseball... "We had two poopers!".

I'm very pleased to announce that my "therapy" is working. I'm really enjoying my sports time with Averill and Fern. My blood pressure is down and I lack the dreadful "morning after" feeling following a Red Sox loss. I have not watched or listened to a Red Sox game now for two weeks but from what I'm hearing, they're worth about as much these days as my dogs' final score! Oh brother...I'm starting to get shook up... "C'mon guys. wanna play ball?". 🍁

Horn of Therapy

The one thing that gets me off the farm a lot in the summertime is my horn. I've always played the trombone and probably always will, but sometimes I feel led around by that cussed thing much like a hound dog being led around by his nose. So far this summer I've traveled to points all over Vermont and New Hampshire to play for village concerts, wedding receptions, funerals... you name it...and it ain't all fun. Sure, there are occasional high points but between the carrying, the setting up, the tearing down and the driving, sometimes it seems like I'm experiencing drudgery in the "fortissimo" range.

The other day, I faced a long day of work on the farm followed by a trip clear to Monroe, New Hampshire to play in a big band that night. I was viewing it with kind of a "hound dog" attitude when all of a sudden my son, Tommy, came rattling over the potholes in our lower drive with his pickup truck. He pulled up to where I was and I hardly let him get out before I started bitching about my day ahead. "Wait a minute" he said, interrupting my rant... "if you're going to New Hampshire, you might as well take the trailer and pick up a scraper blade from my old buddy, Amos Locke. I've had it with those potholes, and Amos and I have already talked price." Tommy seemed to know just what would bring me out of my funk. He suggested I get ready and leave early.... "Make' a day of it", he said. All of a sudden, my attitude changed for the better; I got the stuff ready for my two varied tasks and headed east toward New Hampshire.

I found Amos Locke's place on the north side of Lisbon, within sight of busy Route 302 but slightly set off by small hayfields and the Ammonoosuc River. His buildings were old and weathered, remnants of a 60s working farm which now sits suffering from disuse and lack of economy. As I pulled into his yard, a collection of new but weathering farm equipment bearing names like Hesston, Woods and Bushhog lay scattered on an old cement slab. He might as well have displayed a bronze plaque saying "Yankee Trader" but instead, there were only the words, "honk for service", hand painted on the side of a barn. I got out of the truck, ignored the words, and headed, like that proverbial hound dog, for the collection of machinery.

I was down on my knees, studying the linkage of a certain cultivator, when Amos Locke came limping across the yard. "Make ya a good deal on that" he said in lieu of introduction. I chuckled and said one scraper blade was probably all I could handle today. He pointed to a trailer parked in a nearby shed piled high with more equipment... "blade you want's on the bottom". He limped in the direction of an ancient John Deere that sat in another shed, started it up and backed out through the cloud of black diesel smoke. When he approached on the John Deere, I noticed he had a cloth breathing protector stretched over his nose and mouth. He drove up to the trailer, positioning the bucket loader over the items to be picked off. I climbed up and fastened the chain to each piece of equipment in turn as he lifted them off and set them aside. We finally exposed the scraper blade and we loaded it onto my trailer.

After I got the blade cinched down, Amos beckoned me into his house where he removed the breathing protector and introduced me to his wife, Thelma. The three of us sat at their kitchen table and I wrote him out a check. After I handed it to him, we talked about everything from the weather to the low price of milk to my trombone playing. Just before I left, I asked him if he had "farmers' lung", a condition that plagues certain farmers from years of breathing barn dust. I told him that I had always worried about getting it myself because of years spent battling both hay fever and mandatory barn chores.

"Ya know" he said, "they ain't sayin' I got it yet but I think I do. My wind's bad...some days real bad". I looked beyond the aging couple to a lifetime of dusty memorabilia in an ancient house thinking "There but by the grace of God go I.". Just before I got up to leave, Amos looked me right in the eye with wisdom written all over his face... "Say you play the trombone?.. y' know, I think that must be good for your wind...don't evah stop playin' that horn!"

I shook his huge cow milkin' hand, thanked him for his advice, and headed toward my big band concert in Monroe. His last words hung in the air like mist in a New Hampshire valley... "good for your wind. Don't evah stop playin'". I knew my music would be different from that point on, not just tones from a horn's bell but therapy, and piece of mind, and hope for strong "wind" and a long life. ✤

Friend Wayne

I've recently been autographing lots of my new books, "Golden Times" and for a country boy like me, that makes my head swell bigger'n a prize-winning turnip. One of those folks was Wayne Richardson, a great friend and fellow country boy from over in Worcester. Wayne and his wife, Dolly, came into my store a couple days ago to pick up a copy of the book. While they were here, Wayne said he had just received his "million board foot" pin as a part-time sawyer of logs. Although there's no one more deserving of an honor like that, it was over a totally unrelated and much less glamorous endeavor that I first got to know him. He used to drive truck for Maxham Supply Company, a Worcester company involved in the pet food industry...enter the "less glamorous"...we're talkin' expired animals from farms all over Vermont, scraps from meat markets and some mighty awful offal from huge packing plants. Wayne used to haul it all. Back when I was young, I'd go over there during my offseason and drive the smaller trucks.

I've always had "truckin'" in my blood and still do. There's something that intrigues me about the distinctive drone of a diesel engine with gearing that can propel 40 tons along the open road on 18 wheels. I once had a chance to drive one of those beauties, thanks to Wayne Richardson. Employees of a huge national rendering company had gone on strike down in the greater Boston area and Wayne was being sent down with a crew of scabs from Maxham Supply. They would stay in a motel, rent trucks, and take over the routes picking up meat scraps from stores. They needed a trailer full of empty barrels hauled down and dropped off, and Wayne selected me to ride "shotgun" and bring the rig home.

We took off early one morning, Wayne and me in the big truck with the van full of scabs travelling behind. Over the years, Wayne had taken on an image as the most hard luck driver of all. Those rigs have dozens of lights, an intricate braking system, multi mirrors, mud flaps, and umpteen other features necessary for road worthiness and safety; to cops, trucks are little "pots of gold" because they know they'll always find a deficiency or two and Wayne Richardson drew their interest like flies to a gut wagon. That morning, sure enough, Montpelier's pre-dawn Main Street brought a piercing blue light in Wayne's mirror. He stopped and we both exited the huge road tractor. We walked the truck's 60 foot length to where the cop had stopped the guys following us in the van for speeding.

I was flabbergasted when Wayne walked up to that cop and let him have it. "See here" Wayne shouted. "You're buggin' me all the time with picky little things like lights out...you've collected enough fines outa me to pave this street... it's four o'clock in the morning and there's no traffic on these streets... give these boys a break!" The cop finally did let them off with a warning and our caravan continued on to Boston. After we had unloaded the barrels, Wayne "turned over the reins" to me. That was back in the days before special licensing was required to drive one of those things, so I simply started her up, put her into gear and headed out. I was never so proud as the day I drove that truck home guided by "a wing and a prayer" and my love for big rigs.

Speaking of "wings and prayers", Wayne told a story the other day about driving that same rig to pick up a load of rather foul poultry pieces at a huge slaughter plant up around Montreal. It was the day before Thanksgiving and Dolly went along with him. "Things were a little tight that year" he said "and we hadn't bought a turkey". They had an uneventful trip up I-89 to Swanton, across the Rouses Point Bridge and through the customs at Champlain, New York. Wayne said back then Customs was not as tough as it is today but his magnetism for hard luck kept him on his toes, nonetheless. That day, he and Dolly passed through with no problems and arrived on schedule at the Montreal poultry plant. As he backed the rig up to the loading dock, Dolly suddenly exclaimed, "Wayne, there's a turkey out there!" Sure enough, a huge turkey had somehow escaped the guillotine and was strutting around the yard. "We both got outa that truck quicker'n blazes." Wayne said. "It was quite a circus catchin' that thing but we finally got it cornered between two trucks. I grabbed it, flutterin' and squawkin', and wrestled it back to our truck. Dolly opened the passenger door and in it went!" He said it first flew around the cab and made a bit of a mess but settled down once they got back on the road. Wayne said he prayed the bird wouldn't make a fuss at the border crossing and when they got there, sure enough old 'Tom' was roosting silently back in the sleeping compartment. They passed through that day without a hitch... "didn't even have to declare that extra passenger", he said "and the next day, by golly, we had fresh turkey for Thanksgiving!"

Wayne's no "spring chicken" anymore so his days of truckin' are over. There'll be a huge void out on the road without Wayne. He was a great, mild-mannered truck driver, the most innocent guy ever haunted by cops, and, yes, always good at bringin' home the bacon...uhhh...turkey! 🍂

Dreams of Motoring and Music

I've been a farmer for so long that I'm not bothered by "ups and downs" business-wise, weather-wise or otherwise. I'm willing to work seven days a week when necessary to keep this patch of land green and open. There were, however, a couple of things I wanted to do with my life that got tabled a long time ago when circumstances and these 240 acres found me farming. Those two things, although as varied as sour pickles and sugar-on-snow, are now 57 year old dreams. I've never actually done either one, but they're as much a part of me as this Vermont countryside.

I've always wanted to be a long distance truck driver. When I was a boy, my uncle, Bernard, had three trucks that ran between Vermont and Florida. To a farm boy infatuated with anything that rolls, huge tractor-trailers were the greatest thing since sliced bread. There was usually one of those beauties parked at our farm and I remember spending hours in its cab. I'd marvel over the array of gauges, pedals and levers inside and beyond the huge windshield, I'd imagine Stuckeys billboards and peanut fields instead of Vermont's Green Mountains. The air horn pull-chain hung temptingly from the ceiling but I never pulled it—pulling it would have drawn discovery and a forced return to my farm duties. Sometimes I'd even crawl up into the sleeper compartment feigning blurry eyes from a hard day on the road and actually grab a few winks.

Yup, I've got truckin' in my blood; can't help it, can't shake it. I notice every truck out on the road and know their make and model. Where some folks "count sheep" at night, I count gears—I run the gears of a 15 speed Roadranger, ridin' high in an 18 wheel Kenworth. Usually I'm somewhere in the Midwest, just going into gear 12 when sleep takes over.

The other thing I always wanted to be was a professional musician. My mother says when I was young I'd lie on the living room rug in front of the Lawrence Welk Show, point to the brass section and announce: "That's what I want to do when I grow up." I've been playing trombone ever since those days but, alas, my skill is far short of professional level—trumped, most likely, by lazy practice habits and those 240 acres of land.

I play third trombone in the Vermont Philharmonic Orchestra, the nation's oldest community orchestra. Our conductor is Lou Kosma, a professional bassist for the Metropolitan Opera. Lou regularly makes the six hour drive from New York City to Vermont for our rehearsals and concerts. He's a great guy and, being a professional musician, commands our total respect. Professional musicians, like Lou, rank highest on my list of idols, well maybe except for truck drivers.

Recently I had a musical Epiphany, thanks to Lou Kosma. I had just flown up three flights of stairs at the Barre Opera House with all my trombone paraphernalia, thinking I was late for a rehearsal. When I got to the lobby, there stood Lou with his usual warm grin. I put my stuff down and shook his hand.

"I've been thinking of that picture on your farm brochure—the one of you holding a maple syrup dipper," Lou said. "You don't look right holding that dipper—I don't think of you that way—I picture you holding a trombone."

His comment, although routine for him, brought me a couple octaves off the Opera House floor and ready to conquer the world—Lou Kosma thinks of me primarily as a musician!

I still felt like a musician on my drive home from that great day but the next morning brought back the reality of my job—maple syrup canning day. Our much used dipper hung conveniently on the wall and I grabbed it instinctively. It felt natural in my hand and as the heavenly aroma of warming maple syrup rose from the vat, I knew my chosen vocation was just right—my place, by day is on the farm. The rest of the time, however, is when I do my dreamin'. Dreams can be anything. 🍁

Awkward Ag

I got an email the other day from my cousin Wayne that kind of "struck home" in light of the work I've been doing lately. The gist of his message was about "the automation of farming" and the reason it struck home was because we've been out in the sugar woods tapping trees and repairing tubing to get ready for our upcoming sugar season, our version of farming this time of year. As I read his message, these old bones of mine were "talkin' to me" in good shape because of the week I'd put in and it had even been brutal for the younger guys I work with...whew...sometimes it seems like it's even harder than the old days of buckets and oxen and "wintahs th'way they used t' be"!

Here's Wayne's message:

"I have wondered if you detected that Cousin Robert was a prophet? In early June of 1940 or 41, I was walking with Robert as he drove the horses using a spike tooth harrow to get the weeds just as the corn was emerging, a practice Uncle John employed. Robert prophesied that the day would come when a farmer could set in his living room and direct the fieldwork. It amazes me that I have lived to see that come to pass that a farmer can, by remote control, send the tractor out for planting, tilling or harvesting and control that equipment within 1 or 2 inches of accuracy!"

Amazing I say! And I certainly believe cousins Wayne and Robert; they're both savvy of things agriculture and no doubt glad as hell they aren't still out in that cornfield with those horses! I'm just a bit puzzled about why more of this armchair agriculture hasn't seeped into the world of maple sugarmaking? It sure would be nice to sit in my living room, manipulate a keyboard, and make the maple magic happen but I somehow know that will never be the case. Here's my theory: agriculture has two major ingredients, machinery and nature. Machinery is the easy part; if technology can put a man on the moon and develop computers that are smarter than people, it's a "no-brainer" to make a remote control tractor. The complications arise, however, when "nature" is added...nature, the "tough nut to crack", always calls the shots, and always will!

Farming "out west" (and for a Vermonter, "out west" starts around Syracuse, New York) involves square, flat, pliable fields. I assume those are the places Cousin Wayne was talking about and expect those fields'll "tame up" pretty good (at least until the first tornado comes along). Here in Vermont, on the other hand, we're dealing with wild trees that grow on very inhospitable countryside and require frigid winters as part of their life cycles. A frigid winter's footprint, three feet of snow, is usually still right there necessitating snowshoes, the most Neanderthal of all footwear, when we begin tapping our trees.

Some folks ask "do you have to drill a new hole every year?" and our answer is "yes" with the precision of a surgeon. "Can't you use a snowmobile to make getting around easier?" they persist... "heavens no" we say... "It'd be like that surgeon makin' his incision with a dull ax instead of a scalpel!" We've got to get right up to those maples and find the perfect place to tap all while working around the "spiderweb" of tubing that stays in the woods year round.

Lest I've upset farmers "out west" by suggesting that their job is easy and ours is hard, I don't mean to do so. I'm aware that farming is never easy but that there are certainly easier places to farm than here in Vermont. Our trees are now all tapped and we're waiting for the freezing and thawing weather that will finally release the only ingredient for our crop of liquid gold. Until that happens, I'll include a couple quotes that sooth my wary bones:

"Adopt the pace of nature: her secret is patience." Ralph Waldo Emerson

And my very favorite one of all is by e.e. cummings:

"The world is mud-luscious and puddle-wonderful"

...sounds like sugarin' in Vermont to me! 🍁

Clip-Clop with a Volt

I've recently been committing the unspeakable by running my chainsaw without ear protection...and, yes, I probably should know better. No doubt my excuses rank from the "feeble" to the "ridiculous" but: number one...I'm of the old school; number two...after all my years of doing stupid things, I can still hear; and number three...I can't find my damned ear protectors! Besides that, I really hate to be denied the finer "whirrrs, putt-putts, and vrrroooms" of life today. I personally love the "lulling" of a tractor's engine while on rendezvous with forty acres. And while playing my trombone in a big band is pure ecstasy to me, to an otologist I'm nothing but "cannon fodder" for the drummer to my right and the trumpets blaring from behind.

It came to a head for me when my trombone playing buddy Walter stopped by the other day. I shook his hand and had addressed both the weather and salutations of "long time, no see" when he palmed a "time out", reached in his pocket and donned some sort of hearing device. It seems Walter's years of being "cannon fodder" has rendered him about deaf. "Yikes" I thought... "I'm not that much younger than Walter.". The next` day I went down to our local tractor store and bought a twenty dollar set of ear protectors.

Although we all recall images from the past of that quintessential grandpa holding a trumpet to his ear, it seems most of our audio-zapping culprits these days are matters of modern living. Modern living, however, can be fickle; yup, electric cars with names like "Prius, Volt and Leaf" are surging along our highways these days trying to help Mother Earth stay "green" but there's a downside...they'll sneak up on you! I recently heard that our bureaucrats, pros at legislating the subtraction of sound in workplaces, village squares, and neighborhoods, are actually thinking of adding sound to these stealthy little rigs! Yup, more than a few pedestrians have been hit at intersections and crosswalks because they expect cars to make noise.

Now don't get me wrong...I'm all for saving human life but would urge caution in adding "voice to the Volt". Our world thrives on practicality and this entirely "artificial" project, if done wrong, could make a mockery of modern transportation. One way to proceed could be as simple as stealing an idea from our kids and their bicycles: apply a flapper that would rub on spokes and make a "whirrrring" sound. The downside, of course, is that it would be silent when the car stops and pedestrians expect to hear engine noise even from stopped cars. Then there's the same old repeating horn solution... "honk,honk,honk,honk,honk", and to that I say "OVER MY DEAD BODY!". This leaves what will surely be the solution: creating a simple recording that plays through a speaker on the car's front end but the question begs, a recording of what...the rumble of an idling eighteen-wheeler? a variation of a child's tale?... "I think I can, I think I can, I knew I could, I knew I could", or maybe just a practical message ala cigarette disclaimers... "caution, electric cars can be hazardous to your health when walked in front of".

After more thought, however, there is a way to proceed tastefully with an eye toward historical correctness; let's give those cars "horse and buggy" sounds. For instance, when an electric car slows to, say, 25 mph, a soothing "clip-clop, clip-clop" mixed with occasional driver "clucks" will begin. When the car continues to slow and its GPS senses a stop sign, traffic light or crosswalk, the "clip-clops" will decline and eventually stop. While it waits, there will be gentle "nickering and foot pawing" and then a stern "Giddapp, cluck, cluck, heah, heah" will bring a return to the soothing "clip-clop, clip-clop".

Many times these days, historic bridges and buildings are replaced by "historic" replicas so why shouldn't we do the same in the field of transportation? At the risk of self-righteousness by the wagonload, I think it's a great idea and no doubt Ford, GM, Nissan and Toyota will steal it some day. That's OK because our cities desperately need to be slower, safer, and more soothing. Just remember...you heard it here first. ❧

All Puffed

I was over at the pen barn getting some lumber for a small project the other day when I saw it at the edge of the door. It was as big around as a basketball, white as the driven snow, and pocked and crevassed like the surface of the moon. Finding puffballs, although never as huge as this one, has become an annual event for me in that same barn over the years. They've always prospered there because years of young stock being housed there have left the barn's dirt floor 'flavored' with everything positive for a puffball. I had given up on finding them this year because Betsy and I had been packing out junk all summer and lately packing in a huge pile of firewood; with all of that traffic, we had rendered the very place they most relished almost as hard as blacktop. This monster, however, had crept to the edge of the door where the dirt was still loose and pliable, and sprouted up overnight, as mushrooms do.

I used to find the other kind of puffballs out in the pasture when I was a boy. They were brown, light as a feather and exploded with clouds of deep brown dust when you stepped on them. It was fun to sneak up on people with a palmed puffball and suddenly explode it in their face. Pastures were usually abundant with puffballs because of another thing prevalent out there: cow plops...cow plops are puffballs' favorite meal.

A few years ago, a fresh puffball appeared in that same barn where our lumber is stored. All of a sudden there it was, white, big as a grapefruit and obviously some kind of mushroom. I took my jackknife, severed the single stem and took it up to my naturalist friend, Paul Cate.

"Calvatia gigantea" he said in the language a naturalist uses... "giant puffball...wonderful eating". I immediately thought of brown, exploding dust and cow plops.

"You're serious...you can eat these things?" I asked. Paul assured me that it was, indeed, the immature form of an exploding puffball and that, for a mushroom lover, it was exceptionally good eating. I had read about the agonizing death in store for anyone who eats poisonous mushrooms; words like "liver damage, gastrointestinal upset, kidney and respiratory failure, and neurotoxicity" came to mind. I wouldn't have trusted just anyone but knew I could trust Paul Cate. Paul acted like I had stumbled across the fungal equivalent of the crown jewels and sent me home to slice it thin and fry it in butter.

I did just that and when, with apologies to those who have unfortunately inherited the flawed gene for "mushroom hatred", those morsels came from the frying pan, they were pure ecstasy! The meat was sweet and succulent, like the best darn lobster caught west of Wiscasset. Yes, to me it tasted as heavenly as that sea delicacy and a heck-of-a-lot cheaper. In fact, as I re-member, I ate way too much just as I've done a few times with lobster...and regretted it just as much!

When I found the giant puffball the other day, I quickly harvested it and rushed up to share it with my sister Susie who likes them just as much as I do. She took half of it and will, no doubt, eat a reasonable amount and freeze the rest. I knew better than to take the other half home because of my habit of gluttony. Instead, I set out to parcel the rest to other folks around the neighborhood. That proved to be an exercise in futility; it seems most folks around here either have no stomach for puffballs or worry too much about that slow, agonizing "death by mushroom". I ended up taking all of my half home and eating too much again! Like the times I've eaten too much lobster, I'm presently feeling a little "puffed up" and slightly queasy from my over-indulgence of butter-battered Calvatia gigantea.

It's a long year, however, and I'm sure by next September, when I happen across one of those beauties down there where the barn floor is flavored with everything positive for a puffball, I'll do it all again in the very same way. Maybe I can get one of my neighbors to try some by then and help save me from myself! 🍂

Dairy Dilemma

I've always felt that the expression "you gotta do what you gotta do" is a little bit trite but lately it has gained some momentum in my mind. I'm thinking about our local dairy farmers, or lack there of, and the terrible shape they're in these days; it seems they've been "straight-jacketed" by a federal milk market pricing system that's paying them about $11.00 for every hundred pounds (called a hundredweight) of milk they sell, the same amount of milk that's costing them over $17.00 to produce! It seems like a crime to make these beautiful farms suffer through such a depression but it's a problem that neither consumers, marketers nor politicians (especially politicians!) can figure out.

Although we stopped milking cows here on the Morse Farm some 43 years ago, there's still a part of me that wakes up every morning thinking about a herd of critters and what it takes to get 'em fed, milked, and cleaned up after. We still have a couple dairy farms here in East Montpelier and I get to watch them from my comfortable position as a non-dairy farmer. One of those local farms is huge. The folks who run it have followed the agricultural "path of least resistance", taking their cues from a society which hypes big farming as the only way to go.

Those big farmers, the Halls, are reaching out all over Central Vermont for available cropland. To use a couple of my Grandpa Morse's favorite expressions, they "strike while the iron's hot" and "do business with a large auger". A couple of the fields they hay are right here on the Morse Farm; they bring in their equipment and cover the same land in just a few hours that used to take us all summer long! I recently found myself sitting close by goggle-eyed as a huge machine gobbled up grass from a windrow and belched it into a trailing chuck wagon. Two big trucks, a Kenworth and a Freightliner, stood nearby waiting to receive tonnage from the chuck wagon and whisk it away to a bunker silo. The thought of those trucks backing up and dumping out green silage suddenly darkened...green...dumping...I left, thinking of the money those poor farmers are losing these days.

A few days later I happened past the smallest of our East Montpelier dairy farms. Just before I got to the Butlers' weathered homestead, something caught my eye in a hayfield to my right. "What the..." I thought stopping my car in the middle of the road. Out there, obscured slightly by the mixed vegetation growing along a stone wall, was an ancient truck being loaded with square bales. I got out of my car, made my way through the hedgerow, and approached Gary Butler, most recent of the multi-generations who have worked that land.

"What year is that truck?" I asked Gary, who had just thrown the last bale up on the truck's plank bed. "1928 Chevrolet. My grandfather bought it brand new." Gary said, proudly.

What was most striking about the scene before me was that this was not their "show truck" and they were not making a "statement" by using it...it was just another of the tools on their farm that was owned free and clear, and ready to help. The truck had obviously not been pampered; the cowling had been removed over its grease coated engine, exposing a slow water leak from a failing gasket. Its open doors revealed a seat with torn fabric and springs popping out, no doubt home to multi-families of mice down through the years. Gary was cordial with my questions but obviously needing to pick up the rest of the hay being baled by his father nearby. I stayed long enough to hear the old thing "prrrr" to life and head toward a ledge lined field road and a distant barn.

Recently I happened across the Agricultural Marketing Service website sponsored by our U.S. Department of Agriculture. Its words of introduction struck me like a blow in the groin from a long-legged Holstein: "Dairy Programs assists the dairy industry by providing stability and orderliness in the dairy marketplace, while at the same time assuring the availability of an adequate supply of high-quality milk and dairy products for U.S. consumption." We certainly enjoy the second half of their pledge every time we open up an inexpensive container of milk but they are failing dismally with the first part, to provide "stability and orderliness in the dairy marketplace".

My snapshot of two farms here in East Montpelier reveals a passion certain folks have to work the land and milk the cows. In that respect, the Halls and the Butlers are equal members of the same "club", a club that has served faithfully for years and years but has recently been failed by a flawed system. I feel especially for the dairy farmers who have had to drop out but also for the ones still "hangin' on by the skin of their teeth". It matters not how they operate, the size of their herd, the shape of their machinery...they are all "salt of the earth" in my mind, "doing what they gotta do" until some day they can be paid fairly for the job they love. 🍁

Furnace Figurin'

Recently my son, Tommy, and I made a mini-pilgrimage to the Northeast Kingdom in search of information about alternative heat for our store. We had been told that there was a Greenwood Wood Boiler in operation at the maintenance building at Lyndon State College and the Greenwood is the latest of many units we have been studying. Our country has been hooked on liquid fuel for so long now that most of us have forgotten the days of Sam Daniels furnaces and wood cook stoves. My own memory, in fact, is getting a little 'smoky' but sibling squabbles about whose turn it was to go feed the furnace stand out fresh in my mind. And then there was the constant emptying of the ashes and the brushing of the flues. Yes, it was a great day when we went to an oil burner back in the 1950s.

Because we Americans are so hooked on ease, it's little wonder $5.00 per gallon oil is pointing toward something 'pourable' as a replacement, like wood pellets. That's where our quest started back a month ago but we quickly excluded any kind of pellet burner when we realized the fuel would be very expensive and "scarce as hens' teeth" this winter. One expert explained that the only plants making pellets are way up in Canada and will not be able to serve all the hungry stoves being installed south of the border. Because of that, we turned our focus toward a unit that burned chunks of wood, a fuel 'free' for the taking right here on our farm.

Tommy and I located Lyndon State's maintenance building and a friendly guy named Art. Art spent an hour with us explaining the Greenwood from its huge firebox to the top of its tall chimney. When we left, we felt assured the Greenwood was far superior to the ravenous beast that my siblings and I fought about back in the '50s. From Lyndonville we headed north to Lemington to visit our friends Luc and Jacinthe Marchesseault. Our drive through 30 winding miles of the Kingdom's unique countryside brought the relief we both needed from our grind at the Morse Farm. It also revealed large numbers of Kingdom houses hosting five ton lots of white, plastic bags on their porches and breeze-ways...wood pellets... "guess we know where the world supply of pellets is", I joked to Tommy.

Thinking of all those folks slingin' wood pellet bags this winter reminds me of the day when all farmers around here bought their grain in 100 pound bags. That grain came into the E.W. Bailey Grain Company down in Montpelier on train cars. E.W. Bailey's grain elevator, Montpelier's only skyscraper towered over a long warehouse with loading docks for farmers' trucks like ours. There were huge piles of fat grain bags waiting to be slung onto hand trucks by muscled men and the place smelled heavenly of molasses. Mike Brunelle, one of those muscled men, threw 100 pound bags of grain around like they were balsam pillows. I remember Mike and my father "comparing notes" one time about grain-toting feats. My father told of carrying a 'hundred' of grain 1/2 mile on his shoulders while skiing through two feet of fresh snow. Mike, not to be out done, boasted of carrying a bag on each shoulder and one in his teeth! Tales in the Bailey warehouse were taller than Montpelier's only skyscraper!

Yesterday I visited a neighbor who burns pellets and asked if I could look at them. She pointed to her garage and said I was in luck unless I needed more than 150 bags. I went to the pile and lifted one, surprised at how light it was. When I flopped it back onto the pile where I could read the print, strange language jumped out at me... "18.12 Kg...Granules de bois...La foret pour tous...Des produits qui respectent l'environnement". I was half way home when I suddenly made the connection: Wood pellets have a lot in common with another heating fuel that we're all too familiar with...pourable, very expensive, getting scarce and comes from a foreign country...OYEEE... OIL!!!! When I got home, I immediately went to the phone and ordered that Greenwood Wood Boiler. Yes, I know it'll take some work but at least the fuel will be measured in cords, not Kgs, and best of all, it'll grow free for the taking right here on my farm. 🍂

More "Wisemen" Needed

It's post Christmas and here I sit spiritually full but physically wounded... wounded by a Christmas tree. Yup, that's right, the cussed things are bigger than me these days; I was hefting this one bugger up onto a trailer, my right hand cradling its butt and my left hand a ways into its branches for better leverage. All of a sudden I felt my left bicep, my loyal partner all these 61 years, rip away from its bearing. I knew immediately that I was in for a long siege...felled by a Christmas tree. The doctor says it's normal for my whole arm, from the shoulder down to my wrist, to be swollen and black and blue from this type of injury and that it'll heal over time.

As I said, I feel in much better shape spiritually. Time, it seems, and lots of hard work, have brought me to a place where I can appreciate the "Christ" in Christmas and minimize the "mas" (as in "massive amounts of gifts and hype"). Do I object to the gifts and hype? Heck no...my business depends on Christmas sales and I'm thoroughly convinced that Christ looks down with understanding; he accepts both plastic Santas and Nativity scenes. Recently I picked up a magazine called "Reminisce" and the first thing that popped out was a story by Joanne Weintraub, a Jewish woman from Milwaukee, Wisconsin. I found her description of the holidays of her youth very eloquent and meaningful in this day and age of skepticism and fear.

She wrote: "Growing up in the 1950s and 60s in the New York City suburb of Syosset, I was an enthusiastic second soprano in several school glee clubs and choirs. My favorite part of choir was Christmas, when we got to sing Silver Bells, Joy to the World and, in our best Latin, Adeste Fideles (O Come all ye Faithful). At home, though, my family celebrated Hanukkah. And my favorite memory of that holiday? Not the songs, not the presents, and not even the lighting of the Menorah candles, lovely as that ancient ceremony is. No, it was my grandmother's potato latkes."

Joanne Weintraub went on to describe how her grandmother prepared the latkes (potato pancakes in Vermont lingo), and how scrumptious they were. Here I beg your permission to break a tradition of my own...my tradition of barring "politics" from my writing...but Christmas should be free for everyone to enjoy in their own way with only one stipulation: its name should never be changed. We all grew up with Christmas, regardless of our religious affiliation, but now in this new-fangled world, words like "holiday" or "season" are being substituted in its stead. I say "bah-humbug" to that... there are lots of holidays and four seasons (some say five here in Vermont) but there is only one "Christmas"!

Ah the 50s and 60s...years when our fears were balanced by our faith. There really was some "good" in those good old days, you know! I think folks these days have just let their fears get the better of them and I have faith that society will heal just like my Christmas tree injury will. Yup, the black and blue recedes a little every day, the muscle is slowly reattaching, and the songs of pain I've been singing will turn more upbeat. We're about to start a new year and, like a big truck, the seasons will slowly shift from gear to gear. As the yearlong run approaches its end, I hope it brings you a spirit more worry free and lots of folks wishing each other "Merry Christmas".

Shine On

I went out yesterday for a very invigorating cross-country ski. I like to ski alone so that I can stop when I darn well please to commune with the trees, the hills and valleys…the countryside of my ancestors. Yesterday I spoke to two soft maple trees that I've been threatening to cut for years; "this year I'll cut you for sure!" I passed the remnants of an ancient sugarhouse that only I know about. No doubt, it was once someone's pride and joy but now rests a ghostly hummock beneath the thin snow; strange where those folks tucked their sugarhouses. Was it because that's where the trees were, or did they just want to, maybe, get away from it all? Sugarmakers are "private" sorts. Our Agriculture Department has been trying for years to register them all and there's a few who just ain't talkin'…kinda reminds me of another industry, one with some striking parallels. I received this email a while ago:

"Burr, I'll have you know that the fine batch of Maple I had you ship to me the other week down to (-------) was bartered with my neighbor in the county for some of the finest damn (------) Smokey Mountain moonshine. The Light Amber Maple got me a half gallon of Peach Brandy, the Grade B got me a gallon of Corn Shine and the Dark Amber got me a half gallon of Apple Brandy. Now, just so you don't think all that good Maple of yours went to waste, I'll assure you, this ain't no dirty water, rusty radiator mountain jack juice'…these are some of the finest examples of the ancient art…kinda like your Maple…clear and pure as mountain spring water, the bubbles are tiny and spin up to about 190 proofage by my eye…done right by families that have been making it up here for over 150 years…but then, you all know about family businesses, traditions and getting' things right, I see.

So sometime if ya'll would like a Mason Jar of something homemade and authentic from down here as a thank you for your good work, well I'd be more than happy to get some up to ya'll in Yankee land this coming month.

You just let me know and thanks for some great cooking and table Maple.

Bye, (------)"

Needless to say, I ain't-a-goin-ta tell you his name but, you know, his daughter drove all the way up from (-----) to bring me some; came lugging it in a shoe box with a note titled "Mason-Dixon Exchange." I came in from my ski yesterday thinking about the two industries. The shoebox with a jar each of corn and peach shine sits amid papers and miscellaneous chainsaw parts on my cluttered desk. Close to it, coincidentally, sits a quart of maple syrup. I lifted the jars of shine out and set them down beside the maple syrup—striking, I chuckled, country cousins, they are. One product is made from nature by time-honored folk traditions. The other is, well, made from nature by time-honored folk traditions. I do understand the drawbacks of making too close a comparison: We encourage folks to use our "time-honored" product everyday and parcel it out liberally to their kin. Theirs … wellll! And as my new friend pointed out, "ya'll can throw a label on yours and sell it public…we cain't." Let's not, however, dwell on negatives. We all go to work in the woods and hold what we make up to the sun. The clarity and the economy shine through. We roll it on our tongue and feel proud. We talk about it…or we don't. Cheers. ❧

Only in Vermont

I'm going to dedicate this writing to a couple things that can only happen in Vermont; the first is about the autumn "brush stroke" that nature reserves exclusively for this place we call the Green Mountains. This tale comes, admittedly, from the heart of a seventh generation Vermonter who's biased and righteous...hell, I'm just right!

Being in the tourism business, I have limited access to Vermont's complete Autumn show, a show available to anyone who can hop in a car or bus and travel around. Like a stagehand, I'm confined behind the scenes right here at Morse Farm. Sure, the view out front of our place always presents a spectacular spectrum of early reds to late golds but I always wonder what the leaves are doing in other places. I will admit the so-called 'peak' colors of Peacham and Manchester featured on calendars and Vermont Life centerfolds are truly beautiful! I'm going to go out on a limb, however, as the sort of "foliage misfit" that I am...Vermont offers a late Autumn gold that's unequivocally nature's best show anywhere (and I ain't talkin' about the 'gold' left behind from thousands of leaf peepers!).

Like the very lifeblood of foliage season, photosynthesis, I've found that nature's lighting makes all the difference in my kind of foliage viewing. There's a point at the end of the day, when the last remnants of sunshine still rule, that those golds jump out with a special magic. One recent night it was so stunning that I set out to capture it for the rest of the world to see. I grabbed the digital camera, worked the buttons so that it would perform in "high resolution" and snapped away. Unfortunately, my limitations prohibit me from plugging the thing into a computer and actually looking at the pictures I've taken. The next day when our tech guy, Claude, came in and performed that duty, he quickly found that I had jiggled the camera and my pictures were wavy phantoms instead of the "world's most beautiful golds".

I'm convinced that it's our Vermont sugar maples that make all the difference. In other places too many oaks stand in the way of golden perfection. Sure, oaks and sumac are pretty but only in Vermont, at a certain time of day, do the sugar maples "perform their 'Stradivariesque' music". No, I can't prove it any more than I can prove the existence of God or that I love someone... enough said...I know!

The other tale I have to tell is of a more personal nature; Vermont is such a small place that whispers can be heard from border to border and you never know who'll be doing the whisperin'. Back during peak foliage, I was giving my sugarhouse show to a bus full of folks and when I finished, the group's escort, a man I had never met before, stepped forward to address his group.

"This has been a unique glimpse of Americana" he said about my explanation of the maple process." He went on to praise me for my country charm and hard work but it was something he said about my musical life that must have made my mouth open wide enough to insert a cup mute... "Oh, I almost forgot...besides being a maple sugar maker, Burr is also a jazz trombone player." I found the build up to be way too generous but was especially curious about how he knew I played trombone. As his group left, I asked him. "Hmmm" he puzzled. "It was someone along our route who told me.... let's see...it wasn't at our morning stop in Stowe...oh, I remember", he looked pleased that it had finally come to him... "it was the governor... I ran into your governor when my group was touring the statehouse and he told me"

There are a couple ironies in the two tales I tell today: one is that the governor would be keeping track of little old me in this election season when I'm supposed to be keeping track of him! The other is that the best of our foliage occurs after all the tourists have been here and gone home; this last point, of course, you must accept from a self proclaimed "foliage misfit" who can't prove a thing except seven generation roots in a place where three words bound down the mountain sides and echo through the valleys: "only in Vermont". 🍁

Contrasting Comforts

Sweet and sour, hot and cold, muddy and snowy—being a maple sugarmaker, my life is plum full of those little contrasts. Another favorite contrast of mine, although hot, has nothing to do with maple syrup. It's the sauna. My friend Paul pronounces it "sow-na", stressing the "sow" with a funny little nasal twist. He's been to Finland where they do them right, as opposed to the cedar-clad cubbyhole in the corner of your local health club, where they do it all wrong. The fact is, any sauna worth its sweaty salt involves a walk in the woods, a long wait for a fire, and hellish, "vein popping" heat and when it's over, it's soooo good.

It took me a while to warm up to the idea. My maiden voyage was in Paul's sauna, which sits in a clump of maples a short distance from his house. I must admit that hanging around naked with a bunch of guys sort of butted heads with my modest, Vermont upbringing. The worst of my fears, however, had to do with boiling alive—Paul said the temperature sometimes reaches 210 degrees! When I finally made the plunge I did so clad in my baggy swimming trunks. I remember feeling conspicuous in a reverse sort of way, when my four bare-assed companions assessed me with lowered, judging stares. That was my first sauna.

The temperature was frigid last night when I returned to Paul's, now a seasoned convert. Paul had started the fire two hours earlier and the inside temperature was finally up to 160 degrees. I wasted no time in transitioning from the 10 degrees outside, this time au natural, to the heavenly ambience that awaited me. We sat, Paul, his two sons and me, on the smooth cedar shelves, savoring the goodness. It's a wonderful place to bare (quite literally) everything that's been bugging you lately. It also physically draws out all the poisons that have been festering in your body—sort of a way to purge things both physically and spiritually. When we left the sauna that night,

Paul and his boys rolled in the snow. I did not. I did, however, feel euphoric and physically young again. I thanked them, got in my car and drove back down County Road, singing at the top of my lungs "AH FEEL GOOD---WOOH"—thank you, James Brown!

My other sauna experience was not a sauna at all, but a banya. That's what the Russians call them. My family has been to Russia a couple times, visiting a big family we've accepted as ours. We received the whole gamut of warnings and advice before we went: don't ride the trains, don't drink the water and for God's sake, refuse the vodka. The first night I found myself comparing notes in a language I didn't understand with the friendly grandfather, Alexei. He had a private stash of vodka in his cellar, which he accessed from a trapdoor in his living room; he poured, proudly, like it was a "national" thing. Somehow I couldn't find it in my Vermont cordiality to refuse. Needless to say, it became an "under the table" situation quickly, Alexei the viktor. It took gallons of Russian water to get me through the night. I arose the next morning to a very angry wife and a head bigger than a May Day Parade. I remember facing west, toward America, expecting to die.

I'm convinced my agony would have gone on much longer than it did, had they not hustled me off to the banya by mid-morning. The idea of a stifling steam bath battled with my present state of health and the hot August temperatures. The Russians, however, seemed to know what I needed. I sat, shoulders stooping, between Alexei and his son, Vladimir. They took turns flailing me with a soggy bouquet of birch leaves and when the temperature seemed unbearable, they poured water on a tray of hot rocks, making it even hotter! They kept a bucket of cold water within reach and I survived by splashing it on my nose and mouth. With every agonizing minute, I felt the poisons of the night before rushing out of my pores, down over my soggy body and through the cracks in the plank floor, back into the Russian soil. I gained a lot that day—I learned to love the banya. I learned the Cold War is, indeed, over and when it comes to vodka, I learned a new word—nyet! ❧

Russian Rides

A few days ago I had occasion to travel east on Templeton Road early in the morning. Templeton Road is a gravel thoroughfare up past our place. That morning, winter had returned and Templeton Road's mud season quirks had been frozen into a rutty still life. I don't know if it was the direction I headed (east), the terrible condition of the road or the starkness of the Vermont countryside that time of year, but something made me think of Russian roads that morning. I've traveled Russian roads before and, believe me, their maintenance has received a giant "Nyet" for so long that Vermont mud-season roads look well-honed and spruced up by comparison.

Betsy and I, our two boys, and their friends were there back in 03 visiting our friends, Tanya and Genia Novosyolov. It was then 19 years after Perestroika and the whole country had opened up for unrestricted travel. We took the train from Moscow to our friends' city of Kirov, about 600 miles to the northeast. Our first few days were spent walking and riding the bus around Kirov, a city a little smaller than Boston.

Our friends rolled out the red carpet for us with food, drink and a special camaraderie that seemed pleasantly at odds with the cold war that had previously haunted our two countries. Their hospitality peaked one night early in our visit when a reception was thrown in our honor at the palatial flat of Tanya's boss, Alexander. Alexander had recently prospered in Russia's post Perestroika construction boom and we Vermont "yokels" were feted with caviar, the finest of wines, and a Balkan singing quintet brought in just for us! It was a magical evening capped with the announcement that we would travel the next day to a place called the "Great River". Alexander explained that the Great River carried water that had been blessed by Christ and insisted that my wife, Betsy, who had recently been through breast cancer treatments, should go there.

We woke early, a little "groggy" from our festivities the night before, but excited about our day ahead. Our hosts rushed to prepare a picnic lunch and we then assembled outside where two Russian cars, a Volga sedan and a tiny Lada waited along with Alexander's plush Mercedes. Besides the six of us Vermonters, there were enough Russians to fill all three cars to the maximum. We loaded up and headed out, the Mercedes with Betsy and me aboard led the way.

We passed stately buildings and a huge Russian square in the center of Kirov. The streets were a mish-mash of trolley tracks and brickwork but had been relatively well maintained. It was in the suburbs where we entered the "major league" of bad roads, however. As our caravan proceeded past whole cities of drab, Soviet era tenements, our cars began bobbing and weaving to avoid the punches of bulging frost heaves and cavernous potholes. It was out in the flat Russian countryside that I suddenly realized we were traveling for long distances at odd angles; our drivers were driving in the ditches because they were smoother than the roads!

After 100 kilometers of that frenetic obstacle course, we arrived at the Great River, shaken like paint from a hardware store and very glad to be back on our feet. Our hosts seemed bent on only one thing...getting Betsy blessed so that her cancer would not return. They rushed her to a small outbuilding that turned out to be the ladies bathhouse for holy dunking. The females of our contingent guided her in, stripped off her clothes and ushered her into water. Those of us outside heard her scream like a Russian banshee when she hit that frigid water of early June! She was a deep blue when they led her out but had the smile of a saved person on her face. We had our wonderful Russian picnic and stayed several hours before heading back to Kirov.

The trip back delivered the same bumps and ditches but, like the proverbial horse returning to the barn, our three Russian drivers drove faster than they did in the morning. The Lada had all our young people in it and Genia Novysyolov drove it like a mad man. Betsy and I held hands in the Mercedes and, appropriately for a return from the Great River, prayed like hell!

My father always thought frost heaves and pot holes had therapeutic value and I believe he was right; after all Betsy has been almost ten years cancer free thanks to modern medicine, a wild Russian ride and a brisk dunk in God's frigid water. 🍁

BURR'S ADVENTURES

Gettin' They'ah from He'ah • No Place like "Home" • Old Kentucky Home •
Woodchuck Day • A Springtime Song • A Day Off the Farm • Happy Sailin'
• Let Joy In • Bye to a Great Friend • Another 'Burr' • Welcome to "Moose"
Farm • No Bull • DNA Project • Personalities and Change • Born Again
Baseball • WEATHER ! • "Grave" Situation • Inner Strength • Chip Chat •
Tree Psych 103 • The Personality of Machines • Two Friends of Mine •
A Sweet Trip to Iowa

I've never written to some one 'famous' but I was touched by
one of your recent stories. My Vermont trip was with a friend
who writes young adult literature. She came for a week's study
and I came for the opportunity to see Vermont. The Morse
Farm was a highlight. I've enjoyed all your stories since and
often repeat them. You see, I am a pastor. Presbyterian. Your
insight and stories often fit into the theme of the service soon
after I read them. This letter helped me. I try to encourage
folks to not be afraid. And where would we be if God decided
to hunker down. Thanks for the continued entertainment and
inspiration. Blessings for the holidays to you and your family.

- Emily Barker, TN

Gettin' They'ah from He'ah

Between all the shoveling of snow and cutting of hay, real Vermonters don't necessarily get away very often but when we do, it's usually a memorable affair. Take for instance the time six of us headed for Russia one Tuesday morning a few years back. It was a "trip of a lifetime" sort of thing that we had saved and saved for...Betsy, me, our two boys, and their significant others all crammed into our Morse Farm van and headed for Boston's Logan airport five hours before flight time. I, trip planner extraordinaire, had figured three hours would get us to the airport and allow two hours to get on the plane. As luck (and total ignorance) would have it, the slow roads we encountered all the way culminated in absolute limbo somewhere in Boston's infamous "Big Dig". We finally rolled into Logan that morning with just ten minutes to flight time. Somehow thanks to cell phones and our airline's superior customer service, we were met by a large golf cart at the parking garage and whisked through the process. The whirlwind we had been in soon fell away as we lifted off and headed up the Atlantic coast, frazzled but in store for an extremely memorable trip to Russia.

My friends Steve and Martha, like me, are real Vermonters but are somehow much more refined travelers. They recently returned from a well-planned trip to England but you know what they say about "the best laid plans...". They were due to fly out on September 8 and it so happened that Hurricane Irene made her angry visit just days before that. Steve and Martha are from the town of Chittenden, which is in Rutland County, down in the very hardest hit region of Vermont. Although their home was untouched by the storm, roads and bridges all around them were wiped out. Their planning originally included traveling to the White River Junction area to board the Dartmouth bus that makes a regular run to Logan Airport. There was, however, no way to get from Chittenden to White River. Suddenly the tiny Rutland airport seemed to be their only hope. They called and found a flight that would work and on September 8, went to the airport.

Once there, they found out that yet another storm had changed priorities at Logan and their small plane would be denied permission to land there. The airline at Rutland, though, said "not to worry...we'll taxi you to Boston!". A taxi immediately showed up for them, another passenger, and all of their luggage. The Vermont driver said "Yup...we can git you they'ah but if yer willin' t'do a little walkin', it'll save ya some time." Since they were down to about five hours till flight time, they were all for it. Their anticipation over the "walkin'" part only grew as they headed out through the city of Rutland and proceeded north right back toward the wilds of Chittenden... Chittenden, mind you, is at best the antithesis of Logan Airport and now thanks to Irene was totally shut off from the rest of the world by washed out roads and crumpled bridges! They held tight, though, as the driver somehow kept exuding an air of confidence. The taxi made several turns and finally ended up on a rough gravel road designated by the locals as the Hillbilly Highway. At last, almost at the top of the mountain, their driver pulled off the road and sitting there idling was the conveyance for the next leg of their trip to Boston, a four-wheel ATV pulling a tiny trailer!

"Mike'll shuttle ya to the other side th'valley" their driver hollered as he rushed to transfer the luggage onto the ATV's trailer. Steve and the other passenger crowded on the ATV behind Mike and Martha, smallest of the group, piled into the trailer with the luggage! Once aboard, Mike put the machine in gear and they slowly headed out across hill and dale, forest and riverbed to meet a Boston-bound cab where finally the roads were okay.

Just like us during our adventure to Russia, they made their flight but with not a minute to spare. They're back now and it sounds like they had a wonderful time. We're lucky in this day and age that our airlines are expedient and honorable. It's rare that folks miss out on the wonders of world travel but it's so nice to know that on the rare occasions when Mother Nature shows her ugly side, even from a place like Vermont, one way or another, you can usually get "they'ah from he'ah.". 🍂

No Place Like Home

A while back, I wrote that Betsy and I would soon be going to England to trace my Morse roots back across the "pond". My people came from the small East Anglican village of Dedham where the River Stour separates Suffolk and Essex Counties. In that writing, I wondered if deja vu would "slap me in the face like a challenge from an English duke". Now that the trip is over and we are safely back in Vermont, I'll answer the question "straight away" as they say in England... deja vu appeared much more like a gentle hug than a stiff slap. No, I learned from our voyage that Vermont is my only home but it did prove to be a world-class trip...I'm still high, in fact, on "bangers and mashed", patchwork countryside, and most especially, the royal quality of treatment we received.

Infrequent and nervous flyers that we are, we had been booked on British Airlines since January. As our flight time approached, it seemed "Murphy's Law" threatened us every step of the way with repeated cabin crew strikes and then that Icelandic volcano. When the day of our flight finally arrived, even though everything was "a go" right to the boarding gate, we worried that Murphy might be traveling with us. Luckily, he remained subdued and our plane left on time. No sooner had we landed at Heathrow and breathed collective sighs of relief, however, our flying "companion" Murphy started in again; the news reporting flight disruptions on both coasts would have us worried that our nine day visit would become twelve or fifteen, or maybe even a permanent return to the English countryside.

We were met at the airport by a pleasant looking young man named Steve Wood from the tour company, Classic England. Steve whisked us off through frenetic London traffic to the Cumberland Hotel where we met Carl Morse from Havertown, Pennsylvania and the other members of our tour. Carl, who would prove to be the Albert Einstein of Morse genealogy, and his lovely wife, Rosemary, had worked with Steve to plan a first ever England bus tour of all things "Morse". Our group seemed friendly enough but we had the usual concerns about "chemistry".

The next morning, following the first of many breakfasts highlighted by seemingly mandatory English sausages (bangers), mushrooms and baked beans, we boarded a modern tour bus to see London. Our escort, Robert Sitwil, set a tone of precision, eloquence, and dedication right off the bat... the word, "smashing!" comes to mind. On that first day, Robert showed us quintessential London sights like Buckingham Palace, London Eye, and Westminster Cathedral, but day two of our tour started the Morse "nitty-gritties" we had come for. On our way out of London, we passed Tyburn Gallows where a "long lost cousin" named Henry was hung back on January 20, 1644; his sin?...being a Catholic, a government no-no at the time, and ministering to children who had survived the recent plague.

Our ancestors, in fact, had left England back in the early 1600s because of frustration over religion. It seemed totally appropriate that the rest of Carl's tour would include visiting churches, ancient twelfth century churches, churches way out in the sticks where our 40-passenger tour bus caused many a motorist to gasp and then back up a half a mile. Our "chemistry" grew with each humorous incident and was aided and abetted by our hilarious driver, Paul Smith. By the end of day three, we were 19 Morses headed for the time of our lives. There's English "fodder" for several more stories but for the sake of brevity, I'll pick a few highlights:

Current parishioners of the Church of Stratford St. Mary, the likely church my ninth great grandfather, Samuel, attended before he came to America in 1635, feted our entire group with a supper in the parish hall. The hall was adorned for the evening with red, white and blue crepe paper and flags of both countries. Strategic seating placed us Americans with our English hosts and there, Betsy and I met a wonderful man named Chris Griffin. Chris insisted that we spend the following morning strolling his woodlot where "Bluebells", the wild flowers of Scottish fame, stood out like a blue ocean beneath six-hundred-year-old oaks.

We were invited for teas at the elegant country homes of three "well attended" English Morse families, David and Katy Morse of St. Mary Hall, Pat Mosse (a derivation of "Morse") of Mendham Priory, and Jeremy and Belinda Morse of Barrington Downs. Sir Jeremy, past head of Lloyds Bank, and inspiration for the series "Inspector Morse", and Belinda, noted author and board member of the Globe Theatre, also feted our group with a formal dinner at the Theatre on our final night! The elegance of those Morse estates and the royal receptions we received were truly the work of fairy tales!

An overnight at the Shakespeare Hotel in Stratford on Avon and a requisite visit to Stonehenge brought us toward the end of our journey and the tearful goodbye we all dreaded. Yes, by that time we were all best friends and bonded forever! Steve Wood drove Betsy and me back to Heathrow on Thursday of our trip week, where we remained nervous about potential "road blocks" for our return back across the "pond". It was only, in fact, when we presented our boarding passes at the entrance to our plane that we knew there were no glitches in our return flight. We bade a ceremonial goodbye to flying companion, Murphy... "Get out of our lives you son-of-a-gun" we said. "For you we wish a return of the Tyburn Gallows!". For us, we prayed for a safe return to Vermont, our home, and shouted a loud "here, here" for the England we had seen, loved and would remember forever. 🍁

"Old Kentucky Home"

Betsy and I got on a plane a few days ago and headed out for Bowling Green, Kentucky. It was only a three-day trip and, in spite of chilly weather and troublesome airline delays, we chalked it up as a great time. I was asked months ago to be the keynote speaker for the "Kentucky Farms are Fun Convention" there in Bowling Green. I felt honored to be asked but viewed the task as a bit daunting, thinking of vast rolling fields, million dollar horses, and miles of white board fences.

It all started with a visit by a couple gals from the Kentucky farm community two years ago. They stumbled across our place while on a fact-finding trip to Vermont and asked for a tour of our sugarhouse. I remembered talking to them about their state's special agricultural problems. It seems the flame went out a while back on Kentucky's tobacco economy, leaving tobacco farmers with sagging markets and the need to quit. Vermont, they knew, was a frontrunner in this sort of thing because its dairy industry started drying up like a sagging udder many years ago. They were impressed with the array of agri-tourism ideas that had sprung up in little old Vermont and were apparently convinced that I had something to offer because of my experience at Morse Farm.

Recently they put me in touch with Stephen Yates, Director of Agri-Tourism at the Kentucky Department of Agriculture. Stephen and I emailed back and forth about the logistics of my visit and I soon learned that this guy was a bureaucrat with a farmer's work ethic. He asked me to kick off the convention on its opening morning with high motivation, using my talents in marketing and syrupy PR...when I said that my talents were more aligned with "BS", he seemed OK with it. Through my dealings with Stephen, I knew that my reception would be with a "Y'all come on down" style of friendliness.

After our grueling trip to Nashville on cramped and tardy airplanes, we finally arrived in Bowling Green at midnight the night before my presentation. A few hours of shut-eye brought us, sleepy-eyed, to the Sloan Convention Center and the Kentucky Farms are Fun Convention. We were royally greeted by Stephen and given a few minutes to mingle with the attendees before I was ushered to the rostrum. After a few words by Kentucky agriculture officials and a very generous introduction, I took my place in front of 80 farm folk who I would soon find to be the friendliest and most receptive crowd I've ever spoken to. The true satisfaction for us, however, was at the noon hour when Betsy and I "broke bread" with individual Kentuckians. One man, Lee Blythe, greeted me with a small glass jar of Kentucky maple syrup! I was amazed that maple syrup could be made in Kentucky and, thinking of the frigid temperatures back home, a little jealous that Lee had already had the thawing weather necessary for a sap run. His family runs a bed and breakfast close to Bowling Green and Lee taps 15 maple trees. My thoughts went back to a trip I had made to Cedar Bluff, Iowa a few years earlier where I was equally amazed to find maple syrup being made. I returned home from that trip joking that I had found "the last sap bucket west". Suddenly another sweet milestone added to my library; I had now found "the last sap bucket south" in Auburn, Kentucky!

Another man explained the demise of Kentucky's tobacco industry. I was struck by his positive attitude when I asked if there was any bitterness among the farmers. His answer was clipped, more like a long word than a whole sentence... "Weget t'use ah tobaccahbahns f'somethin' else now." Betsy and I met apple and peach farmers who give orchard tours, dairy farmers who make ice cream, fish farmers and goat milkers, all with their own unique spin on the concept of "value added". We left knowing that these farmers would not only survive but they would eventually find their way into a thriving "farms are fun" market on old Kentucky tobacco land.

The flight home, once again, brought the disappointment of late airplanes and long airport stays. It was well after dark when we finally reached the East Coast. The night was perfectly clear and our pilot had pointed out landmarks along the way. When we flew over Philadelphia, I remarked to Betsy about the vastness of the city that seemed to go on forever. Our approach to Newark International Airport, in fact, confirmed that thought; I suddenly realized that Philadelphia had never "ended" but had just merged with New York's metropolitan area! When our jet banked and turned sharply a few times, I assumed is was to accommodate the dozens of other jets that dotted the sky like lightening bugs in July. On our final bank, I gazed vertically down on the lights of a world that may have overstepped environment's welcome. My thoughts went back to Bowling Green, Kentucky and those farmers who I knew were doing it right. 🍁

Woodchuck Day

Groundhog Day is a special holiday because it contains a strange magic that I've never been able to understand and it's one holiday that doesn't involve a lot of falderal. There are no gifts, trees, door hangings or lights. Groundhog Day never floods the airwaves with obnoxious ads or affects the economy in any way. There are no colored eggs (from a woodchuck...c'mon!), no green beer, and no songs about goin' "over the river and through the woods". On Groundhog Day we just sit quietly in our living rooms listening for rumors of shadows seen or not. Best of all, the state hasn't changed Groundhog Day from its day of origin to a Monday or a Friday to accommodate another long weekend. No, Groundhog Day rests on February 2 every year...always has... always will. Or will it?

Tom Beardsley over at Radio Vermont would like to turn those down country dens upside down...punch out Punxsutawney Phil, he would. Tom wants to wrest Groundhog Day from the Pennsylvanians because, number one, whatever weather the "groundhog" forecasts in Pennsylvania has nothing to do with weather up here in Vermont and, number two...they ain't groundhogs... they're woodchucks! And being a Vermont "woodchuck" myself, I kind of agree with him (for my out of state readers, native Vermonters are called "woodchucks") A few years ago, Tom went to the press with his concerns. He said a reporter from The Times Argus called down to Punxsutawney and got met with a sharp slap in the face... "Groundhog Day is ours. You Vermonters have no right to tamper with our day so just BUG OFF!". Never a quitter, Tom took that curt rebuff and ran with it. Every year since, he has staged the Vermont version of Groundhog Day over at the Rusty Parker Memorial Park in Waterbury.

On that day, Vermonters show up en mass to honor the woodchuck. In Waterbury, there are no top hats or furry fakes in presence; just real folks in various arrays of orange hunting hats and worn out Carhartts. The ceremonies always culminate in naming "Woodchuck of the Year" to chants of, what else, "BUG OFF!". Even though taking the internationally-hyped theme away from Punxsutawney, Pennsylvania remains an uphill battle, Tom Beardsley is determined to keep up the fight. However this feud plays out, thoughts of the day recently came back to me by way of my son Rob's girlfriend, Miriam Bernardo. At the same time that Tom's event was winding down over in Waterbury, Miriam described an experience she had on the theme of Vermont woodchucks. She and her dog, Tia, went for a winter walk that morning. They ended up at an old abandoned farm in our neighborhood. She said they had wandered out beyond the farm buildings and settled by a huge old maple that grew at the edge of a steep bank. All of a sudden they heard a frantic rustling and there, mere feet away, a woodchuck was attempting to climb the steep bank. She said the woodchuck was ancient, a "grandpa woodchuck with frosted whiskers and eyebrows", in her words. "Tia was afraid" she said. "She's usually ready to take on any wild animal but this time, she just cowered behind my back. The woodchuck was trying to get up the bank but kept falling back...I could see that he was angry and after several attempts, he looked in our direction."

For the rest of her story, it's necessary to point out that Miriam is one of these people who can scrunch up her face into a sea of expression and twist her voice accordingly. She described the encounter, giving voice to the woodchuck:

"What the ##*!//! you lookin' at...I'm havin' a damn poor day 'n you two ain't helpin' a bit...now be gone with ya 'n let an old man be!"

Miriam brought that old Vermont woodchuck completely to life and had Betsy and me in stitches the day she told us her story. Although the coincidence of encountering that ornery old guy on Groundhog Day was striking, I wasn't surprised that one of the beasts was up and around here in Vermont that time of year. When we are working in the late-winter sugarbush, we often see dark spots in the snow where woodchucks have dug their way out of their winter dens. As far as the Pennsylvania event goes, however, I think it's long on fable and short on substance. My guess is you could not pay a Pennsylvania groundhog enough in green clover to be out that time of year checking on the weather!

I wish Tom Beardsley well with his campaign. This year his event benefitted the families of our soldiers and the Vermont "woodchucks" came out in droves to support that truly genuine cause. I love Vermont because things here are real...woodchucks, walks in the woods and knowing winter'll end when winter ends, groundhogs or woodchucks, shadows or not. 🍁

A Springtime Song

One day a while back I put on my other hat as a jazz musician and made my annual trip up to Johnson State College to be a judge for an elementary/middle school jazz festival. It was a rather unorthodox ride up this year because of the route I took; normally my "one track" mind leads me on the dirt road short cut to Route 12 in Worcester but I exercised my one once-a-year exception on dirt roads that day: "never in mud season"! I got in my car and turned left, down County Road to Montpelier where I took an "all blacktop" ride up toward Morrisville. Just before I left, Betsy asked if I wanted a great music CD for the road but I turned her down... "CD player's busted" I said, which was the truth but I had a different sort of "music" on my mind.

Lately I've been thinking a lot about spring peepers because their music just started here in Vermont; In fact I was right there for the downbeat. It happened recently in the middle of the morning when I was out on our acreage with the tractor. We had gotten a permit to burn a pile of brush. I had just reached the pile and shut off the tractor's engine. As you may know, we have had way too much rain around here lately but at that point in time, the sun had made a momentary "surprise appearance". Instantly my mind went from the doldrums into a state of peak awareness. I remember looking at the nearby trees and seeing the beginnings of leaves and hearing from a couple crows somewhere in the distance. "This is good" I thought... "can't wait till summer blossoms". And then it happened...like the Mormon Tabernacle Choir on steroids... "HAL-LE-LU-JAH...HAL-LE-LU-JAH... HAL-LE-HAY-LU-JAHHHH!"...the world was ALIVE with peepers! Their burst of song came in triple forte and not just from their usual swamp but from all directions...hell our whole farm is nothing but a swamp these days! They continued all the rest of that day and were still at it when I woke up the next morning.

This puzzled me because I thought Pseudacris Crucifer, our common spring peepers, were nocturnal; had they suddenly changed their modus operandi? If they had, I was OK with it because I love those little buggers. I decided to start early and dedicate my day in Johnson to the peepers as well as the students. As I headed up Route 12 from Montpelier to Morrisville, I celebrated my "day off the farm" with wide-open windows, the radio turned off, and an ear peeled for peepers. It seemed, in fact, that their song followed me right up Route 12 past Wrightsville Dam where water was critically high, and on to the brooks and swamps north of Worcester. I stopped at a pull-off by wetlands on both sides of the road up close to Elmore. "Should get 'em in stereo here" I thought, but when the car stopped and I shut off the engine, there were no peepers. Strangely, when I continued on, they started up again. I was almost in Johnson when all of a sudden I socked myself hard in the forehead. "Hell those ain't peepers at all", I scolded myself; I had been warned at my last car checkup of a noisy left front wheel bearing!

As usual, I was very impressed at the quality of music coming from those students at Johnson. While there, I did poll several people from different areas of Vermont about the presence of spring peepers in their communities. Some said they had heard 'em; others had not but all of them looked at me a little strangely as though I suffered from some kind of Springtime malady... maybe a bit of "post sugaring stress disorder".

I came home through Stowe because there are some big swamps in that neck of the woods. My trip was largely uneventful ; the only "peep" I heard, in fact, was from that front wheel bearing...Argh...stupid, STUPID! I fully expected the creatures to be singing when I drove in to my yard but they weren't. "They must have declared a 'weather' day" I thought as I zipped up my jacket and went out into the atmosphere which had turned bitter cold. The next time I heard them was a few days later when our temperatures turned warmer but their song was much less raucous. These days our neighborhood Pseudacris Crucifers are lulling me to sleep every night but have silenced by morning time. They are, indeed, nocturnal. The more I think of it, their raucous, twenty-four hour debut was quite predictable; just like the rest of us, it's a long, cold winter and when the first warm sunny day of Spring comes along, all God's creatures come alive with exceptional vitality, even the spring peepers... "REJOICE" they sing. " WINTER'S OVER"! 🍁

A Day Off the Farm

I'm suffering from a drought of creativity this morning as the rain comes pouring down on yet another day...what in the world should I write about this time? S'pose I could simply call it a vacation and "blow off" my deadline two weeks from today but I'm not very good at vacations. Speaking of days off, I'm off the farm today playing music starting with a 10:00 AM parade way down in Walpole, New Hampshire...hmmm, by golly, I think I've got my title: "A Day in My Life Off the Farm".

Before I get started, Betsy envelopes me with a huge raincoat, seals the front Velcro like a Ziploc bag and finishes with a stern pat... "now don't leave it anywhere like you have all your travel mugs!". I say goodbye and walk to the car carrying my horn and accessories plus a full, uncovered cup of coffee. "Keep the raincoat on till you finish that coffee" she hollers. I pile all my stuff in, drive off, and as County Road's frost heaves and potholes kick in I think, "God, she's smart"!

I twist and turn through an early morning Montpelier using my favorite shortcut for I-89. The wipers make an annoying "shhhhishhh...KLUURBB...shhhhishh...KLUURBB...shhhhhishh...KLUURBB" leaving only a tiny fan-shaped hole that I can see out of way down low. I scrunch down and kick myself one more time for not replacing those blades. At the cloverleaf I-89 south, I glance to my left and there, standing high on the unmowed bank, is a group of Black-Eyed Susans. Even at my ripe old age of 63, Black-Eyed Susans symbolize the beginning of school to me and school just ended a week ago...what's going on with nature these days? I merge with the traffic, turning my thoughts to Buttercups instead, the true "end of school flower" (and to be fair, the Vermont world is full of Buttercups these days). As I get close to Randolph, the billboards warn: "Sharon Southbound Rest Area Closed, I-91 Hartford Southbound Rest Area Closed". Even though that coffee hasn't started "speaking" to me yet, I stop at the Randolph Rest Area. As I enter the small, well-appointed building, I think it a pity that the economy has caused the shutdown of so many public rest areas...the economy of bladders...I chuckle at the thought! It seems in Randolph, the state is allowing the emptying of bladders southbound but not northbound. Just down the road in Sharon, it's just the opposite with the lavish Vietnam Veterans Welcome Center on the northbound side right across the highway from a demolished southbound rest area. Before I leave Randolph, I draw a cup of the Green Mountain coffee that's always available at these Vermont facilities and stuff a dollar bill in the donation box...rest areas may die but hospitality lives on!

By the time I get to White River Junction, the coffee has definitely kicked in. I get off the highway, head directly to McDonalds, and rush for the Men's room. On my way out, that same old "economy of the bladder" leads me to the counter (rest rooms need to be paid for in one way or another you know). "Number four with OJ please" I say to a sleepy looking counter girl thinking of it more as accounts payable than food. It does, however, taste great as I head out on the final leg of my trip to Walpole. Contrary to Central Vermont, Walpole is blessed with sunshine and is bustling with flags, folks in uniform and an expectant public starting to line the streets. I go to the elementary school and find East Bay Jazz Ensemble's Gerry Grimo somewhere in the confusion of a parade forming up. Gerry has hired me for three different gigs that day starting with a Dixieland quintet aboard a Ford Ranger pickup. After the parade, we join Gerry's full big band to play a concert in Walpole's village park and then another one ten miles down the road in Westmoreland, New Hampshire.

The concerts are over by mid-afternoon. I pack up my horn, say goodbye to the guys, and head north. Most of my trip home is accompanied by southern New Hampshire sunshine but rain rejoins my day as I approach Central Vermont. That's OK though...the music, as always, has brightened my attitude and I'm ready to go back to work on the farm. As I turn toward Montpelier at Exit 8, I glance to my right...yup, the rain's pouring down but that's just part of life, a life full of flukes and short summers where even Black-Eyed Susans and Buttercups can both blossom at the same time on the same roadside bank. ✤

Happy Sailin'

What's in a name? If it's 'Montpelier' the capital, it originated from a combination of "mont - hill, and peller - bare or shorn" according to Wikipedia. If it's 'Montpelier', the boat, it originated from the Los Angeles class of nuclear submarines that always get named for state capitals. Cities... boats...you might write off any further connection as just too 'fishy' but hold on just one minute. You see, the USS Montpelier's crew has been coming to its namesake city for years to march in our Independence Day Parade. They're such nice guys that Montpelier, the city, rolls out the red carpet and on occasion, even sends them some maple syrup. Although a little sweetening never does any harm, it's not necessary in this case...our relationship with these guys has always been like a gentle sail on a calm sea. That, in fact, is just what a few of us Montpelierites did the other day. Our journey began at Burlington International Airport where seven of us met for a flight to Jacksonville, Florida. The Montpelier's commanding officer, Christopher Harkins, had extended us a VIP invitation to come aboard and we were psyched. By the end of the first day, two things had been confirmed: the weather would be perfect for our sail the next day and the chemistry of our group was as wondrous as the weather.

Early on June 17, we joined a dozen other Vermonters and boarded a tugboat for the five mile ride out to where the 362 foot long Montpelier floated. Part of the way out, the huge submarine appeared as a tiny spear. The spear got bigger and bigger until we could see it was supported by a bridge and below, a huge dark body lurked mostly under the surface. As we slowed and approached the monolith, we were each handed a life jacket to strap into while the tug jockeyed around for the transfer. Half a dozen friendly-looking sailors stood on top of the main body, close to a hatch just slightly bigger around then a basketball hoop. The rail-sided ramp we walked down was steep and moved with the ocean. Once on the Montpelier's surface, the sailors helped each of us into the hatch. Climbing the vertical ladder down to the bowels of the craft reminded me of navigating our old Unadilla silo.

Once we were all inside, we were led a short distance to the mess hall which looked like it had been built for midgets. We were welcomed, briefed, breakfasted and divided into groups of six to spend the next 11 hours walking painfully narrow hallways and loving every minute of it. The Montpelier's technology was, of course, mind-boggling but even more impressive were the young sailors from the boyish-looking Commander Harkins on down to each and every seaman aboard. They were all extra courteous, willing to explain the ins and outs of running a submarine and proud of their mission.

While the ship sailed 80 miles to the Continental Shelf, we all had a chance to don heavy duty harnesses and climb 30 feet up to the bridge. Standing leashed to the bridge's rounded surface was like standing on a giant beach ball. In front of us, the sub's mammoth snout parted the Atlantic waters at 25 knots and turning around carefully...very carefully...we witnessed a Niagara Falls-sized froth spewing from the aft. We all agreed, being up there on a glorious day in the blue Atlantic was one of the most unique experiences possible on planet Earth.

It took us three hours to reach the Shelf and then we did what submarines do best...we dove to a depth as deep as the hills that surround Montpelier, the city, are high. First to 150 feet and then down to 700 feet we dove. We did, in submarine lingo, some "angles and dangles" which required bracing against something solid as the floor below us sloped and banked. Some of us even had a turn at the wheel (I'm an expert tractor driver but proved a dismal failure at driving a submarine!). We lingered in the deep long enough to witness 146 professionals run an amazing course with their amazing machine.

Our return to terra firma included a sad goodbye to the crew and another tugboat ride. As though on orders from the US Navy, a happy committee of porpoises appeared portside and escorted us into the harbor. We faced a return flight to Vermont early the next morning and were tired from our long day at sea. It was a perfect North Florida night, however, and our hotel's poolside begged the lifting of a glass or two...here's to a long and loving relationship between our two dear Montpeliers. ❧

Let Joy In

This morning I saw a cartoon in the New Yorker magazine that not only made me chuckle but relates to a couple of experiences I've recently had. Although I usually try hard to avoid subjects like politics, religion, or anything else that might put me on "thin ice", I'm a Vermont farmer with a mind of my own. So, I s'pose you wouldn't want me to "blow my cork" just tryin' to hold somethin' in, would ya?

The cartoon was captioned "Great-Great Grandson of Godzilla". It pictured a very embarrassed looking Godzilla "pussy-footing" among people, cars, and miscellaneous collateral he had crushed while strolling through New York City. There's two dialogue "bubbles" above him. In one, he says "Oh God! I'm so, sorry!!" and in the other, "I'm such a klutz!!". Obvious meaning: our modern generation is "kinder and gentler" sometimes to the point of silliness. Although "kinder and gentler" works for me to a large degree (seems as though the violence and the wars we're seeing these days are way out of control), I believe that some of our modern day thinking lacks a bit of common sense.

My first experience: I was traveling to the Mount Washington Hotel the other night to play music with the Swing North Big Band. My route took me through the quaint village of Bethlehem, New Hampshire. Bethlehem is a typical New England village with just one exception...there's a summer population of Hasidic Jewish people there who are very "front and center". They walk the streets of Bethlehem in their somber black garb and having seen them several times now, I've taken them on as a Bethlehem "trademark". Just for fun, I googled them to get a little more familiar; I found that they come from New York City and have been summering in Bethlehem since 1916. Their black apparel originates from an 18th century decree and the unique sideburns they wear are called "sidelocks". Early in my research, the descriptive word "joy" popped up which surprised me. Their black attire speaks of piety and spirituality, and I was glad to know they are "joyful" as well. I'm also glad to welcome them as part of the public scene in Bethlehem, New Hampshire.

My second experience: On July 3rd, I was popping kettle corn down at the Montpelier Independence Day Celebration. From the vantage point of my tent down on State Street, I could see a large group of folks all clad in sky blue performing way up on the Statehouse steps. I was impressed with the precision of their choreography and, thanks to amplification, realized they were singing a joyful mixture of Christian and patriotic music; "Perfect for this occasion" I thought, as my popper reached a crescendo and I poured out yet another batch of steaming kettle corn. All of a sudden a red-faced woman approached... "It's wrong that they're allowed to sing their Jesus stuff on the Statehouse steps!" she shouted in my face, spitting the word "Jesus". I wondered why she chose me as a sounding post and considered giving her a "pass" with a simple shrug of my shoulders but my own emotions erupted like a bottle rocket... "Ma'am, you're talking to the wrong person...I LIKE it!". And there we stood nose to nose for what seemed like ages until she finally did an about-face and stormed off grumbling.

I'll never forget my little episode of personal "fireworks" on that July 3rd. Thankfully we live in a country where freedom of speech and religion is allowed. Yes, the "separation of church and state" is important but we need to be realistic with it; whether its religious messages at the dooryard of our statehouse or on the public sidewalks of Bethlehem, New Hampshire, I LIKE it...we need more joy in this world wherever it pops up and whatever form it takes. 🍂

Bye to a Great Friend

There's never been a time in my life when there wasn't a "Barn Across the Road", except for now. It started earlier this summer when my son, Tommy, looked the old thing over and concluded that it was 'terminal'; time to salvage the few timbers that were still OK. He began the process of clearing out the accumulated detritus of the past century, much of it thrown in haphazardly during my tenure at the Morse Farm. By mid-summer, Betsy and I had joined in the effort, 'mucking' out alternating trailers loads for the scrap yard and the landfill.

The old barn was born of hand-hewn timbers and wide, Hemlock boards shortly after the Civil War. Even though its original purpose as a hay barn had evolved to wood chip storage at the end, there were still two hay scaffolds separated by a wide open path for wagons to enter one side and exit the other. The barn originally had a hay hoist system consisting of a steel track bolted to the heavy-duty ridge pole, a trolley, and huge steel claws which were suspended by ropes. The claws would swoop down, grab huge clumps of loose hay from waiting wagons and then whisk them away to different points in the scaffolds. It was a perfect system for the times but systems, like people, change, get old, die.

Tommy started disassembling the barn, "peeling it like an onion" from high on its roof where modern sheet aluminum covered aged cedar shingles. Betsy worked the narrow clapboards that had been nailed weakly to a layer of barn boards. The barn boards had weathered to about one half their original thickness, telling us that the old structure had spent much of its life without the clapboards. Betsy remarked about the number of shims and the jagged cuts on both layers of its siding but as we exposed the posts and beams of its frame, we were struck by the quality and workmanship. I suddenly realized why the term, 'framing', was used so much back in the old days...those folks put their "heart and souls" in the frames of buildings but shortchanged the facades...hmmm...sometimes it seems the opposite in our artificial world of today. We marveled at the old barn's multiple personalities and the secrets that seemed to offer with each board we took off; we even found liquor bottles stashed deep within its bowels, no doubt left by some hired man long forgotten!

We finally talked Tommy into abandoning his work high up on the steep roof when several people stopped and warned us of the danger he was in. One neighbor said he lost a whole night's sleep worrying that the barn would collapse and Tommy would end up badly injured or worse. Suddenly our strategy changed from "rescue to recovery" and we made plans to pull it over with our tractor. On the appointed day, Tommy climbed a ladder and hitched a chain to a key timber about half way up the barn's south side. I positioned my tractor at a safe distance away, put her down into 'grandpa' gear, threw her into 4-wheel drive, and crept ahead to tension the four chains that were linked together.

On the first few pulls, the tractor just "snorted and pawed" like a bull getting ready for some real action. The old barn offered little more than a few creaks and a scattering of dust. I kept backing up, setting over, and nudging the accelerator toward more horsepower. Finally there was a key cracking sound and some real movement. Knowing the next pull would end the life of the barn that had served nobly for so many years, I paused out of respect. Tommy stood a distance away, seemingly at attention. From the vantage point that was so familiar, the farmhouse across the road, my brother recorded the scene with his camera. Finally I inched ahead. The old barn made one last groan, flexed in the middle, and gently bowed to the ground. We inspected the remains and found much more rot than we expected. The last of the old barn's secrets came out; somewhere back in time, it had spent a few years with a leaky roof.

We all went home with a "rained on" feeling ourselves, knowing that it would take time to heal our grief. In the meantime, my thoughts go out to old barns everywhere. I know you're being slowly replaced by a motley collection of flat-roofed and plastic covered wanna-be's but times are pointing to the possible resurrection of your kin. Until that time, I'll just say "Well done good and faithful servant...rest in peace, dear Barn Across the Road." 🌿

Another 'Burr'

Vermont is full of contrasts, like maple sugar and dill pickles, high peaks and deep valleys, winter and summer, smart folks and, well...let's just say the "judgmentally challenged". This writing concerns the latter group; my good wife, Betsy, is smarter'n a whip most of the time but once in a while she has a lapse that comes outa nowhere and affects you like a slap in the head. First of all, she's smart enough to work in the field of mental health which brings, in addition to a fair salary, a sense of sanity-by-osmosis...yes, I know, some would argue that point in my case. She's also great help on the farm thanks to a Mount Holly, Vermont heritage. Mount Holly, Vermont is a place where the work ethic grows on trees and common sense is in the water. Betsy's never happier than when she's out in the woods with me and our Black Lab, Averill, throwin' wood onto a trailer. But once this summer, I also needed her help canning syrup.

Although I'm sure she would rather have returned to the woods, that Mount Holly work ethic led her, uncomplaining, to our canning room which is deep in the bowels of our store. She settled into canning like a duck floats on water but there was something about the murky pool at her feet that bothered her.

"You got a drain problem?" she asked. "Yes" I said... "damn thing's been bothering for years. I've run a small hardware store snake down there several times. Once I even hired that professional guy with his special roto-tool. It was a "monster snake" hooked up to a motor that propelled it, pulsing and twisting from the bottom end up the entire drain system. He really worked that thing hard, repeating the process several times before finally shaking his head in defeat and handing me a bill for $200.00."

I could see that Betsy wasn't buying a word of my suggestion that the drain couldn't be unplugged. When she asked if I had tried a plunger, I gently replied that I didn't think a plunger was the right tool for the job. "Plunger indeed," I thought, "real men don't use plungers!" The next thing I knew, she had 'flown' upstairs and returned with a plunger from the utility closet. She positioned it over the drain and began pumping like a mad woman. All of a sudden, she lifted the plunger and there, right before our eyes, one loud 'slurrrrp' took away both the problem drain water and my pesky male righteousness! That drain has worked great ever since, thanks to one determined woman and a simple tool that "real men don't use!".

Before you assume that Betsy's intelligence is indelible, another of our recent workdays revealed her "judgmentally challenged" side.

We started the day by working on the barn across the road that we've been tearing down. By mid morning we had had enough of the barbs and slivers of old boards and beams and decided to head out to cut wood. Betsy worked relentlessly, tossing the smaller blocks and rolling the larger ones that I bobbed off with my chainsaw. After we had accumulated several sizable piles, we shifted our efforts to splitting. Betsy lifted the blocks onto the splitter while I worked the lever; converse to my plunger theory, "only real men handle hydraulic levers"! About halfway through the day I noticed her limping slightly. She quickly passed off my queries saying, "I'm alright...got some kind of 'burr' in my sock...no big deal...I'll tend to it."

Toward the end of the day, we got a call that there were 300 bales of hay to pick up over at the neighbor's place and time was of the essence...rain was heading our way. We left the woods, hitched onto the trailer, and headed toward our next endeavor, lickity-split. When we arrived, we drove slowly out into the sea of square bales; you guessed it, I drove and Betsy threw 'em on! Her limp seemed to be worse but the approaching rainstorm chased us to finish. After three trips, we were finally done and ready to go home to hot showers and blessed rest.

As we entered the house, she went immediately to the chair close to the door. "Balls on a heifer, will you look at that!" she said, using a good old Mount Holly expression, as she whipped off her sneakers. There, protruding up the inside of her shoe, was a good sized nail that she had picked up earlier in the day while working on the old barn. Her face showed embarrassment as she showed me the bane of her workday. She threw the sneaker into a corner and carried on almost euphorically. "Boy" she said... "Life is really good without that nail sticking into my foot!".

We went on to other workdays after that, resuming the barn destruction and building bigger woodpiles. Betsy and I laughed often about that 'nail' episode and ended up accepting it as a metaphor for life; sometimes the obvious eludes us...a drain stays plugged for years in want of a simple plunger and work schedules sometimes trump pain. It's all part of the 'recipe' here in Vermont, right along with the maple sugar, dill pickles and a dash of "judgmentally challenged". 🍂

Welcome to "Moose" Farm

Having been in the Vermont tourism business for a long time, I know what our visitors come here to see. Of course "maple" tops the list...woe to any Vermont tourist who fails to return home without a few containers of our famous liquid...but I bet you'll be surprised at number two. If you happen to be thinking "Sound of Music, Ethan Allen or the Jersey cow" you'd be wrong. No, those things have all had their "day in the sun" but tourists follow trends wherever they go, even coming to Vermont. Give up?...it's the moose...that's the guy everyone wants to see!

We get all types here at Morse Farm and more than once, we've had folks roll in thinking they were coming to "Moose" Farm! One European woman, in fact, got downright ugly the day she came:

"But you promised me a Moose" she said, raising her voice.

"I...I...don't think so" stuttered our young female employee.

"It's right here!" the woman shouted to the girl, violently rolling her "Rs" and stabbing our brochure.

"Uhh...madam...that says 'Morse', not 'moose'" said the now confident girl.

The woman, seeing no humor, quickly about-faced, retreated to her car and headed down the road caring less about maple syrup tours and the like... more than ever, she wanted to see a moose!

Yes, folks from away all crave a viewing of Alces alces, the animal that looks as foolish as its Latin name sounds. How do I describe a moose...God's mistake?, A cartoon character come alive and gone berserk?, A horse wannabe on stilts? Moose are more awkward than Seinfeld's Kramer, possibly dumber than Gleason's Kramden, and as sought after as Nazareth's Christ...I hear beseeching words everyday, "Where do I see a moose?".

I always tell em "the woods are full of moose" but to be careful and not meet one the wrong way. Twice, I've had "close encounters of the moose kind" on my way home from a music gig at night. I was lucky both times, unlike many humans who lose their lives in moose/car collisions. One time, my friend Harl and I had played with the Vermont Jazz Ensemble in Rutland and were returning to Central Vermont well after midnight. We had just passed over Mendon Mountain and were entering the big woods in Killington. I usually drive at a good clip through those woods but that night, a combination of light fog and heavy conversation had slowed me right down. We had just rounded an S curve when all of a sudden a dark form filled the windshield. "What the?" I exclaimed punching the brake pedal and thinking UFO at the same time. It was only after my car stopped inches from the huge obstruction that we realized it was a moose, biggest moose I had ever seen. Sometimes moose hang around for a little "get acquainted" session but this one was on a mission. It moved off as quickly as it had appeared, back into the woods on the other side of the road. Harl and I continued our journey home, slowly and feeling very lucky.

The other moose incident happened just recently over in Sugar Hill, New Hampshire. I had played a community concert with the Swing North Big Band and had headed west toward home on windy Route 117 when I passed a mailbox being held by a carved bear. "That's cool", I thought, and then directly around the next corner stood the silhouette of a moose in the same position. I had just begun to think how creative those New Hampshire folks are when suddenly that "mailbox" walked out in front of me! Luckily I was able to stop the car in time and, unlike the Killington moose, this guy stood there seemingly insistent on a little "quality time". He nosed my Honda for a spell before he slowly turned and ambled away, unfortunately choosing the "path most followed". My escort led us along the next few miles at a snail's pace until something else took his fancy. As quickly as he had appeared, he exited left and disappeared back into the wilds west of Sugar Hill.

Yup, we're lucky here in the North Country to have natural phenomena like maple syrup and moose, things that draw tourists like oceans and Disney Worlds do in other states. Sometimes I feel we have maligned these beasts with words like "stupid" or "goofy". They're actually quite dynamic...they're elusive like movie stars, they never mean harm, and they work to keep our countryside neat and trim. All my "encounters" with moose so far have been positive (including some mighty tasty moose stew that Betsy recently made). As far as my most recent moose encounter...the one in Sugar Hill...I'm glad the guy wasn't a mailbox. No, he made my trip back home more interesting than even a creative mailbox could but since moose are never "stayed by snow nor rain nor heat nor gloom of night", you better watch out for them on our roads and always drive slowly. 🍂

No Bull

Roy and Molly were over at our place a while back helping us out with a problem. I was very impressed with the job they did and hinted that I might write about it. Roy, the modest one, said to write about Molly and not him but I couldn't do that...they're a team, madly in love with each other, a match made in heaven. One morning each week they have a date for breakfast at Joe's Pond Cafe. Roy says he always orders the same thing for her, scrambled eggs, and she dutifully cleans and returns her plate. Roy's wife, Jackie, probably doesn't know a thing about it but, you see, it probably doesn't matter...Roy Folsom is a dairy farmer from Cabot and Molly's a McNab Shepherd. For those unfamiliar, a McNab Shepherd is a cross between a Border Collie, Fox Shepherd and a Whippet...just think "Border Collie" but even better.

Back in early summer, our son Tommy fenced in an area out front of our place and brought in two Herford beef critters. They were pretty out there in the green countryside and when he approached me with the idea of getting them bred, somehow memories of the days when my dad and I once had 60 of the high-strung, labor intensive beasts eluded me. Tommy became discouraged when he checked into artificial insemination...it seems those outfits required everything from his bank balance to his grandfather's sperm count before they would provide service. I suggested he call my friend, Roy for advice...enter a handsome Holstein fella that soon arrived in Roy's pickup-pulled horse trailer.

Ferdinand spent the late summer grazing with the girls and when a veterinarian gave us two thumbs up for pregnancies in November, we knew he had done more than graze. Roy couldn't pick him up until after Christmas but that wasn't a problem for us; he was a well-behaved guest and there was plenty of hay. It was only when those three critters figured out that snow had grounded out our electric fence that things started to change. Their daily jaunts across the fence and out onto our acreage wouldn't have been a problem if they hadn't coincided with the beginning of cross country ski season. In the winter, there are 15 miles of groomed ski trails rolling gently over our land and those three critters seemed determined to try out every inch of them!

My house overlooks the beginning of those trails and one morning, I woke early to witness a sleekly dressed skier doing battle "ski pole to snout" with a threatening Ferdinand. I jumped into my outdoor clothes faster'n a Boston fireman and headed out there with a bucket of grain. Thankfully, the man was forgiving and Ferdy quickly turned his interest toward the contents of my bucket. He and his two girlfriends gladly followed me back to their enclosure. The following days delivered many more of those return jaunts which were always complicated by our skiers trying to help; it takes real skill to herd cattle and those neophytes were reeking Holstein havoc.

When the day arrived for our "guest" to be picked up, old Ferdy was on the loose again. Roy was clearly frustrated as he pulled in with his horse trailer full of steel gates and other paraphernalia designed to coerce a critter into a crate. "Not good!" he grumbled, just before going into drill sergeant mode. Ferdinand stood at a distance, skeptically watching us fasten the gates into a temporary chute leading to the trailer. Once finished, Roy ordered Tommy, my brother Elliott and me into positions outside the corral and then went for his best weapon, Molly. That's when the real magic started.

Molly followed her master to a stone's throw distance of Ferdinand and froze at his icy command to sit. Then Roy crouched down, patted her back and said something to her softly. Suddenly they were complete, two parts of a whole... they had a plan. He barked his final order and she darted for the bull. Molly was like a tumbleweed with a brain, one millisecond ahead of Ferdinand's every move to escape. From our battle points we witnessed the huge beast drawn irrevocably, like water in a vortex, into the chute. Miraculously he bounded up the ramp and into the security of the horse trailer. The three of us Morses stood, mouths agape, at the professionalism we had just seen.

I recently stopped by Roy's farm over in Cabot to thank him again. He and Molly came out from the milk house, Roy in a much more relaxed mood than when I last saw him. Molly greeted me exuberantly and then insisted that I participate in the 'toss" portion of her ball game. In chatting with Roy, I learned that one of Molly's brothers is employed at an Air Force base in Maryland. His job is to herd wild geese, while discouraging them to fly, off the runway...wow, such a family...now we know how old Noah filled up that ark; he had a couple'a McNab Shepherds! 🍁

DNA Project

This morning Betsy and I were in a descending elevator at the Fairfield Inn in Amesbury, Massachusetts. The same elevator carried two Asian businessmen and a chambermaid with a cart full of cleaning supplies. Being a slow elevator, there was plenty of time for us to "size" each other up as folks do in those situations. The two businessmen seemed to be alternating quick sideways glances at my front with questioning looks at each other when suddenly Betsy figured it out. "My God Burr" she blurted. "Take a look at that name tag you're wearing." I reached down and fingered the plastic sleeve that introduced me as "Burr Morse, DNA Project"! Ice broken, the two slick-suited businessmen were still laughing when the door opened and we all spilled out onto the ground floor.

We were at a convention of the Morse Society and the exact words on my name tag were "Burr Morse, Samuel Line, DNA Project"...translation: I descend from a Samuel Morse who immigrated from England in 1635 and I am participating in a DNA project to determine if my Samuel is related to a Joseph of the same era ; to a layman, however, my name tag could well have meant "this guy is some kind of a Frankenstein wannabe" and in my pre-coffee state, I'm sure that I "looked" the part!

Betsy and I are new to the field of genealogy so, to fortify us for the day ahead filled with seminars and God only knew what else, we were heading to the hotel's Continental breakfast. Although my immediate needs included only a cup of strong coffee, for some reason Burr Morse, "DNA Project", headed straight toward a waffle iron that sat on the sidelines. Oddly, instead of tending to my coffee needs, I filled a cup with the mix and started fumbling with rest of the waffle-making process. I had poured the mix onto the griddle and clamped the machine together when somewhere in the two minute wait, it hit me like a ton of bricks...I, Burr Morse, maple sugarmaker, had never before been in the position of having to use artificial pancake syrup! I knew it was time, however, when Betsy, always the mother, chided "now Burr...you got yourself into this...now you get yourself out of this!"

Figuring I might as well be "hanged for a murderer as a thief", I picked up two little peel-back plastic containers, one labeled ""*Smatter's' (name changed) Sugar Free Breakfast Syrup" and the other, simply "House Breakfast Syrup". When the machine beeped, I unclamped it, lifted out a perfectly formed waffle and headed to the table where Betsy sat grinning like a Cheshire cat. To insure a true "apples to apples" experience, I spread out a generous layer of butter and then emptied each "syrup" on different sides of the waffle. Finally, like a fraternity novitiate about to swallow a live mouse, I sliced off a piece from the "House Breakfast Syrup" side, closed my eyes, and popped it in my mouth. In fairness to the process, I will say it was not terrible, just "terribly sweet with a non-descript flavor" and much thicker than pure maple syrup (think 90 weight gear lube on a January morning). I swallowed, took several gulps of water, and turned to the sugar free side. I closed my eyes again, braced myself for that "live mouse" which by this point was squirming and squeaking, and "in she went". All of a sudden, the contents of my mouth became a weapon...spwhew...the projectile flew across our table and splatted in Betsy's lap. Instantly all breakfast-nook eyes turned to Burr Morse, "DNA Project", whose face was as red as a strawberry tart...all I could think of as we emptied our refuse and left the breakfast area that morning was a new and modified slogan... "With a name like Smatter's, it's got to be disgusting"!

I finally got my coffee and we ended up having a wonderful time at the Morse Society Convention. At home the next day, I decided to "close the book" on my little foray in artificial syrup land by testing that new "Log Cabin" syrup that has recently been in the news. I went down to our local supermarket and, sure enough, quickly located it as reported, bumper-to-bumper with the pure maple syrup (Canadian). Feeling like a thief, I looked both ways, quickly grabbed a pint of the stuff and hurried to the checkout counter holding it close to my body. I placed it and a ten dollar bill directly into the cashier's hands, hoping that would expedite my little secret when all of a sudden the words boomed, "Burr Morse...What are you doing!". I looked around and there stood my cousin Pam "Morse" Everingham just two people behind me. Knowing I had been foiled, I announced to the immediate surroundings "just research Pam", and in as official a voice as I could muster, "We're going to get to the bottom of this."

Once home, I unbagged my purchase and placed it on the kitchen counter.

In corporate marketing excellence, the New Jersey company that makes the stuff chose a real maple syrup jug for packaging. The jug's front prominently boasts words like "family tradition since 1887" and "all natural"...hmmm.... strikingly similar to our own "pure maple" language. On the back, microscopic print used words like "xanthan gum", "citric acid" and yes, "Maple [4%]"... translation: this stuff is no more related to pure Vermont maple syrup than a strip mall is to a lemonade stand! Turned off, I quickly opened the jug and tasted it...you guessed it...absolutely putrid! Lastly, I walked to the kitchen sink and dumped the $5.49 jug full down the drain...case closed.

I'm proud to know my immediate "line" back to 1635...Old Samuel put out some good genes, he did! It'll be interesting when the results of that DNA test come in and the "Samuels" find out a possible relationship with the "Josephs". In the meantime I'll be content in a world of "givens" where a "Morse is a Morse", justice always prevails, and there ain't nothin' like pure Vermont maple syrup! 🍁

Personalities and Change

Livestock, just like people, have to change their M.O. this time of year and with the snow we've already seen, they already have that "I'm ready" look in their eyes. November grass is but a meager "appetizer" for the beasts so Tommy is now feeding out hay and I sure like his system. Compared with the old days of a dusty mountain of square bales under a huge roof, his modern hay system is as simple as opening a bag of sauerkraut. Sauerkraut, you say? Yup, where we used to fight mother nature all summer long trying to get hay bone-dry, modern farmers like Tommy put it up full of moisture and enclose it in a giant baggie. Forage hay, as they call it, sits and sours in those baggies that stretch out in fields like huge white worms.

Another contrast between my era and modern times is the method by which the hay is fed out. All that is necessary these days is a circular frame where the thousand pound bales are placed and a bucket loader fitted with a medieval-looking spear to place them there. The circular frame stands out in the open air where critters are happiest and is stocked with hay twenty four-seven for buffet-style feeding. Believe it or not, bovines can be very fussy eaters; back in the old days they'd pick at dry hay like children pick at vegetables but sour smelling forage hay is "filet mignon" to them!

The other day Tom was away so I took my turn at feeding his hungry beasts. I opened the baggie, put the tractor into "grandpa gear" and stabbed into the first bale. A simple nudge on the hydraulic lever removed the bale from the bag and I drove with it a short distance to the pasture. Tom's beef cows crowded the tractor as I approached the circular feeder, lifted the bale again and carefully lowered it into place...voila....simple as that the feeding was done! I drove away thinking of the old days; much of my youth was marred by violent bouts of snuffling and sneezing because of my allergies to hay dust but feeding had to be done at both ends of the day, allergies be damned. Another contrast to my old days is Tommy's system of handling his cows.

He built a small barn close to the hay feeder so when he needs to catch any of the critters, he simply leads them with a bucket of grain into the barn's gated area and slams the gate. Bovines spend 99% of their lives dumber than a stonewall but the remaining 1%, the period where they figure out some human wants to catch them, finds them "Einstein" smart. In my time, we never had a good cow catching system. We'd lead them with grain up to a point but they'd always reach that "Einstein" stage at the last minute and scatter quicker'n a fallin' cow plop. Having been around critters my whole life, I know the look of that sudden wisdom. It starts with a slight stiffening of ears and tail followed by a change in their eyes; their eyes instantly go from dumb cow-eyes to piercing lasers, a universal sign that the game has been lost. Lunging for them or any other fast movement will always result in cows heading for the county line and the only antidote is time. It takes only a short amount of time for them to dumb down so you can always try again.

We recently had to catch two critters of a different ilk here at Morse Farm. Every summer a farmer up in the Northeast Kingdom loans us two Alpacas to serve as "ambassadors" for children who come here. We have to return them to him every fall and this year, we had a particularly hard time catching them. Over the years, we have found Alpacas to be quite docile but this year, it was almost like one of them had learned a few tricks from the beef cows. Three of us, my brother Elliott, Tommy and I approached the long-neck critters with halters. We caught one of them easily and tied him to the board fence but the other one got that "laser" look in his eyes. Finally after giving him a lengthy "dumbing down" period, we got him in the corral area that, in romantic, cowboy terms means "roll up yer sleeves pardner n' rope 'im"...to three Vermont woodchucks it means "git ready for the beatin' of your life!". After several painful attempts, we got the beast cornered. Elliott said "heard once th' way t'catch a 'paca' is t'grab em around th'neck" and I, point man, was the logical one to leap. Not wanting to lose this rascal again, I simply ignored that inner voice that screamed "Don't!" and lunged, fully prepared to be sent "alpackin'". I locked my arms around the soft, fuzzy neck and just like that, his huge kind eyes looked into my own as if to say "OK fella, I give up."

We easily loaded them into the truck and as Elliott drove off toward the Kingdom with those two Alpacas, I chuckled over the differences in personalities of critters. "A beef cow would'a killed me" I thought, gazing across the fence at the cows happily munching from their sour smorgasbord. I thought also of the dusty hay from yesteryear and was grateful for another farm personality, the personality of change. ❧

Born Again Baseball

I've got a confession to make but before I make it, you need to understand where I'm coming from and for a full understanding, you'd need to have been brought up on a farm...a place where cows have to be milked two times a day, every day, 365 days a year. And lest you think the job ends there, I'll point out that between those twice daily milkings, there's plenty of other farm work to do; farmers make "one armed paper hangers" look like slackers.

Because of this, most farmers have no use for the pastimes that non-farm folks are attracted to, like sports. The practical reason is that we never had the time to practice. Because of this, in fact, I'd as soon catch the moon as any other type of ball coming at me. What do you do with it once you've got it?... yeh, I'm the kid who always ran the wrong way with the football and threw the baseball like a girl. To be honest, though, my ineptness with sports goes deeper than a mere lack of practice or effort...I've had an 'attitude'; I took an old adage, turned it on its back and waved it like a pom pom... "if I couldn't join 'em, by God I'd beat 'em"! When other folks speculated on upcoming games, I'd glibly say, "hope both teams lose!" When the game was played and the winner was decided, I'd walk away grumbling...if there were an Olympic category for "worst attitude of all", I'd have been there for the gold.

A couple years ago, however, it suddenly changed. I woke up one morning, rose out of bed, and realized there was something radically different with me. It took me a while to realize what it was but I knew the change was etched indelibly into my being; as shocking it was as if I'd woken up craving a sex change operation...sometime in the night, I had turned into an avid Red Sox fan! From that point on, I started to learn all the players' names and positions. I'd listen to every game on the radio, even the "red eyes" that went to 13, 14, 15 innings and left a drought of hours before worktime started at 6:00 AM. When the Sox won, I'd thrust my fist in the air and holler 'YES!'. When they lost, I'd walk around like a stockbroker on a bad day.

I kept it under my hat pretty well but Betsy knew. She accepted my change with gladness, thinking that the Red Sox would be harmless compared to all the addictions I might have taken on...alcohol, horses, perversion or just remaining a closed-minded farmer. My son, a born Red Sox fan, also knew. We work together and although the old "farmer instinct" generally forced me into silence at work, I'd occasionally loosen up to Tommy about an especially exciting play the night before. One night he called and said "Dad, don't plan anything for the night of September 22 because we're going to the game." He meant, of course, making the three hour trip to Fenway Park, something he'd done several times but an adventure I held cached in my "wildest dreams" file.

Tommy held firm in spite of my list of reasons why I shouldn't go (another farmer thing). "I've already bought the tickets and we're going" he said and secretly, I was excited. When the day arrived, we headed out in my aging Nissan, Tommy, our friend, Nat Winthrop and me. The trip down was full of baseball talk between Tommy and Nat. I mostly kept my mouth shut but listened intently, anxious to learn every possible thing about my new 'addiction'. We arrived at Fenway after a very enjoyable trip and walked into the bowels of the famous park. Tommy led the way past hamburger stands, beer joints, and souvenir sellers, all with prices designed to make my farmer eyes bulge as big as baseballs. We finally got to a place where a left turn and a rapid ascent brought us to an instant panorama of the magical field where my team performs. Banks of lights shone down on a manicured greenness interrupted only by the earthen diamond and the likes of my heroes right there on the same acreage that we sat!

My mouth was agape the whole night, not only because of the momentum live baseball provides but just seeing the people around us...wow, I never realized the crucial role beer plays in running a ball game.....bucket brigades of it went past us into the stands! And then there were the peanuts and Cracker Jacks, "get yer Crackah Jacks heahhhh!" It was a wonderful night, even though the Sox lost to the Indians. We stayed till the very last pitch, joined the 'rat-race' streaming out of the park and finally headed north, full of baseball talk. In fact we were so "wound up" that we got on the wrong highway in Manchester, New Hampshire and when we finally got righted, we proceeded to drive into the EZPass-only lane at the Hooksett Toll Plaza (my excuse that Vermonters don't know what a Toll Plaza looks like didn't 'fly' when I later appealed my $25.00 fine!). We finally got back to our homes at 2:00 AM, tired but still excited. Yes, the trip netted a couple of errors but for a baseball neophyte like me, it was a grand slam.

I sit here notching off certain milestones: Christmas tree season is upon us once again. After a considerable fight, the EZPass people finally declared my case closed just days ago and we look forward to another fierce winter here in Central Vermont. The change of seasons seems to go a little less smoothly the older I get. Some folks say I should be slowin' down but life just seems to be adding to my plate; now I've got yet another season to worry about... baseball season! 🍁

WEATHER!

Yesterday I had a bus full of folks from the Lancaster, Pennsylvania area in our sugarhouse. It was great having them for two reasons: this is a slow time at our farm and I knew they'd take quite a bit of syrup home and, well, I just plain like people from that part of the country because the Lancaster area has a lot in common with Vermont; open farm land and farmers with a "slow moving" way of life...life is good around Lancaster.

I showed them slides of our maple sugaring process and when I got to the one that shows sap dripping from a spout one drop at a time, I "milked" it as usual. "Sap never flows...it just drips one drop at a time", I told the group of wide-eyed Pennsylvanians... "I've seen a three gallon bucket fill up before in eight hours...why, don't y'know...things get pretty damned excitin' here in Vermont!" I went on to describe our need for perfect weather, freezing nights and thawing days but not too cold and not too warm; I punctuated that idea by saying we usually get that perfect weather here in Vermont. Less than eight hours later, all hell broke loose.

That was Thursday night, May 26, and Betsy was at work. The black dog Averill and I lounged in our living room, I watching the news on TV, she on the rug nearby. The weather guy talked of pretty violent storms approaching from the west. He mentioned places like Essex County, New York and the Northeast Kingdom of Vermont but suggested no hint of anything that would affect us. "Guess you're spared the agony tonight Avie" I said to Averill but I could see a bit of disagreement in her eyes; Averill hates storms and being a dog, forecasts pretty darned well. The angry sky outside our window seemed to agree with her forecast and then the rain started like a hydrant opens... instantly and violently. Somewhere in the middle of "Jeopardy", our local TV weather guy Tom Messner broke in; this time he was talking about places like Barre, Montpelier, and East Montpelier Center, just one mile from our place. And it wasn't just heavy rain and thunder storms on his mind....he was talking possible tornadoes!

Yup, Tom Messner was slightly wrong in his original placement of the storm but what the heck does he know...he's not a dog! In the meantime, Averill had become a "basket case". She leapt up on the couch and snuggled tight against me, shivering like a jackhammer. I pulled a blanket over the two of us, put my arm around her, and used words like "We'll be OK Avie" but she wasn't "buying" it. The TV soon snapped and sputtered to a standstill so I turned it off and flicked on the radio. Our local radio station WDEV had gone into emergency mode and Roger Hill, Central Vermont's maestro of meteorology had taken over. He was reporting floods and evacuations in Barre and Montpelier but no tornadoes yet. I wondered where our sons were and worried about Betsy at work but there was nothing I could do but pray and stay close to Averill's quivering warmth.

I had never seen rain come down like it did. Just outside our living room window is a place where water sheds from a "valley" in the roofs. The torrent from our valley that night would have filled a bathtub in five seconds. Bombarding rain mixed with snapping lightning and thunderous BOOMS. It brought a feeling of Armageddon and I knew that Averill felt the same. After what seemed like an eternity, the rain subsided but not before there was a huge amount of damage to our Vermont. When folks are forced from their homes and roads wash away, it's hard to talk "silver linings" but we were, indeed, much more fortunate than many recent tornado victims around the country. My sons and Betsy were all OK and after a fashion, Averill breathed a sigh of relief. It's hard to be a dog in a storm. I'll no doubt go on joking to folks in our sugarhouse about sap "drip, drip, dripping" and boasting of our perfect Vermont weather but for every "rule" there is an exception like that Thursday night when, announced by a black dog and completed by nature, all hell broke loose right here in our neighborhood. 🍁

"Grave" Situation

Meet Elliott and Allen, two cemetery guys. They haven't always been cemetery guys. No, Elliott spent most of his work life tinkering Volkswagens and Allen donned a tie and spent 34 years working for the State of Vermont in various agencies including the Department of Health from which he retired. Although they both raised families right here in East Montpelier just around the corner from each other, they lived in two different worlds with no real connection except maybe an occasional wave. Then, of course, they ended their working careers and began searching for their next adventure.

Elliott followed his heart and the "path of least resistance" to Morse Farm Maple Sugarworks where he became chief candy maker and bottle washer. Elliott Morse is one of those guys with maple in his DNA so he took to the job like bubbles take to boiling sap but there was not enough work for him full time. Enter the cemeteries of East Montpelier. He says it was just a job that needed to be done but I know differently; Elliott wears "dignity" and "respect" on his sleeve... "bury 'em proper n' don't forget 'em"...so he took on our local cemeteries with a "can do" attitude.

Allen approached Elliott one day and said he'd recently joined the ranks of the retired and would be willing to help in the cemeteries. Although Elliott agreed to give him a try, he had monumental doubts; "T' tell y' the truth" Elliott said, "I didn't really know if a hot cemetery would be the right place for a guy who wore a suit for thirty years.". That was ten years ago and Allen Ploof knew better. He grew up in the northern Vermont village of Highgate Center and although he refers to himself as a "city kid", worked on a farm up there and loved working in the outdoors. Yes, he got waylaid for part of a lifetime "pushin' pencils" but always knew he'd return to his roots in one form or another.

The first day Elliott handed him a string trimmer, Allen started a long-lasting battle with the witch grass, dandelions and bed straw that threatens

East Montpelier's thousand plus granite, marble, and slate markers. Those markers stand in nine different cemeteries and range in age from the early 1800s to two weeks old. Despite the best of human intentions, grave stones eventually get forgotten and abandoned...not, however, on the watch of Elliott Morse and Allen Ploof; those two guys fuss over their cemeteries like "old mother hens".

We recently had a terrible nighttime storm here in this area. There was plenty for all Central Vermont residents to worry about that night but Elliott Morse's "tossing and turning" focused on one major thing; his beloved cemeteries! We all woke up the next morning to face massive damage to roads, homes, and businesses. The roads were so bad that Elliott and Allen couldn't even get to some of their cemeteries for a few days but when they had finally inspected all of them, Elliott came to me with some good news. The cemeteries had suffered no major washouts. All were secure except one of the oldest, the Cate Cemetery over on the east side of town. Elliott said when he approached that historic gravesite, he immediately saw a sizable tree had fallen into its oldest section. As he walked toward it, he no doubt envisioned toppled and irreparably damaged stones but was amazed at the "respect" that big Cherry tree had shown for the departed. It's primary crotch lay straddling the Holmes family monument that bears the names of Captain William Holmes who died in 1873, his wife Margarete, and their children. The children, four of whom died between the ages of four and eleven, also have tiny stones lined up with the six foot tall Holmes monument. The fallen tree gently blanketed all eight of the children's stones without damaging a single one. It's largest limb simply "dusted" the marble marker of one "Melvina A, DAU'R of Coolidge Desire", who died in 1864, and its top lay inches from the lichen covered memorial to Angeline McConihe, age four, who died in 1842. The day Elliott came telling me this happy story was May 30, Memorial Day.

Last week, Elliott and Allen had to hand dig a grave in another of East Montpelier cemeteries. "Hardest gol dang diggin' we ever saw...only went an inch an hour" Elliott said. He went on to say it was impossible to reach the "deep six" that day but they were able to get it just barely deep enough. "Nobody'll mind" he said with a twinkle of his eye and I'd say "here, here" to that; by now it's all covered over and grass is beginning to sprout around East Montpelier's newest monument. One thing for sure, it'll be well cared for as long as Elliott Morse and Allen Ploof are able to pull the starter cord of a string trimmer. 🍁

Inner Strength

A couple weeks ago I was asked to be an adjudicator at a festival of the Vermont Association of Jazz Educators at Johnson State College. I felt honored to be asked because, although I play in the same groups with many of northern Vermont's music teachers, I'm not one myself; I'm just a farmer who happens to play the trombone. I rode up to Johnson with my friend, Rich Davidian, who has taught music in Montpelier since Methuselah played the Miraphone. Going back to Johnson brought back memories of the days when I was there as a student.

The VtAJE was a grand opportunity for elementary and middle school band students from all over Vermont to "strut their musical wares" to the critical ears of seasoned jazz musicians and "strut" they did! Rich and I worked as a team in the acoustically perfect confines of Dibden Auditorium, where six different groups set up and played jazz pieces they had worked up. Our job was to critique their performances which, I might add, was easy to do in a positive way; these young Vermont musicians were good!

At noon, Rich and I went over to the modern dining hall which stands in striking contrast to 1967's Martinetti Hall where I first got fat. Yup, contrary to most of the complaining college students of that time, I loved my Saga Food and always went back for seconds. We stopped at one of several stations that offered such modern fare as burgers, pizza slices, and personally styled sandwiches; I noted a complete absence of salmon pea wiggle and chipped beef gravy. We selected from the sandwich bar and took our trays to a small round table in the dining hall where we sat overlooking the beautiful Sterling Range to the west. Our fellow diners consisted of mostly Johnson students, sprinkled with an occasional professor. The students, although very well mannered, were distinguished by an array of backwards caps, beards in all stages of growth and clothing approaching the "grease rag stage".

"Wow" I said, eliciting a laugh from Rich, "I remember being called on the carpet once on this very campus for having my shirt untucked!" Yup, back in 1967, my math teacher, Miss Biallecci, turned from the blackboard one time and said "Tuck in your shirt, Mr. Morse"...times, they do change!

The week after my experience at Johnson State, Betsy and I traveled to New York City to see our son, Rob, who is attending City College of New York as a music student. In his two years there, we had never been down to see him and we were surprised at the beauty of the CCNY campus. It stands in a comely part of Harlem, distinguished by fieldstone buildings and ornate gates. On our second day, Rob took us a short distance from where he lives to a city park right on the Hudson River. It was a beautiful late afternoon and as we strolled across a pleasant walkway, the George Washington Bridge, a short distance to our right, carried two levels of bumper-to-bumper rush hour traffic. All of a sudden my thoughts turned toward "suspension wonders of the world"...and I wasn't thinking of the bridge. There in front of us strolled a young local couple. The boy was thin as a rail and walked along holding the hand of a shapely girl. She was dressed like she had just left her office job but his apparel was all oversized, rag-tag, and most strikingly, every stitch of it had "gone south" by exactly one degree. His oversized ball cap lopped down over the tops of his ears. His stained jersey hung down beyond his midsection and his pants somehow miraculously stayed suspended, waistline somewhere sub-buttocks, crotch down at knee level; an overage of pant cuffs "shoooshed" along, two crumpled masses on the street surface.

We followed them silently for a while and when I quietly suggested that we tell the boy his pants were falling down, Rob responded sternly enough to have woken up General Grant who lies in a crypt in that same neighborhood; he chided me in no uncertain terms that when in the city, one minds his own business!

The last night we were there, we went to a concert of Rob's big band. They played a mixture of old jazz standards and more avant-garde material and made both styles sound full and wonderful. They had worked hard all year just like the younger students back in Vermont; they "done" their generation proud! We went back to Vermont the next day feeling much less critical of backwards caps and saggin' pants...discipline and great art always comes from within. ❧

Chit Chat

Well here it is almost sugaring season and we're "scraping the bottom of the barrel" for wood to heat our houses... used to be quite universal that Vermont farmers would feel this "drought" on the home front while sitting on a woodshed chalk full of dry wood for the sugarhouse. These days sugarmakers have "stretched the limits" fuel-wise; though they may still burn wood at home, many maple folks are burning oil for boiling sap. While the temptation is sweeter'n ever to go this route, those old family ghosts hanging out in our ancient sugarhouse would never allow us to burn oil. We've gone to a rather unorthodox fuel for sugarmaking, woodchips.

A while back I made my annual call to Joe Gagnon at his lumberyard down in Pittsford for a load of chips.. "Yaw...probly could...be Sat'dy maybe seven-seven thirty in th'mornin 'less, o'course th'roads're too bad." he said, which interprets in native Vermont talk: "You best be ready at six 'cause I'll be early and there ain't no such thing as roads too bad t'travel!". I got up at five that Saturday morning and had my coffee early in anticipation of Joe's arrival. As I sat in our living room, though, the weather outside did look a little "iffy". Snow was comin' down sideways and the view we normally have of the valley to the south wasn't there at all. "Hmmm" I thought. "Maybe even Joe will call it off on a day like this."

It was about 6:30 when I finished my coffee, put on my winter garb, and headed down the driveway toward our sugarhouse. Driving snow pelted my bare face and my hands felt the raw wind right through my thick gloves. When I got to where I could look down County Road toward our distant cow barn there, parked on the roadway in the distance, was the looming ghost of an eighteen-wheel Freightliner; I chuckled to myself thinking "God I'm smart. There's Joe down there a half hour early puttin' on his chains!"

Joe was born on the same Pittsford, Vermont dairy farm that had been in his family since 1880. He grew up like every other farm boy doing the thousand-

and-one things necessary on a Vermont dairy farm but he was always happiest in the woods cutting trees and workin' them up into firewood or sawlogs. His son Ken recently told me that his dad had a secret hankerin' to work fulltime in the woods and finally saw his chance when dairy regulations changed in the 1960s to require the installation of expensive bulk milk tanks. "He sold the cows and built a sawmill" Ken said leaving out the conventional ending to that thought, "that he never looked back". Joe Gagnon "looks back" all the time to his farming roots, to when he learned "biblical-scale" things like buying the best equipment, maintaining it, and using it. One thing in particular that's universal among farm boys is the ability to "back up" farm implements and trailers and Joe's no exception; Joe Gagnon could back a camel through the eye of a needle! Today Gagnon Lumber Company is a sizeable operation and Joe, quite logically, gravitated toward its huge tractor trailers years ago.

The day of the delivery I went down the road toward the big truck and Joe was just chaining up the last of eight huge drive wheels on his road tractor. "God I thought maybe even you'd call it off today.", I shouted over the howling wind. "Oh no" he shouted back. "Weren't that bad...just had to slow down a few times...couldn't get by the snowplow, y'know". He had traveled the sixty miles to Montpelier from Pittsford (one of those routes you can "hardly get theyah from heah" in any weather) and droned up the steep hill from Montpelier. As he approached our wood chip barn, however his common sense kicked into high gear. He knew it's a "trucker's nightmare" to back into our place and careful planning, including chains, is just good insurance. Satisfied that all was ready, he climbed up into the cab, continued the short distance to our barn, and backed the behemoth in; a one-shot deal!

As I stood watching the self-unloading trailer disgorge 30 tons of freshly ground wood chips, you might think I was contemplating our coming sugaring season and all the syrup we'll make from that fuel but I wasn't...I was reveling in watching the machinery work and secretly wishing I had been the one to back that big rig into the barn! Yup, you see, I'm a native Vermont "farm boy" just like Joe and I, too, would have driven up in that storm. My friend Gerald Pease oft used the expression "load light n' go often" which means "don't ever carry more than you can handle even if it means makin' a couple extra trips to the barn." The day I talked to Joe's son, he chuckled about his dad coming up in that storm. "Heck" he said "a couple Mondays ago we got 24 inches of wet snow, Dad made two trips to Middlebury and one to Bennington...had th' road all to himself!" I had no trouble believing that of my friend Joe Gagnon, a true "load light n' go often" sort of guy. 🍁

Tree Psych 103

I can't let a Christmas season go by without writing a story on the "psychology" of Christmas tree shopping. Over the past four plus decades, I've accumulated a whole forest full of stories (yes, it was way back in 1966 when Dad and I loaded our first retail Christmas tree onto an aging Studebaker!). And speaking of stories, I walk a very fine line these days being both a writer and a Christmas tree salesman. A few years ago I wrote about a couple of gals who used to buy their trees from us. When they failed to show up one year, I asked around and found that out that my words had offended one of them and, you know, when I went back and read it, I had to agree...although I was just trying to be funny and meant no harm, I, too, would have been offended. I started that story by crediting my father with getting folks to our farm with "suaveness and charm" and went on to say that "It was my job to figure out what they wanted, make sure there was plenty of it, and then stay out of the way." I'd say that offending someone publicly was hardly "staying out of the way" and so I'll make a public apology to "Karen" right now.

That brings me to an end of an era...no, I'm not giving up selling Christmas trees but, mark my words, I'll never use anyone's real name in a Christmas tree story again! So today I'm thinking of the "Balsams", a local family whose history of tree shopping brings a whole new meaning to the term "family tree". This couple started coming up here when their kids were just saplings and they required the real deal: no selecting from our displayed, pre-cut trees for them; they always brought their own saw and only needed access to the Morse wilds and a promise that there were big ones, huge ones out there.

I especially remember one of their treks. It was snowing hard that day and the Balsams had been gone a long time when the father suddenly emerged from the blizzard hunched over and looking stressed. "We're having a terrible time gettin' that tree down. Got a sharp saw we can borrow...and, oh...mind if I take th'Subaru out there?". I said "Hell, I don't care if y'go out with a bulldozer just as long's you fix up the mess". He thanked me, got in the Subaru and drove slowly back into the blizzard.

I was busy with other tree customers when suddenly a huge, prostrate conifer appeared in the distance. It seemingly moved without the aid of human hands or machine power and as it crept toward us, folks gasped like they were seeing a yuletide Trojan Horse about to invade the Morse tree lot. It had come out of the deep woods, following a path that is normally only tractor accessible but I knew it could only be the Balsam family. As it pulled up, a hand holding some cash reached out through massive boughs. "Keep the change" said a tired-sounding voice... "I can't get out." I knew there was a Subaru in there somewhere and in the Subaru were a family of wide-eyed "saplings" who would always cherish the experience. We all watched as the "tree" turned south on County Road and headed off toward Montpelier.

The other day a young couple drove into our yard in a Saab with Massachusetts plates. I could see from a distance that the young man was one of the Balsam "saplings" now grown up and married. When they went to select their tree I backed off, extending them proper "Balsam" reverence. I only approached when I noticed they had made a selection and he was in the process of tying the large, perfect Fraser Fir on to the Saab's roof (no easy matter on a car with no roof rack). We exchanged pleasantries but I offered no help...offering Christmas tree help to a Balsam would be like asking Santa if he might prefer oxen to reindeer. I did note that the young man's wife remained rather aloof to the process and when he asked her for help, she declined...that's where I almost stepped in: "See here young lady" I would have said. "You're a Balsam now and Balsams support each other in this sacred process". Instead I made a joke about how it's always the passenger's job to reattach trees that fall off travelling cars; she smiled and then began helping.

No, I kept my mouth shut as I wish I had with "Karen's" story. They say that "practice makes perfect" so I truly hope that my writing gets better with every story and that I never offend anyone again. I won't, however, stop writing Christmas tree stories because, damn it all, I enjoy it! Like my last customer yesterday: The woman had "very specific" requirements of her Christmas tree and she had me twirling just about every tree in the yard. She kept coming back to one in particular, however, but said "the top just doesn't 'work' for me...it's too sparse at the top". I developed my most angelic smile, tipped my hat and said "me too but folks can still enjoy me". She laughed and bought the tree. With Christmas trees, there's a tale in every sale. 🍁

The Personality of Machines

It's Farm Show time again here in Vermont and I've just returned from my annual trek over to the Barre Auditorium. I will admit that this year it was largely a "fact-finding" venture, a matter of desperation...I needed a story! Over the years, I've found that show to be little changed. Sure the tractors these days are bigger and the equipment a little more intricate but the premise is the same: it's a chance for farmers and farmer wannabes to wander the aisles like cows on a country lane checking out everything brightly painted, proudly grown, and engaging in personality.

Looking back, I realize my quest was a bit too panic-driven; I went right after the "engaging in personality", thinking surely any story worth its weight in corn silage would come from a person, a character, someone to quickly and efficiently spew fodder for the best column yet. My first cursory walk through the equipment displays netted sideward glances at massive tractors and haying machines but brought a complete drought of characters. "Maybe I'm trying too hard", I thought as I sulked to the refreshment area for a steaming cup of coffee and a greasy donut. I sat there watching a fair sampling of Vermont humanity stroll by...a leather jacketed mega-dairy farmer, a couple of aging hippies, and a scruffy logger, knowing each had his own personal reason to be at the Farm Show. Somehow I felt different when I returned to the displays, coffee still in hand.

I stopped first at a gaped-mouthed monster, the bottom of which resembled a giant blueberry picking rake. "Valley apples", I chuckled to myself, instantly knowing the thing was designed to pick up rocks in plowed fields. My friend, Gerald Pease, used to call rocks "valley apples" because rocks on a Vermont farm are as predictable a "crop" as apples...they appear every time a field is plowed up. "You pick them stone ("stone" is plural in Vermont lingo) every time you plow for sixty years an' you get the same amount on year sixty as you did on year one," Gerald used to say. As I bent down to examine the thing more closely, my back reminded me how many of "them stone" I've picked the hard way!

The rock rake, like all the other brightly colored implements I passed, drew out my love for machines...machines that I neither need nor can afford. More appropriately, they drew out a thing called nostalgia...nostalgia began leading me for a second, slower walk down the equipment aisles. I passed the Kubotas, the John Deeres and the Hestons but it was a video showing a "land clearing" machine that drew me in and held me captivated for several minutes. On the video, a jagged-toothed cylinder whirled like a giant dentist drill on the arm of a 20 ton excavator. The thing resembled a tree devouring dinosaur grazing through the wooded countryside. It started at the tops of the trees and left nary a twig intact. "Fun toy" I chuckled but probably not too practical in this day and age of environmental controls and anti clear-cutting laws!

Just around the corner was a booth that featured a modern variation of the old fashioned scythe. That booth also offered an action video that showed a man swinging the simple tool toppling grass and briars from a patch of land. It reminded me of the days my grandpa Sydney covered our entire farm mowing the nooks and crannies that were inaccessible to the bigger machines. As I watched, I realized that my peripheral vision still held the "tree monster" whacking away in the booth I had just left. "Wow...such contrasts" I thought...two machines so varied in design and magnitude performed the same simple task, clearing the land!

The rest of my day at the Farm Show was thoroughly enjoyable because the pressure was off...I suddenly had the story I had come for. I would go home, sit down and use two more ultra-varied tools at my disposal, computers and words, and focus my next column on the personality of machines. Sure people always make interesting subjects but in their relationship with machines, all they do is move the levers...machines do all the work! Just before I left, I returned to the place where I could view the "personalities" of land clearing in stereo. The term "full circle" came to mind as I cinched up my heavy jacket, headed for the Farm Show's main door, and went on home...back to my farm with its machines and all the work still to be done.

Two Friends of Mine

I just went out the door toward the paper box with seven year old Averill. She went right to a darkish blob of something awful and rolled in it. "Gosh darn it Averill" I said. "That's disgusting!". You guessed it....Averill's a dog, not just any dog, mind you, but my dog! We go back a long way...well, seven years, but it seems much longer than that. When dogs come into our lives, we know we've only got twelve or so years with them so we start maximizing the love right away.

Betsy reminds me, though, that it hasn't always been that way. "Would your Grandpa Morse have been as silly with a dog as you are?" she chided in an "if th'old collar fits, put it on" sort of tone. "Would he have let a dog on his bed, 'cooed' to it like a baby, snuggled with a dog while driving?" I had to admit guilty to all of the above. My grandpa would sit and scratch a dog's ears and talk to it but that's as intimate as he would ever get. And, don't get me wrong...Sidney Morse loved dogs. He always had 'em around the farm and, no, they weren't work dogs. They didn't herd cows, power machinery or even fetch his slippers...they were just dumb dogs who followed him around; an inexplicable part of life for a Vermont farmer.

These days it's downright uncanny how canines can climb the social ladder. For many couples they're the perfect substitute for babies who bring too many complications; no, many folks are choosing the twelve-year cycle of family planning...pick him from a litter, housebreak him, and savor the love.

Betsy and I had two of the human variety but they're grown now and on their own. Now it's just us, Averill, and younger son's dog Fern who gets babysat often at "grandpa's and granny's". Yes, I'm a fool with dogs but there's one little area where I'm more a holdover from the old days: I don't believe in exercising them. Betsy, on the other hand, is out daily with those two black Labs. The threesome always leave our house on a positive note but an hour and several miles later, they may return one bedraggled woman with a hair-raising tale to tell and two lusty Labs ready to go again. On those jaunts where Betsy is not pulled-over or knocked-down, she gets to ponder a little dog psychology: Just up the road lives Bear, a healthy young Rottweiler. Bear, in the interest of domain protection, never lets Betsy and her charges pass that section of County Road without an "investigative" appearance. The three, in fact have "mixed it up" on occasion but our two Labs quickly learned that Rottweilers are the canine equivalent of Mohammed Ali. Betsy said when they near Bear's domain these days, Averill and Fern revert back to a primal survival of the fittest mentality...they both compete for the inside flank which leaves aging, osteoporosis prone Betsy on the outside to fend for the "pack".

After they pass the "Bear hurdle", the three turn right onto Barnes Road where lives Kit, a docile Golden Retriever. Kit's life is narrowed by an underground invisible fence, a situation that Averill and Fern are more than happy to take advantage of. As they approach Kit's place, they switch back into primal attack mode. "Awh-Hawh" they seem to say... "We can take this bloke!". Poor Betsy still bears welts where she was just recently snapped to a full face-plant in Barnes Road gravel. She told of the ensuing whirlwind that quickly involved not only three snarling dogs but three frantic dog owners. She said Kit's humans, Barbara and Allen, were more than cordial under the circumstances...I somehow think that's not what old Robert Frost had in mind with his expression about good fences and good neighbors!

I keep telling Betsy to quit with the exercising... "let's turn these rascals into lazy rug dogs", I say but she keeps returning to the daily battle zone. My style with dogs is strictly domestic. I love the safety of my bed with a good book and two black dogs who jump aboard, circle three times, and find their nests in the perfect place. 🍂

A Sweet Trip to Iowa

It all started a week ago when my son, Tommy, came to work. "The weatherman says there'll be no sap weather for two more weeks—something about what's happening out west." he said. I grumbled as I put the rest of our tree tapping paraphernalia onto the storage shelf: we had just finished tapping all 4000 of our trees. There's been a thaw in early February and we thought sugar season was upon us. Suddenly the impulsive side of my brain kicked in: "I'm getting' outa here," I said. I went home and announced to Betsy that I was leaving at 5:00 AM the next morning for places unknown, and I did.

I drove west, alone and glad to be getting away from it all. I'd always wanted to see Mount Rushmore and my impulsive brain seemed to be leading me there. I-90 took me to a few hours of sleep in Toledo and a snowy wakeup call the next morning. A whiteout of Great Lakes proportions accompanied me almost to Chicago, where it suddenly turned to white knuckles. Somewhere in mid-Illinois, Mount Rushmore started to fade with a sudden brain-shift back into "rational mode".

Iowa looked welcoming in the distance and when I crossed the Mississippi at LeClaire on I-80, I sought out the Mississippi Valley Welcome Center. I approached the desk with that "needle-in-a-haystack" look on my face and asked a friendly looking lady if she knew of a place in Iowa where they make maple syrup. I'd heard of such a place and my hunch that she hadn't was right. After several calls, however, she located Hartman Reserve Nature Center up in Cedar Falls. "They've just tapped their trees and would be glad to talk to you," she said, looking relieved to have solved her problem question of the day. As I left, I stood facing the Great Plains with the Great River at my back. Iowa had already proved to be a friendly place with great variety. It would fill the bill for my much needed change of pace.

Seventy-five pleasant miles and one huge Iowa pork sandwich at a place called the Machine Shed, brought me to Cedar Falls and the warm handshake of Vern Fish, Director of Hartman Reserve. Vern, dressed in a green park ranger uniform, showed me their neat sugarhouse. The unmistakable fragrance of boiling sap still hung in the air. They had already made syrup. He asked me about maple sugaring in Vermont and I told him of our weather woes—said our sap running weather always starts in the West. Vern looked pleased that Iowa might play a small roll in Vermont's maple success and said Hartman Reserve is the farthest point west where hard maples are tapped. He suggested, with a twinkle in his eye, that I had just driven to the last bucket. "Interesting," I thought. "Maybe I've found the source of Vermont sugar weather!"

Before I left, Vern told me about Green's Maple Farm, Iowa's oldest sugaring operation. The next day I followed several state routes from Cedar Falls to Castalia and arrived just as Dale and Karen Green pulled up atop separate John Deere tractors. It was bone-chilling cold and Dale, a huge, bearded man dismounted. I could see him eying my Vermont license plate as he approached. He looked cold in spite of the worn, quilted coveralls he wore. After a quick introduction, Dale offered to show me the Green sugarhouse. Before he got in my car, I heard him say something to Karen about lunch. We drove a short distance toward a wooded hillside he referred to as "the timber." I was impressed by the size of the operation as we pulled into the sugarhouse drive. We entered and Dale explained how the Green family had been sugaring for five generations. Beyond a Vermont-made evaporator, production figures for every ear since 1948 were hand scribbled on the wall. This year they had only boiled once before the weather turned cold, like it had back home—cold, with an added portion of Iowa wind. As we left the sugarhouse, Dale pointed to the surrounding maples, saying sap from 2200 trees was gathered with two teams of horses.

We drove back to yet another homestead where Dale and Karen lived. A dusty pickup truck sat in the yard and beyond, a stock trailer stood outside several full farm machinery sheds. We entered their home and paused at a worn boot-jack. Dale removed his boots and stripped down to the first layer or two. I kicked off my shoes and followed him. Without words, I had just received an Iowa invitation to lunch. A huge pot of homemade soup sat on their kitchen table, along with a pan of freshly baked corn bread. We sat down and began eating. The soup tasted wonderfully like home after three days on the road. We slathered Green Family maple syrup on the corn bread: it was great syrup, not Vermont, mind you, but great syrup!

I had a wonderful time in Iowa, starting at the Mississippi Valley Welcome Center. At Hartman Reserve I saw "the last bucket west" and since that bucket had sap dripping into it, I hereby appoint Cedar Falls Iowa the official source of Vermont Spring weather. I found American farm hospitality at its best with Dale and Karen Green. They allowed me to interrupt their busy day on a farm where all things "Iowa" reign, plus maple syrup. They are surely Iowa's sweetest couple.

Suddenly I was itching to travel again, this time back to Vermont. I drove east on I-90 through places like Chicago, Gary and Cleveland, checking the rearview mirror often. Every time I looked, I saw hints of Spring and the promise of a good sap run when I got home. 🍂

PHOTO GALLERY

Photo by Collin O'Neil

Top: Burr & Tom Morse and the new Leader Evaporator (Burr's third) *Three Evaporator Life* (pg 3)

Bottom: Bulk maple syrup in stainless steel and plastic drums, ready for canning *Bulk Syrup and Booze Bottles* (pg 9)

Nelson Griggs (1914-1971) was father of the modern sap collection system that is being used universally for maple production. The first patent on the technique of linking tapped maple trees together and routing sap directly to the sugarhouse was granted to Nelson in 1959.

A Vermont native, Nelson did much of his research on plastic tubing and taps here at Morse Farm.

Nelson Griggs' contributions to sugaring are noted in Harry's Sugarhouse *A Sugarmaker's Thank You* (page 14)

Burr's greeting, 50 years in the making, to all who visit Morse Farm
OK for a Spell (pg 21)

Ilene, the Very Important Cow, in her place of honor at Morse Farm
Our Newest Cow
(page 34)

Averill and Fern, awaiting the next adventure with Burr
Springtime Pros and Cons (pg 23)

Allen and Gary Butler's 1928 Chevrolet hay-hauling truck
Dairy Dilemma (page 53)

Photo by Collin O'Neil

Two Morse Farm Sugarhouses

Above: The current Morse Farm sugarhouse on the first night of the season
Sweet Trip to Iowa (page 120)
Below: Grandpa Sidney's hand-built sugarhouse as it stands today on other side of
the Morse Farm property
Sweet Beginnings (page 125)

A Vermont sugarhouse and cornfield, both created by man and machine
Awkward Ag (page 47)

A pair of Vermont silos awaiting this year's corn crop
Corn, Corn (page 127)

Burr's early school, Four Corners School in East Montpelier
Beans, Beans, Beans (page 137)

A young Harry Morse Sr. manning the evaporator
Quality Boredom (page 139)

Stanley Morse's family farm as it stands today
Cousins Removed (page 157)

Dean Shattuck, driving force behind the early ski area at Morse Farm *Old Friendships, Sweet Skiing (page 162)*

Photo provided by Susan Shattuck

The Kent Tavern in Kent's Corner, Vermont
Station Identification (page 207)

A bear and her five cubs, an unusual amount, warily being photographed *Forever Hold Your Bears* (page 209)
Photo by Tom Sears

Vermont Statehouse Model, built in 1929, on display at Morse Farm *The Little Statehouse* (page 215)

A new generation begins with a calf's birth in our front pasture.
Smart Calves and Swimming Babies (page 218)

Dot and Harry Morse, sweethearts forever
Lots of Lilies (page 192)

East Montpelier's Old Meeting House, the site of many memorable, joyous and sad events
Ring Me Up by Rainbow (page 194)

Danny Coane in the promotion photo from his local band, Starline Rhythm Boys
Winter Stories (page 213)

Photo provided by Danny Coane

Harry's Sugarhouse

This sugarhouse is dedicated to Harry I. Morse, Sr., 1917-1999, six generation Vermont sugar maker and lover of all things "maple". Our father, Harry, spent a lifetime of sugar seasons boiling sap and "spinning yarns" in this place.

Harry's Sugarhouse sign on display at the Morse Farm
Harry's Sugarhouse (page 243)

MORSE FAMILY HISTORY

Sweet Beginnings • Corn, Corn • Up Clay Hill • Haying Memories • Forever Strawberries • Beans, Beans, Beans • Quality Boredom • Thanksgiving Pigs • Emotions with an Oink • A Different Seed • Plush Plumbin' • Yankee Yahoo • Umbrellas are Swell • Cousins Removed • Maple Misnomer • Old Friendships Sweet Skiing • My Land, Your Land • Wild "Meating" • "It" Happens • Old Haunts • A Happy Blue • Lots a Lawpstahs • Kindness the Vermont Way • Visiting My Grandpas • What's in a Name • Bull Strength and Ignorance • Christmas Scenes from Yesteryear • Mother Knows Best • A Great Spirit • Lots of Lilies • Ring Me Up by Rainbow

When my father died in 2001, I was heartbroken. Over a period of three years, I found myself visited by dragonflies OFTEN while gardening, or biking, or walking the dogs. The dragonflies would land on the top of my hand and rest there. The first time it happened, I was ready to swat whatever Florida insect had landed on me, but I paused when I saw what had arrived. I slowed down to the moment, and had the most wonderful sense of calm come over me. It felt as if my father had a hold of my hand at that moment, and I felt as if I was a little girl, again. That dragonfly gave me a sense of peace I hadn't felt since before my father's death. The wonder was, it didn't happen just that once. It happened so often for the first three years, the toughest years of grief for me, that I became certain it was a message from my father. Over the next few years, dragonflies would continue to land on my person, usually my hand or my arm, and rest there for a minute or an eternity, I lost all sense of time while they were there. One particularly stressful day, a dragonfly found me and landed on my hand in the teacher's *lounge of the school where I work. We were way in the back of the cafeteria, closed in a room in the center of the building. I don't know how it got in there, but I carefully walked it out of the noise and humanity to the field out back of the school, and set it free. My attitude shifted, I continued my day happily. In 2007, my mother died. Hilari and I had been with her constantly, and the night our mother died, she had left, exhausted, to go rest in a comfortable bed while I slept on the sofa next to mom in her hospice room. Just around morning, mom drew her last breath. After she passed, I opened the blinds of her room to let her soul have free flight out of there. Smiling down at me was a crescent Moon, the bottom of the Moon reflecting a grin of light towards earth! It was definitely a smile, and a sign to me that my mom was okay now. Since her passing, when I see a smiling crescent Moon, I am warmed by my mother's smile (she had a beautiful smile) and given a sense of peace that I relish and cherish. It truly seems that our loved ones find ways to "stay in touch" even after they've passed, whether by rainbow, dragonfly, or crescent Moon! Thank you for sharing your own story and for reminding me of the ties that bind, even beyond death.*

So, I read your books, read your "News from Vermont" emails, and find smiles and a sense of peace in your words often. Today, your words moved me to finally write to you. I am forever in debt to your family, and feel confident that your parents are proud of you all! They did a right fine job raising you, and you're carrying on the family name in their honor well. No wonder they send you rainbows! You deserve that and more!

- Jodi Ehrlich Pecoraro, FL

Sweet Beginnings

A while ago Eric, the young man who manages our ski center, asked if he could fix up the little sugarhouse over on the hillside maple grove west of here. "That sugarhouse is still fixable?" I said surprised and flattered at his interest. You see, my Grandpa Sidney had built that sugarhouse a long time ago and although it still holds sentimental value, I had not been over there for a long time. We were standing down in our lower parking lot at the time, a place within sight of both Sidney Morse's original grey farm buildings and that little sugarhouse.

My grandfather bought this farm back in 1948, the year I was born. He viewed it as a flatter, more farmable piece of land than the rocky sidehill place he hailed from eight miles up the road. He immediately started making improvements on both the buildings and the land but buildings were his specialty. The farmer before, Mr. Bliss, had done his best with maintenance but when Grandpa Morse arrived, he left "no stones unturned" with roof repair, shoring up, and applying paint...grey paint, his trademark. He also built a huge new barn and several smaller buildings to support his dreams for farming this place at "high speed". When he was done, the Morse Farm was one of Vermont's best dairy farms...a show place, it was!

Fast forward to the year 2010: What's left of Grandpa Morse's buildings sit begging for repair and new paint, and it all happened "on my watch". I feel especially bad when some old timer comes along and remarks about how it used to be. "Looked like it jumped right outa 'Vermont Life Magazine' it did", he'll say, and punctuate it with a "too bad....tsk, tsk, tsk". Yup, those comments would really get me down but for a soothing feeling that always steps in...a message that I know comes straight from Grandpa Morse. "Don't worry, Burr...times have changed and dairy farming's been bad for a long time. I understand."

That's the way he was, always understanding and accepting of "changed times". Grandpa Morse was my idol, a small man with a big heart and a gait so soft that it seemed his next step would "be on water". He was able to retire early and by the time I joined my dad on the farm in 1971, Grandpa Morse was here doing odd jobs. I remember his love for maple sugaring, the focus of our new diversified farming venture. I can still see him standing over a plank bench using an enamel pitcher to can every drop of syrup we made! He and Grandma tried Florida for a time but he didn't make it as a snowbird, especially when spring approached; the sweetness of sugarin' always beckoned even before its time on the calendar.

One summer he started this project across the field over in the little sugarbush to the west. We'd see him head out early in the morning carrying miscellaneous lumber, tools, and a dinner pail. That was the year he told Grandma he was done with Florida...if she wanted to go, she could go without him. He chipped a shelf into the hillside ledges and then built the sugarhouse using scraps of lumber and flat stones from the chipped ledges. Grandpa sugared there the following spring and had the time of his life. That fall, however, he started having problems with his stomach and by February, he was gone. Except for a couple of minor attempts by family members to sugar over there, Sidney Morse's little sugarhouse has been out of use for nearly forty years now.

Eric, it seems, had an ulterior motive in fixing it up...he wanted to propose to his girlfriend, Heather, there! He spent some time taking out the rusted remnants of an abandoned sugarhouse, put in new windows and battened up the walls but he especially remarked on the floor; Grandpa Sidney had laid up a beautiful slate floor by coaxing large flat stones in with levers, and block and tackle. When Eric described the floor to me, I said I wasn't surprised... "Sidney Morse was a genius with block and tackle. Slowly but surely, he could move anything", I said. After Eric finished fixing up the place, he added some special romantic touches that included spreading flower petals from wall to wall. One moonlit night this past February, he "seeded" the sugarhouse with a few special friends, got Heather over there under false pretense, and popped the question.

I'm convinced Grandpa Morse was watching that night. Yup, we've felt his presence around here since he passed away so long ago. Even though his dairy empire has "crumbled", for some reason his last building project, the little sugarhouse, has weathered the years to serve again. Oh, by the way, Heather said "Yes". I have a great feeling about their upcoming marriage. It'll be blessed with a "sweet" beginning, lots of creativity, and most importantly, by a great man like Sidney Morse. ✹

Corn, Corn

Corn, corn everywhere and not a kernel to eat. That's the way it is here in Vermont this time of year when all the gardens have gone the way of Jack Frost and what's left are only fields of peaked-looking corn stalks saved for the cows. Yup, that's the way cows like their corn, frost-hardened, kernel-dented, and chopped into little tiny pieces. In Vermont, farmers don't pick, harvest, glean, or gather their corn...they chop it. Although corn chopping conjures up nostalgia as big as silos, it's a wonder that anyone ever survived a single season; the history of chopping corn is rife with man-eating machinery and careless ways.

Our Allis Chalmers chopper was connected to an Allis D-17 tractor via a long hitch pole and a brutal power take off shaft. The chopper, resembling a pumpkin-orange Brontosaurus creeping through the cornfield, was followed by our black '48 Ford farm truck with high sides. The person driving the D-17, usually my father, had to somehow "zero" the thing in on a single corn row while using the proper gearing and engine speed. For the duration of chopping season, he needed the pivotal dexterity of a hoot owl; it was essential to keep his eyes on both the chopper's thousand moving parts and the cornrows ahead. The Ford had a jumpy clutch, a grinding transmission, and a flathead V-8 engine that stalled at the drop of a hat. The Ford's driver, constantly blinded by a "sandstorm" of corn silage, had to "match bumpers" with the chopper at 5 mph through mud holes, and up and down side hills. That old Ford had more idiosyncrasies than the cornfield had stalks; a person who could successfully drive it deserved the unofficial title of "master of anything on wheels".

There wasn't a lot of danger out in the cornfield except for the constant temptation to jump in the chopper's opening out of sheer frustration built up from all the breakdowns and plug ups! The real danger came back at the silo with the unloading. It was usually a quagmire out there since "Murphy's" design for chopping season was most always torrential rain. Our silo, an old wood-stave Unadilla, was thirty feet high. It was fed by a ten inch steel pipe which went from the extremely "unforgiving" blower to an opening in the silo's dome. The blower was powered by a slapping leather belt, spun at frightening RPMs by the pulley of an ancient farm tractor. The most dangerous part of the blower, however, was a long trough with an endless chain conveyer. The conveyor had paddles that were designed to convey corn silage, or anything else that might fall in the trough, into the blower.

When the Ford truck was full, we'd drive it to the silo area and ram it backwards, through the mud, to where it would empty into the trough. It had a dump body and after we unlatched the tailgate, we raised the body to an angle that would allow gravity to help with removing the silage but not let the whole load spill out all at once. Then we started the blower tractor and "threw her into gear". One of us climbed into the silo to level the blown silage; the other stayed outside to pull the stuff steadily from the truck with an implement fashioned from a long iron pipe and a potato digger.

To this day, I have nightmares thinking of that moving conveyer; one misstep and the guy unloading the truck would have been drawn right into the blower's gaping maw. My brother, Elliott, said one time the blower "swallowed itself". He was up high in the silo doing the leveling and all of a sudden there was a deafening clatter. "I scrambled to the edge of the silo and stood there with my back pasted to the wall. Shrapnel was sprayin' all around me and all I could do was pray that none of it would hit me!" he said.

It must have started with the conveyer chain breaking and being "sucked" into the blower and up the pipe; it ended with a total voiding of the blower's bowels until there was enough spare parts mixed in with the silage to repair a battleship. Luckily Elliott escaped injury that day but said he and Dad spent several days separating metal from cattle feed and somehow toggling that blower back into working order.

In spite of the nightmares and Elliott's close call, I'm still full of nostalgia about chopping corn. I loved the fermented smell of the puckery ooze that seeped from the silo's bottom. I loved driving that old Ford bumper to bumper with the chopper, guided by "by-guess-and-by-gory" through a tiny hole in its corn coated windshield. I loved the feel of blown silage against my face, danger be damned. We no longer chop corn at Morse Farm so it's a clear-cut case for nostalgia. We do, however, "flaunt" foliage season to the thousands of tourists who come here. I love the crispness of autumn and the beauty that surrounds us; it's almost nature at its absolute perfection. Like an expensive steak, however, there's always room for a little seasoning and from my point of view, autumn is only perfectly "seasoned" when you have a field of corn to chop.

Up Clay Hill

There's something about our Vermont winter that brings total awe from traveling folks; "How do you survive in the winter? Can you get out at all? Do they even try to plow the snow or is there simply too much? Those are the questions they ask in the same tone as if puzzling craters on the moon. I, seven generation Vermonter, am always tempted to "milk" it... "hell no...we just put on some extra fat and hibernate." But, being a Vermonter, I always tell the truth; "Vermonters are pros at winter" I say.

Oh, there are those who use snowstorms as a good excuse to shun work or school, but there's rarely a time when we can't get out and go with the best of 'em. "Snow days" are what they call it when schools shut down but I say "Pshaw" to that! It's an insult to our warriors of the blizzard battle, road crews who fight twenty four-seven and always win! Wintertime in Vermont has a lot to do with motivation, high boots, and physics, the "science that deals with matter and motion". Yes, our partnership with physics is a great winter equalizer, a fact that totally escaped Mr. Henry Ford and all his American counterparts until recent times. I'm talking about the anatomy of automobiles: cars with engines in the front and drive wheels in the back make as much winter sense as shoveling snow with a pitchfork but when I was a kid, that's the way all cars were made.

Memories of those days came drifting back recently when I returned home from Montpelier in the middle of a blizzard. These days we think nothing of Clay Hill, the steep-ish part of Main Street that culminates in a ninety degree curve at the top. In the old days, however, conquering Clay Hill required skill, strategy, and white knuckles. A typical scene would have presented cars queued up at the bottom. Some folks would be under their cars "chaining up", feet sticking recklessly close to traffic. Others would be just sitting, pondering strategy...waiting their turn. Sans chains, our greatest hope of making Clay Hill was sheer speed and to accumulate enough of that, we'd need to start clear down by Kellogg-Hubbard Library. At that point there was a half mile of flat street which would, in the best of circumstances, get us up to 50 mph before the hill started. In the worst of circumstances, however, we'd either "wipe out" on the curve where Spring Street begins or encounter some motorist who would enter Main Street from Spring Street just in front of us. In that unfortunate event, we'd have to abort our "run for the hill", go back and wait our turn again.

My education started when I was so small I could hardly see over the dashboard of our '55 Plymouth. My mother and I were coming home from the A&P with a trunk full of groceries; the blizzard had caught us, pants down, in downtown Montpelier. As we waited by the library, Mom sat as rigid as a bowling pin, white knuckling the wheel. She told me to hang on extra tight (there were no seat belts in those days) and suddenly it was our turn. She dropped the Plymouth into gear and headed out. We "sailed" into the Spring Street curve lucking out with conflicting traffic. Mom skillfully compensated from a couple of skids and shifted into high for the final run on Clay Hill. We were half way up and "just a' smokin'" when she exclaimed "Curses...that pill is pulling out in front of us!". She spat out the word "pill" like the guy had just snatched her purse. Another car had entered Clay Hill from Emmons Street and forced us to slow down; Mom had to "abort" the run and return to the queue line!

I forgot how we finally got home that day but remember being so proud of Dot Morse's skill behind the wheel! I had became proficient at Clay Hill myself when, beginning with the Volkswagen Beetle, cars started being built with engines over the drive wheels. Following the Beetle an array of Japanese front wheel drives evolved and, just like that, the need for skill in winter driving evaporated like snow under a hot iron; fitted with four good quality winter tires, modern front-wheel-drive cars will go anywhere (well, at least when driven by a Vermonter).

In some cases, the advent of front-wheel-drive cars came sooner than native Vermonters' ability to adapt. Betsy and I had just gotten married and had acquired a Toyota one time when Fall brought the need for snow tires. She'd been told that these modern cars needed snow tires all around but I, being a thrifty Yankee and expert winter driver said "Hell no Betsy! You only need traction on the drive wheels." I prevailed; we bought just two and the first time I took that car out on a snowy road, all of a sudden my world started spinning out of control and I ended up off the road with a wrecked car on my hands! To this day, I'll always "wear" four winters and can go everywhere in every storm thanks to the grace of God, a little common sense, and the latest anatomy of automobiles. 🍁

Haying Memories

I'll always remember the old grindstone's song, "SHWSHSHSHSshwshsh SHWSHSHSHshwshsh". It was a "lulling" melody to everyone but me; my ten-year-old arm had been turning its iron pipe crank since section number one of a thirty section cutter bar and felt like it was going to fall off! Grandpa Morse, a perfectionist, wouldn't declare an edge sharp unless he could shave with the cussed thing. He was smart, knew I was bitchin' and moanin' to myself, but was no doubt thinking, "it's good for th'boy". And it was.

A lot of "water's gone over the dam" since those days. I don't feel old these days but the calendar says I am. Grandpa said it would happen... "One day you'll be tellin' folks how things use-ta be just like I am now.". I'm not sure I believed him at the time and every youthful-feeling bone in my body's screaming "no" but, y'know, I guess it really is my turn.

I was born into the age of square bales and long summers. Unlike farmers today, we didn't start haying till almost July. We waited till then because there's a better chance of dryin' weather at that time of year. When there promised to be a good stretch of it, we'd whack down several fields at once... "strike while the iron's hot, b'God" Dad would say. Our Allis Chalmers B had an underslung sickle bar mower with dozens of moving parts. Its "weak link" was a thing called a Pitman Rod which pulsated close to the ground faster'n a "bat outa hell". We learned to be intimate with ledges and outcroppings, enemies of the Pitman Rod. Following the mower was the most dreaded piece of farm equipment ever made, a thing called the Cunningham Hay Conditioner. Its purported job was to take in mowed grass, crush the green stems in its two steel rollers, and spit it out for faster drying but that was just a cruel sales ploy; its real purpose was to tangle up hay and bloody the boy's knuckles who did the untangling. Next came the tedder, a kinder and gentler machine designed to "fluff" the hay for drying and when it was dry enough, it was groomed into fields full of windrows by the side-delivery rake.

Yup, those farm tools all had "personalities" of their own but the king of haying equipment was the intrepid square baler. It moved along clattering and stirring up dust, gobbling up whole windrows and parceling out neat twine-bound packages. When the baler appeared, people also appeared, people willing to work hard in the stifling heat...and,oh, by the way, it was hotter'n hell back then...don't let anyone tell you that hot, muggy weather is only a recent occurrence! We'd begin picking up bales as soon as they dropped from the baler but that scene quickly gave way to one that featured whole dotted fields. Camaraderie was born in a hayfield...dirty jokes, muscle contests, who can build the tallest load...and every once in a while mom would drive up with a trunk full of cold drinks and we'd stop and guzzle Kool Aid, ice water, or switchel (a foul-sounding but extremely thirst-quenching concoction of ginger, water, vinegar and maple syrup) by the gallon.

Wagonload after wagonload went to the barn for stacking but on marathon hay days, our '48 Ford platform dump truck filled the bill. We'd pile it high and then go hell-bent to the barn, raise it up and dump the loads. When the day was finally over, there'd be piles of dumped bales extending way beyond the 100 foot long barn and out into the yard. The job of stacking those mountains of bales would be left for the next day and the youngest of us always got chosen! It was "near torture" in the July heat but we always made a game of it; the boys feeding the hay elevator would always try to "swamp" the boys receiving bales at the top and the "bottom boys" always won.

Grandpa has been gone for thirty-seven years now and I'd give anything to be able to turn the grindstone for him one more time but that's not the way it works. No, life denies us the chance to go back and work and learn from Grandpa again but it does bring certain guarantees; the knowledge, the memories, the nostalgia will always be ours to keep. Oh and one more thing...justice...last year I dragged up what was left of that Cunningham Hay Conditioner and sold the cussed thing to Bolduc's Scrapyard for twenty cents a pound! 🍁

Forever Strawberries

My father went through a divorce back in 1966...oh no, don't get me wrong...it had nothing to do with my mother; it was that smelly herd of cows that had been vying for his attention for his first 50 years. All of a sudden, his mind was made up...no more milkin' on this farm. I think he was open to just about anything but whatever it was had to support the acreage, which he loved, and the knowledge that the "milk check" would no longer appear in Friday's mailbox. Enter strawberries. Yup, strawberries seemed reasonable at the time but we soon found out that they caused more worry and care than a barn full of brucellosis. There was planting, fertilizing, weeding, setting runners, watering, mulching, picking (if we were lucky), and selling. Then there were the strawberry villains like nematodes, cut worms, root rot, leaf spot, deer, woodchucks, frost damage, tarnished plant bugs, cedar waxwings, and slugs as big and fat as the ripe strawberries they devoured. We were particularly cursed with soil that favored rocks, ledges and huge crops of witch grass.

We raised strawberries for years, sometimes getting pretty good crops and other times total failures. Even on the good years, returns came more in the smiling faces of our customers than in dollars; our berries were tastier than others because of our farm's heavy, hilltop soil. On the bad years, some of the hardest work was just keeping the faces smiling...folks got downright despondent without their Morse Farm strawberries. One year, weeds and grass had declared such war on our two-acre field that we came up short of berries to sell. My father sought out replacement berries from a place similar to our own, one that would guarantee that "heavy hilltop" flavor. The answer came in the form of one Hezzy Somers, a farmer from West Barnet, who had a real "strawberry" attitude and, in my mind back then, the worst of both worlds...he managed to raise a few acres of the fussy fruit and milked a high butterfat herd of Jersey cows at the same time! The rest of my story relies on

40-year-old memories.

A half dozen of us had piled into the bed of our pickup and ridden, in the rain, the 40 miles to Hezzy's farm. Although the Somers place looked like it walked right out of a "Vermont Life" magazine centerfold, all of that romance was lost on us pickers. We had come to pick a few hundred quarts for sales at Morse Farm and quickly settled into our task. Hezzy's rows were a mixture of deep green, straw color and luscious red. They yielded full quarts quickly compared to our "weed patch" back home and prodded by a modest per basket payment and my father's pledge of a treat on the way home, we filled our quota and headed back to East Montpelier by noon, drenched and stiff, but done for the day.

Hezzy's "ace in the hole" bailed us out of a few other bad strawberry years and through the process we got to know him quite well. We eventually stopped going up to Hezzy's and gave up growing strawberries ourselves. Twenty years lapsed before I next saw him but one day at a farm auction somewhere in northern Vermont, I leaned against a fence beside an older man. Something about him looked familiar but when the small talk started, I knew from his West Barnet twang that I was talking to Hezzy Somers. We reminisced about the days our Morse gang picked berries in his fields and just before we parted, I asked him a special question:

"Hezzy" I said. "I always envied your ability to keep those perfect strawberry fields and milk cows at the same time...you must really love farming."

Hezzy Somers, wrinkled and stooped from a lifetime of farming, palmed his grizzled chin and went into deep thought. "Gosh" he said slowly and deliberately... "I think I like it...yup, I THINK I like it."

And that was all I got from the man who had spent a lifetime growing sweet strawberries and producing creamy Jersey milk!

One thing I KNOW is that I didn't like strawberry farming when I was doing it! Strawberries, however, have a strange "hold" on folks. Every year when June turns to July in Central Vermont, I can smell strawberries in the air and picture pickers with red fingers and catches in their backs. The nostalgia is alive and well...in my mind it'll always be "strawberry fields forever". ❧

Beans, Beans, Beans

I'm embarrassed to admit it, being an old New Englander, but I really don't like baked beans. It's not that they taste bad...I mean they're sweet and full of carbohydrates, both things I like but...well, I think there's a little "physiology" going on here. It happened way back in the seventh grade at East Montpelier's Four Corners School when my hormones were bouncin' around like Mexican jumping beans...most of them lunged in the direction of a girl named Nancy who had a smile to die for and had recently emerged from her awkward "tomboy" cocoon. Nancy didn't exactly love me back, yet, but I knew it was just a matter of time...well, it would have been but for something else that "jumped around" one day.

My mother had been baking a special treat one cold day in late November. We were all looking forward to it and finished up our barn chores extra fast just to get home and "dig in" to the butter-slathered Anadama bread right from the oven, and baked beans, flavored with maple syrup, salt pork and just the right amount of mother's little spice secrets...ummm, ummm...we couldn't wait! The next day was a school day and I was sitting just across from that "special" girl. It's too long ago to remember just what we were studying but I do remember a lack of talk. We sat, all 38 of us, making only the sounds pencils make on paper. Suddenly there was a break in that silence. It must have been the way I was sitting but it came out more like distant sniper fire than a full-scale assault...pop, pop, pop...pop, pop...pop, pop, pop, pop...pop and, contrary to the common notion that human flatulence is "voluntary", for the life of me, I could not get it stopped!

There's something about deep trauma that holds one's memory in stop time, like Pearl Harbor or when President Kennedy died, and I'm not suggesting my experience that day rates that kind of respect, but I'll never forget those few moments back at Four Corners School. Sometimes when flatulence gets the better of us, there's a chance to feign innocence by just looking around, or "throwing" sounds like a ventriloquist does; that day, however, there was no escape...I had been caught red-handed. At first, my classmates just sat shocked but when the surprise wore off, grins began blossoming like fields of garlic mustard... that is, except for the love of my life. She sat with a distressed, scrunched-up look on her face, her mouth forming the unmistakable word, EEEEYOUEW! From that day on I was a changed person...I had no use for baked beans and no future with Nancy, my fleeting first love.

My friend, Steffen Parker, is a real "bean" guy. He says it's tradition in his house to have baked beans and hot dogs cooked in them every Saturday night...guess there was never any deep "bean trauma" in his life like there was in mine! Steffen's wife, Kathryn, lovingly prepares them, right down to the dark maple syrup that melts in with the bacon, onions and special combination her own little spice secrets. A few years ago the Parkers talked us into holding a bean event at our farm, based on a custom brought to Vermont from old lumberjack days in Maine. Back when the log drives were going on, cooking crews traveled down river, 24 hours ahead of the log drivers. Once camped, they would prepare batches of beans in ceramic crocks, dig holes in the ground and line them with fieldstones. Then they would build up hardwood fires, lower the bean pots into the holes, shovel red-hot coals around them and cover them up with earth. By the time the log crew arrived the next day, the beans would be ready to dig up and serve.

Every summer Steffen and Kathryn, along with their children, Josiah, Molly and Jacob, form their own "log crew" for our bean event. They cook 'em in the ground, just like the Maine lumberjacks did, and when the beans are ready to dig up, there's always a group of folks who have gathered to witness the pot being unearthed and drawn from the hot embers. I'll be there to help out, but when the cover is lifted off for a grand unveiling of the Morse Farm bean hole beans, I won't be in line for my serving. Oh No...although the fragrance will be as heavenly to me as it is to everyone else, those few seconds of "stop time" from way back in seventh grade will come back in spades... "no beans for me, thanks. Please pass the potato salad". 🍂

Quality Boredom

I sure have been spending a lot of time in the sugarhouse lately boiling batch after batch of God's golden syrup. I've got maple sugarin' in my blood, you know, and am as much a part of that old building this time of year as the pins that hold it together and its weathered board siding. Along with that attachment comes an array of smells, sounds, sights and feelings. One of those feelings might surprise you...boredom. Yup, sugarhouse boredom has always been a strong part of the maple tradition and has grown even stronger in modern times with evaporators that require even less tending. All I have to do to fuel our new, modern evaporator is flick two switches that activate a self-unloading wagon and an auger. If the equipment works OK, the wood chips spill into a hopper like Rice Krispies into a bowl. Other than that, and changing filter papers every once in a while, all I do is sit close to the rumbling evaporator watching, waiting, feeling that power right through my wooden chair. It's an odd contrast, all that energy combining with the hundreds of gallons of sap pouring in, only to culminate in a tiny trickle of maple syrup coming out at the end of the boil.

My father was the boiler around here back in the days of cracklin' fires and shed fulls of sugarwood. Even though the wood handling was a big job, there still was a lot of watching, waiting, and feeling the rumbling. Harry Morse was an easy going, mild mannered man but I always suspected from all the Doublemint Gum wrappers I'd see around the sugarhouse that the boredom even got to him. He never chewed gum any other time of year. Once when I asked him about the boredom, I got a typical "Harry Morse" answer. First he cradled his chin in his right hand, thought for a minute, and then slowly admitted... "Well yes...there are times...but ya know, by gory...it's QUALITY boredom". He stressed the "quality" with rumbling energy and a twinkling eye. For the most part, my father spent his lifetime a non-smoker but the few times he started up were, you guessed it, in sugarin' season. Always though, as soon as the last sap bucket was pulled, my mother would step in to quash the nasty habit; Harry Morse was not going to be a smoker and Dot Morse saw to that!

My mother was death on things like smoking and drinking, and if any of us in the family were going to do either, we best hide the evidence. To this day, I never drink a beer without an "eye out" for an emergency exit or a place to stash the bottle! She made just one exception that I know of....my sister-in-law, Annie Parker, tells the story:

Dot Morse and Annie Parker taught school together over at the East Montpelier Elementary School just after it was built. Prior to that, my mother had always taught in one room schoolhouses, workplaces where the teacher not only taught but was sole disciplinarian, policy setter, and plunger of toilets; just to survive, those veteran teachers developed certain traits like intestinal fortitude, individuality and loyalty. My mother was no exception. It was a huge transition for folks like her to be suddenly "transplanted" to large schools but she was such a good teacher that she rose to the occasion. The new school, complete with a gymnasium, commercial kitchen, and library, even had a "break" room for the teachers, a place for planning, copying, gossip, and privacy from students...they quickly became "hooked", in fact downright righteous, about their break room. One day my mother was in there sorting some papers while Annie and a couple other smoking teachers sat enjoying their cigarettes. One thing led to another when someone "dropped a bomb"...the school board was considering a ban on smoking in the break room.

Emotions were, of course, high on the subject because those were the days before smoking had become passé like it is today. My mother continued her paper sorting, staying out of the conversation...up to a point, that is. Annie said suddenly Mom lunged. Her hand shot through the blue haze and snatched Annie's cigarette. "Gi'me that thing!" Dot Morse shouted. She put the cigarette up to her lips and started puffing like a maniac! All at once, it seems, Dot Morse had heard enough...recent changes in education were hard enough, she felt, without teachers being told what that could and could not do in their own privacy!

The policy did change soon after that and Annie and most of the others quit smoking. My mother, one of the best darned teachers that school ever had retired in 1982. She never mentioned the "cigarette" incident but I do remember her coming home one day a bit "green around the gills" and still fuming about something! Both she and dad are gone now. We miss them terribly right down to the principles they believed in. They both taught me that people need to maintain their rights and that change is only good when well thought out...and, oh, that a little "quality boredom" never hurt anyone.

Thanksgiving Pigs

It's time of radical transition again here in Vermont. To be honest, I never enjoy going from October's beautiful colors to winter's drab but am aware that it's just what nature does and we certainly can't fight nature. We've recently moved our goat and sheep from their summer pasture to the dark pen in the back of the barn. If they could talk, I know they would agree with me about the transition. In fact Otis, the goat, fought it for a time as goats will do. She (yes, Otis is a 'she') immediately defied our pen walls and ended up on "Vermont open range" eating decorations, both late Halloween and early Christmas. We didn't worry about the road because she seemed wise about that and was just projecting her goat message... "I only want to be free!". The thing, in fact, that made us tack up some more boards and finally get her confined for good were all the well-meaning people who stopped to tell us our goat was out... "Mercy sakes" we wanted to say... "of course we know...we live here!". Instead we said "Oh thanks for telling us...we'll get right on it." Well, finally we did.

This makes me think of another experience we once had with a different type of farm critter. A long time ago when Dad and I were raising vegetables on this place, we got a couple of sows and turned them into the cornfield. The field had been picked clean of quality corn that we sold by the dozen but still had lots of ears left that were good enough for pigs. "Too bad t'let it go t'waste", Dad said. To a pig farmer, the rest of my story might sound a bit unorthodox but we never let a little "straying from convention" bother us. All it took was a simple electric fence, a crude shelter, and a gentle brook for those rascals to be happier than a "pig in...", well, let's just say they were happy hogs.

Nature gave us an 'open winter' (a Vermont term for a winter with little snow) up to a point that year so we ended leaving them right there when weather got quite cold...they'd cuddle up warmly in their little shelter and look forward to the grain we hauled in twice a day. Along about Christmas time, one of us had the idea that the companionship of a boar would be a good present for those girls so we went out and borrowed one from a neighbor.

Sometime in January, winter finally presented itself. The snow settled with a vengeance onto our little pig community, leaving it unworkable to move them to another place. We just kept hauling in grain and watching to make sure they were making daily treks to the brook; they seemed comfortable. Since a pig's gestation period is 3 months, 3 weeks and 3 days, sometime in late sugarin', those rascals both gave birth to big, healthy litters. They had gotten so used to the great outdoors that they became a little more particular about human company than the average pig. One day my father took my cousin, David, up to the enclosure to show him the little ones. When he went in and reached to pick up a piglet, Mother sat a distance away looking pleased with the world. The first squeal, however, brought her to her feet and advancing like a lion going for the kill. She instantly knocked him down and went right for his throat. Had my cousin, a big guy, not grabbed a stick, hurdled over the fence, and beat that sow off, she surely would have killed Harry Morse Sr. that day.

As the next planting season approached, we somehow got those pigs corralled and moved to a more appropriate area. Summer's harvest led through foliage season and we suddenly realized our pigs were market ready but we had no market...our entry into the project had been too impulsive to include any know-how in selling pigs. Worst of all those devils had never lost their taste for the great outdoors and kept searching for that original cornfield...they were continually on the loose! That year we had all just sat down for our Thanksgiving meal when a car horn sounded outside. I got up from the table and looked out the nearest window. There, in stark contrast to the blacktop highway, were all 15 of our tan colored porkers parading up County Road... we Morses laid down our forks, donned clothing appropriate for the frigid November day and spent the next two hours chasing pigs! Neighborhood scuttlebutt circulated for years after that... "Those damned fool Morses don't have anything better to do on Thanksgiving Day than to chase pigs up and down the County Road!"

We finally got them back in their enclosure and returned, a bit the worse for wear, to our cold Thanksgiving spread. As I remember, it tasted pretty good in spite of our unfortunate and unusual interruption. We ended with the traditional pumpkin pie except that Dad and I had a little extra piece de resistance...a bit of pork-flavored "egg-on-our-face"! 🍁

143

Emotions With an Oink

I'm sure you've all heard about the cow's famous "lunar leap" but I've got a story about two little pigs trotting way up to the Horn of the Moon (for those who don't know, the Horn of the Moon is the western-most section of East Montpelier). The other day my brother Elliott drove in pulling his high-sided trailer. Elliott, East Montpelier's Assistant Animal Control Officer, had been called about two pigs that were on open range up in the Horn. The word was that they had already fully excavated one lawn and were heading for another one; folks up that way were starting to squeal about these potential new "land developments". Elliott had been told the pigs were docile and he thought they would follow grain right into his trailer. "Yeh sure" I thought, recalling a young pig I once found way out in the woods.

Some 35 years ago I was logging deep in the woods with a guy named Levi Gray. We had just had our lunch and were about to resume logging when all of a sudden a little black and white pig ambled up the nearby brook. The fat little guy kept coming toward us and ended up right at our feet, rooting around for bag lunch remnants. We knew the pig was a long way from home and needed to be returned. Although he was quite tame, he shied away when we reached to touch him and repeated attempts made him all the more shy. Pigs'll never run far like a cow or a horse but they're smart and proficient at feinting, bobbing and weaving. We spent the next half hour in a furious bout with the rascal, our leaps netting only fleeting hoof grasps and wild dives into muddy voids; our shouts of strategy echoed throughout the forest. At last Levi, the younger of our duo, made a desperate lunge that enveloped the pig. Quicker'n a flash, I clamped onto two hind feet and raised the beast into the air. Levi rushed to empty our burlap tool bag and held it for me to deposit the screaming devil into. Unfortunately our struggle was not without bloodshed; at some point in the melee the pig had bit me deeply in my left index finger leaving a scar that I bear to this day.

When Elliott asked if I'd like to accompany him to the Horn of the Moon that day, I grabbed two pair of thick leather welding gloves, thinking of my experience so long ago, and jumped in his truck. We knew we were close when we approached a small group of people gathered across the road from a lawn that resembled a war zone. Elliott backed the trailer up to a roadside bank and we joined the group of people. In the group was Sandy Conti, East Montpelier's Chief Animal Control Officer. Sandy, seasoned in cats and dogs, looked rather out of his element holding a lasso and staring down two white pigs. The pigs, one about 150 pounds and the other half that size, were very sociable. In fact when Sandy approached the larger one with his noose, the guy simply accepted it like a scratch on the rump. Having grown up around the creatures, however, I knew the futility of lassoing a pig and I think the pig did, too. A pig's head is shaped just wrong for a lasso to grasp (think roping a pyramid). Sandy's repeated attempts were met with quick circular strolls followed by nonchalant "shake offs" and all the while, Mr. Oink seemed to be laughing at us... "umphumphumphHAWHAWHAW".

We humans were getting down right frustrated with the caper when I finally suggested to Sandy that we make a halter to fit around his neck and in back of his front feet at the same time. Sandy, a complete gentleman, handed me the rope and said, "Be my guest". Remembering how my grandpa would have done it, I fashioned the halter. When I knelt down and fastened it to the pig, the beast's temperament took an immediate about-face; he knew he could not escape this hitch and started screaming like a banshee. Our group, with the addition of a small army of passersby, promptly grabbed hold and "towed" the flailing beast onto Elliott's trailer. Once there, he toppled onto his side and began crying in the most mournful way I have ever heard. The smaller pig, in the meantime, was easily caught and coaxed onto the trailer to be with his wailing friend. The wailing only stopped when we closed the trailer's tailgate and released him from the halter. We transported them to a nearby horse farm for temporary housing until the pigs' owners could be found.

They say pigs are among the smartest of animals and I'll not only agree but would add "emotional" to the mix. I'll never forget the change in that guy's attitude; he went from "Let's have fun with these foolish humans" to "Oh my God, they're thinkin' 'bacon'" in the shake of a curly little tail. If truth be known, in fact, I had to hide some tears of my own over the mournful sounds I heard that day...although I'm a meat eater, I'll no doubt lay off pork for a while! The owners claimed their animals a couple days later (not without, I might add, paying for some re-landscaping and a little pig food!). I 've always wondered how fairy tales get started... "cats and fiddles, jumping cows, falling Humpty Dumptys". Who knows, maybe years from now there'll be one about "the sobbing pig...way up in the Horn of the Moon". 🍁

A Different Seed

Contrary to what some folks think, sometimes it makes great sense to cut sugar maple trees and send 'em off to the sawmill. Yup, I tell folks often that you're either a sugarmaker or a logger. If you're a sugarmaker, you nurture those blessed beings so they'll be trusted servants for over one hundred years. If you're a logger, you cut 'em down systematically so there's always young ones left to grow. That's what my brother, Tick, just did up at his woodlot in Calais on the old Robinson Farm. Tick is trained as a forester so he knows when to cut 'em and which ones will gain from the thinning. He also knows his trees, but black maple, Acer nigrum, is not in his vernacular.

The other day he approached a big maple with his chain saw. Something about its bark made him stop short, however. The bark had a strange pattern to it—this tree had a different attitude from the Acer saccharum, whose language Tick speaks. Since it was prime, however, he revved his chain saw, notched it and felled the giant. When the dust cleared he went back to the stump and counted the growth rings—about one hundred years old, it was. From that prostrate perspective, however, the tree looked even more foreign than when standing. He was anxious to get home and look it up in his old forestry textbook.

I was down at my mother's house the next morning when she told me that Tick had identified the tree he'd cut as a black maple—hmmm—my mind went back to a trip I made to Iowa last spring. In Iowa they tap black maples, not sugar maples. Black maples thrive in the rich soil of northeast Iowa but are non-existent here in Central Vermont. I remembered telling my mother about those black maples. Suddenly we looked at each other, mental telepathy coursing like sap in a maple tree: "We're both thinking about old Irvin Robinson, aren't we?" she said.

My great grandfather, Irvin Robinson was a frustrated farmer. He was born into the hills of Calais, Vermont and spent much of his life working the

147

boney, side hill soil there. Crops on the Robinson Farm were marginal at best; it's safe to say, in fact, that there was only one crop my great grandfather was proficient at—daughters. My great grandmother, Nellie, had seven daughters in quick succession and Irvin got more frustrated with each one. He wanted a son, not only to carry on the Robinson name, but to do the farm work that had never come easy to him. Irvin Robinson spent as much time dreaming about foreign places as he did farming.

One time, in fact, right after Teddy Roosevelt left the presidency and headed east for exotic trophies, Irvin hopped on a train and headed west for trophies of his own. He had always dreamed about the Plains and the open skies out there where the buffalo roam. He ended up in northeast Iowa, ironically in the area where hills and maples abound, much the same as Irvin's native Maple Corner back in Calais. In spite of the sameness, Irvin was excited to be in a new place. He traveled the area by horseback and came across a farm that he wanted to buy.

The rest of my story is, admittedly, speculation but I have a feeling in my bones that it happened this very way: He telegraphed Nellie back in Vermont and told her to pack up the girls and come out. "We're going to relocate in the hills of Iowa," he said, "where a different maple grows and fortunes abound." (I'm sure he was thinking the new life in Iowa would somehow beget a son for Nellie and him, as well.) Nellie's return telegraph was short and to the point: "Irvin, if you don't get your bones back here on the next train, you won't have a place to live!"

Irvin dejectedly placed Nellie's message in the rubbish and bought a return ticket east. While waiting for the train, he went back out into the country. He faced west, breathed in the excitement of a new place, and relished the life that could have been. The last thing he did was to stop under one of those Iowa maples and slip a seed in his pocket.

He came into Montpelier Junction early in the morning and hired a man with a carriage to take him the eight miles north to Calais. As they approached the Robinson Farm, just prior to his reunion with all the girls, he had the driver stop. He got out, walked a ways down over the bank and removed the seed from his pocket. He leaned over, pawed a hole in the Calais earth and planted that black maple seed. He made his way back to the carriage and pointed to the homestead on the next hill. "That's where I'm going," he told the driver. Somehow he felt better on the last leg of his trip—he'd just planted another seed, a different seed this time. 🍁

Plush Plumbin'

I just returned from runnin' the chainsaw all day and it took about as long as a tree to fall for me to shed my filthy clothes and let our powerful shower wash away the wood chips and grime. That glorious feeling hasn't been possible long. No sir, our old shower's pressure would have made a geezer with a lemon-sized prostate look like a spewing hydrant. It was pathetically piddly...hardly better than a trudge to the brook in January...let's turn the clock back 33 years.

I was a frustrated 27-year-old living off a pauper's income and trying to balance the love of continuing this farm with nature's leanings...I wanted a family and for that to happen I needed a house. Thankfully, I was born with a chainsaw in my hands so the task of cutting logs and hauling them to the neighbors to be sawed was the easy part. Somehow I 'worried' the boards into place even though the most complicated thing I had ever built was a calf pen. An older brother helped me with the electrical work but plumbing was another story; I grew up wearing a couple "cup half empty" tenets like a badge...water will always leak and goats will always get out. Thoughts of my rough boarded bungalow, an angry wife and two crying babies were daunting enough without the added the misery of "water, water everywhere".

In spite of my fears, I knew that living without plumbing was not an option. One day I went down to our local creaky-floored hardware store and approached Mr. Ruggles. "S'pose you could teach me plumbin' in ten minutes," I asked, halfway between joking and desperation. Don Ruggles was a typical hardware guy, savvy in everything "door jam, light socket and kitchen sink". He also was a businessman and knew that if he was going to sell me all the stuff to plumb a small house, he'd better honor my request. He took me aside and explained the process of 'sweating', or soldering copper pipes and then started collecting all the tail pieces, half bends and hubless connectors that I would need. At the end of the session (which lasted some more than ten minutes), I took all of the stuff home.

I certainly don't mean to diminish professional plumbers by suggesting that one can learn the trade in a single lesson but somehow I did end up plumbing my house. Lots of human sweat went into 'sweating' my pipes that appeared thoroughly dobbed with silvery pigeon poop, but they held. To this day those pipes deliver water efficiently and without leaks for my family's needs. The one thing however, that has never worked was one tub-shower fixture that I got a 'deal' on way back then. The thing was 'buried' in the wall so, for 30 years, I've thought we had to live with its idiosyncrasies of leaking, belching and piddling. I never dared to call a professional because of the mess my plumbing was. "This time I'll fix that cussed shower," I'd say to Betsy but my sessions always ended with thrown wrenches, more swearing and the thing working a little worse.

A while ago we'd enough. I called David Pope, a neighbor, plumber by trade and nice guy to boot. I figured if anyone would take the job on, he would. Over the phone, I was honest about my situation and joked that if it got any worse, he'd be smellin' us clear up at his place. David, ever the professional, said something like "Oh it can't be that bad" and agreed to come down in a couple days. On the appointed day he came in, flashlight in hand and approached the problem area from all sides, finally crawling under the rough countertop I had toggled so many years ago. "I've seen messes much worse than this," he quickly said, not denying that it was a mess but suggesting that there are, indeed, 'messes of scale'. He told me where he would make a small hole in my kitchen wall and that it would be no big deal.

Two weeks later what had been a huge thorn in my side for thirty years had suddenly been solved by the painless 'household laparoscopy' of a true professional. Yes, I wrote him a good-sized check but it was the best money I ever spent. One time an old plumber told me the downside of his trade was that nobody ever saw his work; it was always buried in walls. Sure, we don't see what's buried in walls but every time I take a shower these days, I feel the result of a plumber's good work wash away the daily grime and memories of a very bad experience. ✹

Yankee Yahoo

I've always felt that the terms "real Vermonter" and "Yankee" could be used interchangeably but a recent incident has led me to a little soul searching. Although the definition of both have been questioned over the years, I feel that the term "real Vermonter" is much easier to qualify; my roots have reached into the same Vermont hillside for seven generations. I constantly crave dried beef gravy, sugar on snow, and peas with new potatoes. To me, splitting wood and hefting bales are the two best exercises (What the hell does "aerobic" mean, anyway?). And my definition of "political correctness" is "a vote for the best American"...I am a real Vermonter! As far as my classification in the phylum "Yankee" goes, however, I seem to lack one of the major qualities...I'm terrible at "makin' deals". Yup, I can get "cheated" by just thinking of getting up in the morning...don't even have to actually rise from between the sheets!

My family has a strong history of proper Yankee horse tradin'. My siblings can pinch nickels with the best of 'em and I've got cousins who not only pinch 'em but still have their first ones! Poor ol' me on the other hand...Old Midas was off-duty the day I was born! The incident that brought me to this point happened recently after I answered a call-in ad on our local radio show "The Trading Post".

That morning, a man named Mac from Williamstown (names and places have been changed to protect both the innocent and the most shameless of horse traders) called in saying he had an onion hoe he'd sell for ten dollars. Because of my "challenge", I'm usually never tempted by Trading Post deals, but that morning the words "onion hoe" struck my fancy. Back when my father and I were eking out our living growing vegetables on this place, we had a whole fleet of onion hoes. A true onion hoe has a narrow, sharp blade that'll chop through the heaviest soil, a long, back-friendly handle, and an endurance that'll outlive season after season of hard labor. When we phased out vegetable farming, our onion hoes disappeared one at a time. Although my days as a produce grower bring back many memories that I'd rather forget, I'll always consider the "onion hoe" a loyal and worthy partner.

Suddenly that simple tool dangled huge before my eyes like a fresh, garden carrot...I had to have that onion hoe! I called the guy from Williamstown and said I'd be right over. I had no problem finding his place and he quickly answered my rap on his door... "yup, I'm the guy with th' hoe" he said, assessing me through narrow eyes as if I'd been wearing a suit and carrying a brief case. "Hoe's right there...good 'un...worth every penny" he said in words that would have sounded alarms with either of my brothers.

The hoe, which appeared to be brand-spanking new, leaned against a nearby wall. From the distance I could see a hand-scribbled $10.00 tag on it, obvious remnants from a yard sale. As I walked over to it, a crusty Yankee voice somewhere in my soul screamed... "looks, by God, like a cheap hardware store hoe t'me. Why's he sellin' a brand new hoe, anyway?...Burr Morse you damned fool...you're about t'get took!". I ignored the voice, picked the hoe up and extracted a ten dollar bill from my wallet. The guy shook my hand and inserted the ten in his own thick billfold. I took that hoe home and proudly gave it to my son, Tommy, who has begun growing vegetables again on our place. Tommy came to me the next day saying it had completely fallen apart on its first "swipe" into our heavy soil... "I'm sorry...total junk" he said.

A couple weeks later, I was at a party at my brother Elliott's house. As folks do at those affairs, we were all sitting around shooting the breeze and, you guessed it, "horse tradin'" was a hot topic. I heard about recent yard sale trophies, everything from rototillers to battery chargers, deals all signed and sealed by the true "Midas touch". I sat contritely for the longest time knowing that I had nothing to offer. Finally, though, be it simple stupidity or maybe even innate honesty (a positive Yankee trait that I do have), I found myself telling the "hoe" story. They let me get only as far as the "ten dollar" part, however, when things changed as suddenly as a torrent in a cabbage patch... "You'd pay ten dollars for a hoe?", chided brother Tick. And then my nephew Brian joined in, "Williamstown?...you'd drive all the way to Williamstown for a hoe?". All of a sudden all eyes were on me, wise, frugal eyes...Yankee eyes. "Uhhh...ya...I...I guess...I did" I admitted, head bowed like a boy who'd just been caught in the cookie jar.

The party had ended and I was back home when the humor of it hit me enough to relate my story to Betsy. "Yup" I said. "I admitted to my own flesh and blood that I got 'walloped' again by a Yankee trader". Betsy, who loves me in spite of my "handicaps", thought the incident was funny... "Burr" she said, "Don't worry about it. You just made a ten dollar installment on your education loan, that 's all.". Oh, I'm sure all those kinfolk love me, too, but part of 'em will always question my pedigree... "guy's good at a few things" they'll say, "but he sure can't make a deal." ❧

Umbrellas Are Swell

I've been a farmer and a Morse for more than six decades now and must admit that both qualities bring on certain little "life disclaimers" like, "men don't wear shorts, farmers hate ball games, and the best forms of exercise are splitting wood and loosening lug nuts". After much soul searching and a little personal therapy, I'm just beginning to work my way free of these matters of previous gospel: I now slip on shorts when the temperature is over ninety; although I still have no use for football, basketball, hockey or group hugs, I've recently become an avid Red Sox fan; and Betsy has even coaxed me onto her stationary bicycle on occasion.

One time Betsy found out about one of my father's little "rainy day" quirks. When our son Tommy was just a little guy, she sent him with an umbrella to wait for the school bus. My father, who lived just across the road from where Tommy stood, decided to have a little fun with his grandson. He went out to where Tommy was and, using his pet name for the boy, announced: "Sir Thomas Iguanas, you know Morse men don't ever use umbrellas!" Tommy, a big-eyed towhead, was too naive to catch his grandpa's wink but, sure as shootin', felt his first testosterone that day...he looked up at his grandpa with horror, collapsed the umbrella, and tossed it aside. I recently asked Tommy if he remembered the episode; "hell yes", the thirty-year-old six-footer replied... "haven't touched an umbrella since!".

Call me a "chip off the ol' block" but you know, at the expense of runny noses galore and hampers full of drenched clothes, I've always resisted umbrellas myself! One day last week, we had buses arriving almost bumper to bumper here at Morse Farm. It was peak foliage but no one would have known it through the torrential rainfall that started in early morning and lasted into the night. I spent much of the day guiding our guests from motor coach to sugarhouse with a big John Deere umbrella. I held it at arm's length so that they would be fully sheltered; after all, it made no difference that I was on its periphery because I am the one who doesn't believe in umbrellas! Yes, I wore a raincoat but raincoats never quite "cut the mustard" in a downpour. Needless to say between buses, I made several "pit stops" home to change into dry clothes.

Probably "punchy" from spending my day like a drowned rat, I did something very out of keeping toward the end of the afternoon, something that had the same effect on my psyche as "my first kiss" or "the day Kennedy died"...I took that umbrella and strolled out into the rain. The feeling of euphoria was instant and explosive...I felt free; a world I had never seen before suddenly opened before my eyes; I stood in a dry micro world while there was nothing but misery all around me and, like a new-born calf taking its first steps, I edged further out in the parking lot to find that my "safety zone" moved right along with me...just like Gene Kelly in "Singin' in the Rain", I was suddenly sky high with that rain storm!

On the subject of umbrellas, my grandparents Morse told me an "umbrella" story one time that has been passed down in our family since the early 1800s. They said that Grandma Robinson (my great grandmother), a prim and proper woman who never used a cuss word, told them a story once about her grandparents. It seems her grandfather always had fast horses. One time they were driving an especially high strung mare to the village of Maple Corner and a thunderstorm suddenly came up. The mare was spooked by the storm and beginning to run out of control but old Grandpa, intimate with his horses, knew that Grandma's umbrella was aggravating the problem.

"Put down your umbrell!" he shouted over the storm.

"Ehh?" said Grandma who was very hard of hearing.

"Put down your umbrell!" he shouted louder.

"Yes, yes, the mare does go well" said Grandma.

At this point, prim Grandma Robinson braced herself and continued her story... "and then Grandpa screamed 'Dammit...dammit to hell, PUT DOWN YER UMRELL!'. That finally got results!" she said.

Sometimes I think native Vermonters are more affected by these "life's little disclaimers" than anyone else. My formative years were rife with stupid little things that "we" weren't supposed to do or like. Who knows, maybe my father's position against umbrellas stemmed from that horse incident so long ago. I know now, however, that these things don't have to be forever... when it comes to umbrellas, I'm cured. I'm free...I'll keep my trusty John Deere "umbrell" handy for the rest of my life! ✹

Cousins Removed

I've got a couple of special cousins up the road. In genealogical terms, they're my "first cousins once removed" but these guys have such a good time when they're together, the question might be "what are they removed from?". Seventy-eight year old Stanley Morse and his brother Kent, 70, live a short tractor's drive away from each other up in Calais on the farm that their great grandfather John Morse worked back in the early 1800s. I expect old John would be proud that Stanley still hays the fields that were cleared way back then. In fact, it was my need for six bales of hay that took me there a few weeks ago. When I drove in the yard, Stanley and Kent were talking with each other out by the newly painted red barn. Somehow the family bickering that haunts so many sibs these days has escaped these two guys although I'm sure they'd never admit it. A visit with them always leaves me somewhere between just feelin' good and "knees slappin' silly".

The two Morse brothers seemed happy to see me as usual and after we got the 'weather' and a couple other expected subjects out of the way, I nudged them toward one of their stories. "Kent...tell 'im about the time I almost killed you with the dump rake" Stanley said, beaming like only an older brother can. "Tell 'im, Kent...he'll get a kick outa that one." Kent rolled his eyes and then got this dung-eatin' grin on his face that made me know the story was on its way.

"Wellll...we went over to David's (another brother) in the truck." Kent said. "He was drivin'"...Kent's rolling eyes beckoned at Stanley "and when we got there, he backed up to the rake. We got out and both grabbed one end...you know, those things gotta tip the scales at more than half a ton...and lifted it up t' the level of the truck bed. All of a sudden he asked if I could hold it alone while he backed the truck up under it. I said 'no!' He said, 'ya sure?' I hollered NO! and the next thing I knew he was on his way to the truck sayin' 'why, of course you can!'"

By that time Stanley was showing early signs of 'melt-down' as Kent continued... "I just knew I couldn't hold that thing but I knew if I let go, it would kill me...seemed like it was takin' forever for him to back that truck up!" Kent's voice rose to a higher pitch and Stanley's laughter got louder. They left the end of the story for speculation but I assumed, since Kent stood before me glaring at the doubled over Stanley, that he and a dose of adrenaline managed to keep the dump rake suspended that day.

The next story they told was about something that didn't stay suspended. Stanley pointed to the roofline of his barn and said "Ya don't see that weather vane up there, do ya?" I remembered a historic weather vane shaped like a horse that had adorned the barn my whole life. It seems one day they decided to go flying in Stanley's airplane. Stanley drove over to Kent's to pick him up and it was such a pretty day, he stopped to take a picture of his farm from Kent's dooryard. Then they drove up to the E.F. Knapp Airport, started up the Cessna and headed north so Kent could take some pictures with his camcorder of the home place. When they got just overhead, Stanley angled the plane to the perfect point where Kent could snap away. Kent said he tried to get Stanley to go lower but he was too careful. "Hmmmm" I considered, thinking of the dump rake!

After a pleasant afternoon of flying, the Morse brothers returned to the airport, parked the plane and returned home. A day later when Stanley noticed the weather vane was missing, he went right over and told Kent. Kent, a retired employee of the Vermont State Police, went immediately into detective mode. "Let's look at that picture you took from my place before we went flyin'," he said. One quick look confirmed that the weather vane was there at that point in time. Kent next suggested they run the movie pictures he had taken from the airplane, "just in case". When they did, Stanley said they both just about jumped out of their skin... "It was a bit blurry" Stanley said, "but there in that footage was a person walking away from my place"... while the Morse brothers were directly overhead in a small Cessna, a thief was just walking away after climbing the roof and stealing Stanley's heirloom weather vane!

I asked if they ever caught the scoundrel and got the weather vane back but Stanley said 'no'...said they weren't quite close enough to get a good picture of his face but that the "cuss knew who he was and would have to live with himself." When I drove from Stanley's yard that day with my six bales of hay, the rearview mirror revealed both a roof line missing a horse-shaped copper weather vane and two guys with hearts of gold...my cousins Stanley and Kent Morse, "once removed" from all the baggage that makes the rest of us so uptight. 🍂

Maple Misnomer

It started with a telephone call I got the other night. The lady said she had a friend from South Carolina who had heard that maple trees could suddenly explode. He wanted to know if it was safe to let his children go near a maple tree. The lady was a little embarrassed, having to seek out an expert maple guy, but she needed an answer for her friend. I laughed, wondering if the guy had been into the sap beer, and considered making up some wise-crack answer. I opted, however, for diplomacy and explained how maples are our friends and would never hurt anyone. She accepted my assurance that the children would be safe.

My brother told me later that there had been an April Fool's satire on the subject of exploding maples on public radio earlier in the spring. It seems some down-country writer had heard the weather up here in Vermont was not right for sap runs. He'd written that the maples were so ravenous to run that they were "exploding." The humor of the piece obviously escaped some listeners, like the guy from South Carolina. Being a bit of a writer myself, I wasn't about to let some down-country guy sensationalize my maple trees better than me. At the risk of perpetuating a falsehood I started thinking up some "explosive" maple language of my own.

In the fall, maples explode with reds, oranges, and golds, and cause major tremors throughout the Vermont economy. In the spring, they explode with the news that winter is over and our immediate future bears lots of mud and, with luck, a sweet sugar season. In the summer they provide an explosive amount of shade to picnic and have fun under. In the winter, well, I've heard 'em crack like a gun at forty below zero. It's a harmless cracking—just their way of complaining about the temperature, I suppose. Then I heard about how my cousin, Stanley Morse, used to split wood using black powder. Hmmm…that sounded interesting, so I drove up to his place.

I found Stanley and his younger brother, Kent, out at an ancient tool shed installing a security light. Stanley and Kent live next door to each other on the farm our common ancestor, John Morse, owned back in the early 1800's. They stopped what they were doing and greeted me wholeheartedly. I told them the nature of my story and Stanley said he had, indeed, split wood before using explosives. He reminded me that hardwood, like people, had different personalities:

"I used to go over to the Creamery Store in Barre and buy these special wedges," he said. "Every once in a while there'd be a tree that was ornery as the devil…impossible to split. We'd drill down through the center of it with a hand auger and pound in one of those wedges. Then we'd pack it with black powder, touch it off, and run like hell. They'd usually split down to a more agreeable state and we'd work them up the rest of the way with a hammer and wedge."

He said one time there was a woodcutting bee for the Maple Corner School. They felled a huge maple that proved disagreeable right from the start. The auger handle broke before they completed drilling but they pounded the wedge in as far as it would go and packed it with black powder. Stanley said when they touched it off the wedge, not being fully anchored, followed the path of least resistance.

"It was a war zone out there," he said. "We all dropped down behind the biggest trees we could find. That powder wedge zinged all around us—sounded like a rocket. It finally echoed off into the hills. We never did find it."

Stanley is 75 years old now and still works in the woods. He said his wife, Janice, bought him a walkie-talkie set for Christmas because she was concerned about him working in the woods alone. Stanley "harrumphed" over the walkie-talkies: "I feel safest when it's just me and the trees. When someone else goes to the woods with me, I have to worry about them doing something stupid and killin' me!"

I said goodbye to the two Morse brothers and got in my car to leave. My thoughts turned toward great, great grandfather, John Morse, as I glanced at the field across the road from Stanley's big red barn. I visualized him looking down at the field that would soon be cut by modern, green machinery. I knew he approved of time's changes and was proud that Stanley still owned and cared for the farm. He especially focused on one thing that hadn't changed—on the hillside beyond the field, maples still gently waved in the breeze. ❧

Old Friendships, Sweet Skiing

Sometime ago our Vermont maple and skiing industries married up. On the surface they seem like strange bedfellows, flashy, spandex skiers and grizzly, woolen sugarmakers, but, really, I say "Why not?" They sure do have some things in common...the snow, the wooded slopes, the special appliances to navigate wintry countryside, and the need to sell their "product" to down-country folk. Toward that end, they have pooled resources and printed a map and guide that'll direct you to the nearest slope and then to a convenient sugarhouse for a container of your favorite grade of syrup, "apres ski".

I got in on the cutting edge of this union. When I was a boy, we had a ski area all our own right here on the farm. It was the brainchild of Dean Shattuck, an avid skier who would eventually marry my sister, and my brother, Elliott, a jack-of-all sprockets, wheels, motors and transmissions. Elliott, charged with the task of getting skiers up the hill, first experimented with powering a rope tow with the wheels of jacked up tractors and cars. When that failed, he retreated to his workshop with a Ford engine, parts of an ancient hay hoist and some Thomas Edison determination. The result was a rope pullin' machine that served our farm slope, and the entire East Montpelier-Calais community for the next ten years.

It was on that old hill and in the accompanying ski shack that many of us had our first love affairs, drank our first beer, and smoked our first cigarettes but we also learned how to ski. Thanks to hundreds of hours and a few tips from Dean Shattuck, I ended up pretty good at the downhill art. My reputation preceded me in 1962 to Montpelier High School and the MHS Ski Team. The ski coach, Mr. Johan Naess, had high hopes for me as a member of the downhill slalom team but that proved short lived; I looked great on a farm slope but was dismal at competition...to me gates were meant to keep cows in and not to "swoosh" through at 60 MPH. Every time I approached a gate,

I became a somersaulting projectile headed for the hinterlands.

Mr. Naess was determined to find a niche for me. He first tried me on the cross-country team but, although I stayed upright, was too slow...doomed by short, stubby legs. The last, and least likely resort for this landlubber non-athlete, was jumping. Coach Naess fitted me with special jumping skis, assured me that I could do it, and took me to a place where there were no gates; just a gaping dropoff interrupted by a brief moment of flight. I was terrified but wanted to do it for Coach, who had stood up for me all along. After my first couple jumps, I warmed up to the sport and began developing good form and flying like a bird.

I would also quickly learn that Mr. Naess was one of the nicest guys in the world. The old cliche, "he would take the shirt off his back", took on a literal meaning one day at a jumping meet up in Newport. My mother had just bought me a new jacket. The jacket, one that I had picked out, was made of a shaggy, synthetic material, colored brown with bursts of vermillion in odd places. It was, to say the least, unique. I had it on that day in Newport and when they cinched the number bib on my chest, the jacket puffed out like an angry chicken. Just before the competition was to begin, Mr. Naess approached me.

"Burr...I'd like you to wear my sweater today" he said as he pulled the sleek-looking ski sweater over his head. I feebly objected, saying that I liked my jacket. "Please", he persisted. It was my last attempt, "why", that put him over the edge. "Because, my goodness, you look like Magilla Gorilla in that thing and I want my jumpers to look good!" he shouted as kindly as possible for "one of the world's nicest guys".

I quickly stripped the thing off, my face probably as red as its bursts of vermillion, and donned the sweater that made me look sleek and helped me win the meet that day.

I recently ran into Mr. Naess at the Vermont Tourism Conference held down in Manchester. The youthful-looking Johan Naess was on a panel speaking as one of Vermont's working senior citizens; ironically I look older than he does these days and we joked about that. We also reminisced about the old ski team days and the strange twists and turns that life brings; both he and I work these days in Vermont's tourism industry. He is a guide over at Rock of Ages Granite Quarries and I entertain many of the same visitors here at Morse Farm.

The conference was both fun and educational. Like Mr. Naess, I was on a panel as well. The theme of ours was "How to Stay in Business Through Tough Times". I was the agri-tourism / maple man on the panel along with delegates from The Vermont Country Store, Green Mountain Coffee Roasters and, what else...Okemo Ski Resort...skiing and maple...a match made especially for Vermont. 🍁

My Land, Your Land

Betsy came back after her walk in the woods with the dogs this morning saying she had an idea for my next writing. She loves to walk the cross-country ski trails and never returns without a story to tell of something new and different she saw out there. The dogs love it, too, but Averill, the older one is a might territorial...if she was human, she would probably tack up "posted" signs along our borders.

The thought of those "posted" signs brings me back to Betsy's idea: She said the old Woody Guthrie song, "This Land is Your Land...This Land is My Land" kept popping into her head out there on her walk. The whole idea that my conservative wife Betsy would suggest using anything from old radical Woody's repertoire as a model kind of intrigued me... "Hmmmm... this could be interesting" I thought. She went on to point out a story about my late father Harry Morse. He was sitting at the breakfast table one time when a family member rushed in saying there was someone down at the farm pond fishing. That family member expected Harry to get all shook up and rush right down there and kick the poacher off the land. Instead, he finished chewing his mouth full of oatmeal, looked up and said: "S'pose he's havin' any luck?".

Although there have been a few times our pond has been fished clean.... nary a single trout left...we still have never posted this farm. As Harry Morse would probably say "Why, we just expect 'em to behave!". There are occasional pitfalls to the Harry Morse "be courteous with your countryside" plan. We've had gates left open, Kleenex and energy bar wrappers dropped here and there, and signs of a few teenage parties held out in our Christmas trees; what I saw the other day, however, takes the cake: Tommy had called me over to where he lives in our old farmhouse to help him with a project. As I drove in, I glanced back at the pasture area over to the east and there, way out in the middle of nowhere, was an SUV pulling a little cargo trailer. It was right on the edge of a vernal pool and I knew even from the distance that it was stuck "tighter'n a gnat's arse". I mean, this was a rig meant to move a college kid home for the summer or grandma from her sprawling residence to a condo but out in the Morse Farm pasture in rain season...no way!

Normally I would have hopped on the tractor and gone over there. I probably wouldn't have "chewed 'em out" but would surely have suggested they were a long way from I-89, hitched on and pulled 'em free. Instead I got busy helping Tom with his project and forgot about what was out in the pasture. In the meantime, Betsy watched the whole process from our house. She said it was a woman driving the rig and the whole situation seemed strange but she's so used to seeing "anything goes" occurrences here at the Morse Farm that she assumed the woman had some purpose out there.

She went on to describe a Triple A wrecker showing up and slowly driving out toward the grounded SUV. "It was quite a process" she said. "I could see the wrecker guy strategizing and finally slogging out through the swampy pasture to hitch his cable on to the vehicle's underside...he had to move his truck several times and re-hitch but finally got the thing out without getting stuck too.". When I came back from Tom's, there were telltale signs on County Road where that rig had finally gotten away; mud was everywhere... the blacktop road looked like a big manure spreader had gone berserk! We never did find out why that woman ended up in our "back forty" with her SUV and cargo trailer. 🍁

Wild "Meating"

Recently my son Tommy's been building a corral out front to catch a couple of his beef cows that are ready for market. By definition, I guess, the beef cow's job is to eat, put on weight, preserve and fertilize open land, and, yes, finally end up on our dinner table. And, I might add, while doing that they sure look pretty out there. I enjoy a good hamburger as much as the next guy and truly believe those critters pass on to the "carnivore's curtain call" without even an inkling of what's happening to them. They do, however, so enjoy the munching part of their existence that they have developed uncanny creativity in not getting caught. In fact, beef cows, although incapable of real "thought", are masters at "thinking outside of the box".

While TV offers generous glimpses of cowboys roping critters and even jumping from horses and tackling them to the ground, none of that stuff really works...it's all Hollywood. In spite of the hype, there's nothing that'll catch a three-quarter-ton critter better than a bucket of grain, a small corral built of strong planks...let's call it a "box", and a lot of luck. The logic is good; you lead 'em to the box with the bucket of grain they can't resist. They go in the box and you close the gate to lock 'em in. It works fine on paper except for the bovine's Murphy-centered ability to "think outside the box". Usually they make a decision just nanoseconds before the gate is closed, opting for continued munching somewhere in the back forty.

I'm reminded of the old days when my father and I had a whole herd of beef cows on this place. Every fall we had to corral a few for market and, no, we never got good at catchin' the buggers. One time we struggled for days to corral a Hereford/Ayrshire cross, the Northern Hemisphere's equivalent to the Tasmanian Devil. Finally we got him into our high-sided Studebaker truck and transported him to the local slaughterhouse. Being Vermont, a place hardly known for its meat industry, our only slaughterhouse was run by a guy who was world-class at skinnin' both cows and customers; I'll always think of him as "the fat butcher".

My father was so leery of him that he dropped both me and the critter off, figuring it wouldn't hurt to make sure only the four-legged of us got skun. As long as I was there, the fat butcher put me to work pushing wheelbarrow loads of offal to a waiting dumpster and salting piles of cowhides. When our animal's number came up, we attached a rope halter to him and led him onto the floor where beef cows enter the last part of their "job description". Although the butcher had led thousands of them to this point, he didn't take into consideration the qualities of a Hereford/Ayrshire cross and their instant hankerin' for the back forty. I was about to draw the rope through a steel ring in the floor when that critter wanted out. He yanked the rope from me like I was a toddler and then all hell broke loose.

I distinctly remember seeing the double doors that led to the "aging room" burst open and hearing heavy, slapping sounds and cries of human terror. I rushed in just in time to see the fat butcher projected like a rag doll up onto a ten foot high freezer. The raging steer did an about-face and headed back through still swinging sides of beef and out the next doors to the meat market. There he ran through a narrow aisle past display coolers full of New York Sirloin and fresh hamburger. The entrance door was open and that critter made his final exit to the great outdoors. He ran through a small field, swam across the Winooski River, and settled in a bigger field way out back. Three of us, a shaken up fat butcher, a very angry state meat inspector, and I stood outside the meat market watching the distant critter, head down, grazing like nothing ever happened!

Thirty years of meat-eating bliss have passed since that episode and, although I swear to God all of the above is true, I've dropped out memory of that critter's fate. For all I know, he still roams the hills between East Montpelier and Barre Town satisfied with the quality of forage. More likely, though, we finally caught him and had him processed to a tamer and tastier state. That fat butcher has long since gone on to the big slaughterhouse in the sky and I'm not anxious to ever repeat the experience I had that day. I'll just encourage Tommy to use extra planks, pray for luck, and be prepare for the inevitable...a bovine's uncanny ability to think outside of the box. ❦

"It" Happens

'Tis the season, the season of spreading good will on earth, and although Christmas is just around the corner, I'm talkin' about something much less sacred but important none-the-less...whittling down th'old manure supply. Yup...if you're a farmer in Vermont, it's time to spread it on the earth and it's going to take a pile of "good will" because of the way it smells! These days farmers are under the gun for disposal of what we used to fling about liberally any day of the year. They store it in huge containers called "lagoons", mix it with water, and spread it in giant trucks with very dirty backsides. The other day I knew they were spreading in the neighborhood long before I saw the big rigs out on our fields...yes siree, there's nothing that'll clear th'old sinuses better'n a good whiff of liquid manure!

The business of spreading in the neighborhood is pretty complicated these days. Farmers have to store it just right, keep it away from brooks and rivers, and get it spread before a certain cutoff date; spreading on winter's frozen ground these days bears penalties "piled higher and deeper" than murder and extortion. I recently Googled "manure laws" to check my facts and found such volumes of red tape that it left my mouth agape and, once again, left me pining for the good old days.

Manure shouldn't be that complicated. First of all there are certain simple tenets to accept: "It" happens, life is full of "it", and "it" must always be conveyed to a spinning object, like a sludge pump impeller or a set of beaters to be broken into small particles that are flung out onto the countryside... hence, "it" hits the fan. I can remember when the biggest complication of spreading, in fact, was driving with crossed fingers (frozen in the winter) in hopes that it would somehow stave off a breakdown of the spreader. Anyone who has ever shoveled manure out of a broken spreader and then repaired it surely knows what I mean!

The traditional spreader is based on a simple principle: a rugged "apron chain" inches manure along the spreader's bed and into the spinning beater where, you guessed it, "it" hits the fan. That old spreader design served farmers very well clear from "horse-drawn" days to when those water-based pumpers recently came in. Nobody ever tried to improve upon that design... that is, till my brother, Elliott, woke up one morning with a "power to the pile" attitude and a design in his head that would revolutionize the world of spreading. Being a genius with things mechanical, Elliott realized the apron chain was the spreader's weak link. His design was based on gravity; instead of inching the heavy stuff backward along a level plane, Elliott's new spreader would dump hydraulically to deliver material to the beaters.

He went to work in the farm shop one January morning and after a whole winter of welding, banging, and cussin', emerged in the spring with this thing that looked like a cross between a dump truck and a wolverine. It hitched to a tractor via a rugged framework that carried a power takeoff shaft from the tractor to a truck transmission. The transmission somehow directed power to a hydraulic pump which raised a dump truck bed and two car tires which, when inflated, matched each other like gears and activated a vicious set of beaters. The thing would have made Rube Goldberg slap his knees, but was doomed by a problem Elliott missed and, undoubtedly, ol' Rube would have, too: the dietary function of fifty dairy cows.

You see, in the summer when cows are out on green grass, their manure is rather, shall we say, "runny". When Elliott loaded up with that stuff and threw his dumper into gear, the whole load poured out quicker than, well, "it" through a sieve. Winter, on the other hand, brought just the opposite problem...cows were locked in the barn and ate dry hay which resulted in manure that wouldn't slide out at the steepest angle. Elliott finally "threw in the towel" one winter day when his load, besides being firm, had sat outside too long and was frozen solid. He raised the dumper to its steepest angle, threw the beaters in gear, and started pounding on the frozen mass with a sledgehammer. He should have suspected trouble ahead when large, frozen chunks broke away but suddenly the whole load busted loose at once. Elliott said the thing sounded like a Gatling gun as he ran for cover, dodging shrapnel from the shattering beaters. He looked back to see the two car tires "smokin'" toward the valley and within seconds, his revolutionary new spreader was history.

We usually don't think of Vermont's four seasons in terms of cow diets and manure laws but it's all part of life here now. Farms are bigger and folks worry about the quality of our lakes and streams. These days we should all hope "manure worries" continue, though farmers are hurting financially and going out of business. If they all go, I'll sure miss the pungent odor of modern-day spreading in the neighborhood, the good old days of clickity-clacking spreaders, and even the occasional break down...after all, "it" happens and life must go on. 🌿

Old Haunts

In just a few weeks, Betsy and I will be heading off the England on a quest to unravel an important piece of Morse "code". You see, I was blessed some 62 years ago to be born into the hills of Vermont to two loving parents, Dot and Harry Morse. Strange as it seems, though, I've always had a feeling that I came from somewhere else...Vermont is just the place where I've spent a lifetime. A woman on my email list recently wrote some wonderfully complimentary words about the stories I send out. She said my words make her "homesick" even though she's "never had the pleasure of living in Vermont." Yes, sometimes when I think of the flat land of East Anglia...the part of England where the River Stour separates Suffolk and Essex Counties, I get "homesick" even though I've never been there before.

I've always had this strange feeling but remained ignorant about my roots until my first cousin once removed, Robert Morse, worked here at Morse Farm some twenty-five years ago. In getting to know Robert, I quickly found that he had a firm grasp on Morse genealogy. During our first talk of ancestry, I went right to the "path of least resistance" and asked how we were related to the famous Samuel F. B. Morse. Quicker n' the rattle of a closet skeleton, Robert said we weren't and punctuated it with "Burr...you're not related to anyone rich and famous!". He said there was an exodus of Morses who came over from England between 1635 and 1639. Although they shared the same name, they weren't necessarily related. They did, however, share such a heated frustration with the Church of England that they were willing to get on small wooden ships and sail across a hostile ocean to a likely hostile land. Because of this association, seven of them are forever grouped on a monument in Medfield, Massachusetts under the heading of "Puritans". My guy from that gang of seven is "Samuel". Samuel F. B.'s guy is "Anthony", again, not related.

My Samuel Morse sailed on the ship "Increase" in 1635 with his wife Elizabeth and son, Joseph. They hailed from Dedham, England and settled in Dedham, Massachusetts. In 1638, Joseph married a woman named Hannah Phillips and on went my line through a couple more Josephs and a Seth. It finally moved up here to Vermont with my great, great, great, great grandpa James Morse in the late 1700s. "Ye olde tymes" have certainly changed since those days, especially in trans-Atlantic travel. Where old Sam and his family risked life and limb to find freedom, Betsy and I will just drive to Boston in our Honda Accord on May 10, stay overnight in a "spiffy" Ramada Inn and then fly to London on May 11 simply in search of a piece of the Morse "code". Once there, we will be whisked away by bus with a group of 20 Morse enthusiasts.

I want to walk the streets of Dedham and stand on the banks of the River Stour. I want to wander the misty dales and inhale some British air. I want to resolve the feeling of being "homesick" for a place I've never been and if deja vu "slaps me in the face" like a challenge from an English duke, I'll know the "code" has been solved. Betsy has no patience with this stuff. She thinks I should put more energy into my relationship with "live" Morses instead of "dead" ones...ya got me there, Betsy! She compares us Morses to a bunch of dogs sniffing each other out! Her purpose in going to England is to see the sights and have a pleasant holiday.

In spite of our differences, we're both looking forward to our trip but are a little nervous about some recent "roadblocks" to international travel. A while back, a pesky strike grounded some of the British Air fleet, but the biggest problem of late has nothing to do with man; a recent volcanic eruption in Iceland has wreaked holy havoc on trans-Atlantic flights, leaving huge numbers of folks in travel limbo. A complete cancellation of our trip might happen but another possibility, being stranded for days at Heathrow Airport, will find me beseeching those old Puritans of 375 years ago... "please dear sirs, give us a good sturdy boat like the 'Increase' to take us back where we belong...home to Vermont!" ❧

A Happy Blue

It seemed an odd time of day for my cousin Stanley to stop and ask if I wanted to go flying but my day had been hectic and I was game. It was pushing 4:00 in the afternoon before we approached the E. F. Knapp Airport and the mystery of the "odd time" was finally unlocked; Stanley wanted me to see the sea of blue lights which highlight the tiny airport's brand new taxi way. The significance of those blue lights "nagged" at me but I couldn't put my finger on what it was. We pulled up to Stanley's aging Cessna and he began preparing the plane for flight. I stood and watched from the sidelines because Stanley, a lifetime farmer and crackerjack with equipment, has an almost sacred routine with his plane. There was still a touch of daylight when we boarded the tiny cockpit and followed the blue path to the runway's end.

The little plane shuddered as Stanley first throttled it up and then accelerated until the open sky above Central Vermont was ours. We headed north above a bustling Montpelier and then over my own farm, always striking to me from that perspective. Morse Farm passed quickly...Tommy's new house, the maple woods, the sugar shack...reminded me of when I was a kid and my uncle Bunny used to fly his Piper Cub up from Springfield, Vermont. Once over our farm, he'd idle the motor down, open the window and holler out: "Come to the airport"...oh the quaint times before cell phones! Stanley and I continued on following County Road toward his farm, the hilly patchwork first tilled by our ancestors back in the early 1800s but Stanley had another place on his mind: he wanted to show me the new maple operation that's being built up on Robinson Hill where my family lived until I was five.

When we reached the spot, Stanley banked the plane and tipped me down to where if I'd been a jelly bean in a jar, I'd have spilled out. Below was a broad slash just barely visible through the early night sky. I could see a large building and a long lane, both replaced what would have been deep woods just months before. The rumor mill has run wild on that project and I was glad to finally see it firsthand...looked like maybe 20,000 to 40,000 trees to me which would be all hooked up by plastic tubing. I thought of the days when my father boiled from 3000 trees on that same spot, collecting every drop the hard way. We circled a few times and then headed back south toward E. F. Knapp Airport and its new blue lights. As we approached I marveled at the site and suddenly realized the significance of those lights ala 2010 Stimulus money: Stanley's wife Janice has had a life-long love affair with the color blue. Janice was once our "bean counter" here at Morse Farm and although she did an excellent job of helping us with the blacks and reds of finance, this time of year she especially had the color blue on her mind. I'm thinking of her blue-lighted outdoor Christmas trees; there were only a couple of them and they were nothing fancy but in my mind, the way they set against her small red house made them spectacular. I never told anyone but every year at Christmas time I would drive the seven miles up the road just see Janice's trees.

My parents, on the other hand, were intimate with lights on a much more "Olympian" scale. For many years they'd plan a pre-Christmas trip down southeast of here to the La Salette Shrine in Enfield, New Hampshire and the Joseph Smith Memorial in Sharon, Vermont. Both places chose to honor the Season and their celebration of Christ with multi-thousands of lights, lights to behold, lights fit for a King! Yes, we'd be "led to the east" by those two places and would, of course, check out some other "oasises" of lighted bliss on the way. I've always felt lucky to have had parents who would treat us kids to those wondrous sights, and would never have told them but, you know, I always liked those two blue-clad evergreens of Janice Morse's best of all. 🍂

Lots a Lawpstahs

It's interesting how we get notions in our heads about certain foods linked to certain geographic areas; like Vermont and its maple syrup...and thank God for that! I remember well the time in Florida when I ate oranges until, as my father would have put it, "had to head on a dead run for the woods!" Then there were the Chinese restaurants in San Francisco that stretched on like the Great Wall, and in New Orleans, a huge bowl of gumbo. One of my earliest and most cherished food associations, though, was Down East where, you guessed it, lobsters became "printed" indelibly in my eight-year-old brain.

Our family was fortunate to know the most quintessential of Down East couples, Gwen and Herb Thompson from South Bristol, Maine. South Bristol is on one of those many "fingers" reaching into the Atlantic from the mainland, this one starting at the mainland city of Damariscotta. The Thompsons had a small farm within a stone's throw of the ocean and what qualifies them, in my opinion, as Maine's most quintessential couple was their long-term tie to both the land and the ocean. They were in the ice business and their biggest clientele were the men who harvested lobsters all over that part of Maine. The Thompson Ice House started in 1826 when Asa Thompson dammed up a brook to create Thompson Pond. Members of the Thompson family annually harvested blocks of ice from the pond in the winter, stored them between layers of sawdust in the icehouse, and sold them all year long. Herb, last of the Thompson "ice" line, sold the final block of natural ice in 1985, ending 159 years of family tradition!

Only a fool would attempt to simulate a true Down East accent on paper, an accent steeped in tradition like 159 years in the same business and location. A true Down East accent has everything to do with the level of face-scrunch and mouth-pucker (think a very troublesome raspberry seed lodged firmly in the front teeth), but for the purpose of this essay, I've got to try.

Poor Herb was a man of very few words, not because he was all that introverted but because Gwen simply wouldn't let him talk! She had a unique way of "involving him but not involving him" every time she opened her mouth... "Went up t' DAMNiscottah Sat'dy t'get a surhtain (certain) paht f' Hurhbbaht's cahr... isn't that right Hurhbbaht?...and on th'way home hit a deeah on a shahp turhn...isn't that right Hurhbbaht?...so when I got back t' South Bristol Hurhbbaht needed the cahr paht plus a new fendah t'boot... remembah that Hurhbbaht?"...and on she went to the next subject never even giving puckered lip service to the possibility of a Herb answer!

I remember our family traveling to Gwen and Herb's one time when I was eight and that's when my lobster "epiphany" happened. The Down East red carpet was already underway as we "VURHmontahs" drove into their yard.

"Hurhbbaht, go get some 'lawpstahs'. I'll go pick some sweet cawhn...the cawhn's just right, isn't it Hurhbbaht? and we'll have lawpstahs n' cawhn f' suppah."

Herb did as he was told, rushed off to one of his lobstermen ice customers and returned with what seemed to my eight-year-old soul a whole bushel of the squirming creatures. I had never seen live lobsters before, much less eaten one. It bothered me a bit to see Gwen drop them, alive, into the boiling water but my compassion evaporated when we sat down at the table and I had my first butter-slathered taste! I remember "digging" into that meal like I hadn't eaten for a week and at one point Herb sidled up to me, proving that he could indeed talk... "Lawpstahs'r richer'n th' devil Buhrr. Don't eat too much."

There was just one other time in my life that I experienced anything similar to that wonderful time at Gwen and Herb Thompson's place. It was over fifty years later and I was playing music for a gala corporate party in southern Vermont. We musicians were treated to the same meal as the partygoers and among the array of delectables was, you guessed it... "all we could eat" lobsters. All of a sudden there in southern Vermont, I became that eight-year-old again, cracking into one lobster after another. It was "hog heaven" all over again which reminds me of another of those "culinary associations"... yup, let's see, it was out in Iowa and there was this humongous pork sandwich.

Kindness the Vermont Way

My mother used to show kindness even to the point of pain. Like the day Mrs. Boast, one of our "summer people" came into our vegetable stand carrying a quart of fancy maple syrup she had bought from us the day before... "This stuff is no good" she fumed. "It's not nice and dark and robust like the real Log Cabin I'm used to!" My mother leapt into damage control knowing darn well the returned syrup would have taken a blue ribbon at any Vermont county fair... "Oh Mrs. Boast I'm so sorry. For the life of me, I don't know what could have gone wrong with that batch...here, take your money back and let me give you a little extra for your trouble." Mrs. Boast left that day happy as a clam, not even knowing she had just been slammed with kindness by Dot Morse. My mother reserved that tactic for even the most hard-core complainers and, you know, it always worked!

Dot Morse's attitude came by way of nine Vermont generations steeped in things like waist-deep winter snow and having to pick summer berries whether "y'want to 'r not". Some call it "fortitude", others, "pig-headed", but my mother's attitude was not unique; it's common to this day here in Vermont. The other day I received a "thank you" note from a young lady who has worked here at Morse Farm for a couple years.

Young Ali said that when she first started working for us she was "kind of nervous about talking to people" but (like my mother in a berry patch) found merit in having to do the job. Among other things, Ali said she has learned about "solving problems and helping people, about taking responsibility to notice what needs to be done and to do it. Most of all, I've learned" she went on "how charming and beautiful the general public is." Wow...I'd say that's "shades of Dot Morse" in spades; my mother knew how to work with the general public and her biggest criteria could be summed up in one word... "kindness". Thanks Ali for "sweetening" my faith in Vermont's youngest generation!

And speaking of good attitudes, I've had numerous emails of concern since our terrible flood of August 28. We here at Morse Farm were among the lucky ones but there certainly has been much pain and suffering among our fellow Vermonters...take Beth and Bob Kennett down in Rochester for instance. A few nights after the flood, it came out on the TV news that Beth and Bob were desperate for people to "hand-milk" their cows. "Hand-milk!" I exclaimed to Betsy... "There must be some mistake. Farmers never hand-milk cows anymore. If they lose power, they simply activate their generator or if they don't have one, they get..." My words tailed off at the end, like the final remnants of a storm. I suddenly realized that Rochester, Vermont had tragically become Vermont's newest island. There was no way to get generators in there or even fuel to run them...Beth and Bob Kennett were truly having to milk their herd of cows by hand.

Suddenly I felt needed. "I can milk cows that way" I told Betsy looking down at my farm-trained hands, but my stupidity continued. I rushed to my computer and sent them an email... "I'll be right down"...and then realized there would be no email in Rochester. I called on the phone only to get the message "This mail box is full. Please try later." There was no way to reach my friends. Heck, there was no way a person could even travel there, except by helicopter. I sadly pictured the whole Kennett herd going down with mastitis and having to be slaughtered...I stayed in the comfort of my unscathed world and did nothing.

A week later just by fluke, I tried the phone again and Beth answered. "This is Burr" I said in a small, disbelieving voice. She projected both gladness that I had called and strength, super strength that can only be achieved through deep trauma. I babbled on that I had been concerned and had wanted to help but she stopped me in mid-sentence; "Burr, we are OK. The cows are fine...no, don't come down. You can't even get here right now." She went on to say the only thing she wanted from me was a big hug the next time we saw each other. It was a short call. Beth didn't dwell on all the heartache down there in Rochester probably because when someone feels lucky just to be alive, nothing else is that important...when the call ended that day, one of us was sobbing deep, wrenching sobs and it wasn't Beth Kennett. ❧

Visiting My Grandpas

Lately I've felt a hankerin' to go walking in cemeteries. It probably just comes with my age, along with an overage of mid-section, an underage of brain cells and a propensity to grope around for my reading glasses. There are, however, privileges that come with this age like my right to brag about my roots. Yup, seven generations of my roots mingle down deep with the roots of the maples in this Vermont heartland. Yesterday, in fact, I visited the graves of multi-grandfathers, right up to great, great, great, greats (hereafter referred to as gggg).

Things were quiet on the farm so I headed out early in the morning. On the way to the Robinson Cemetery I passed the Robinson Sawmill built in 1803 by Joel Robinson, a gggg grandfather of mine. Joel rests in the Robinson Cemetery just up the road from the sawmill. His marble stone tilts at a five degree angle and has been repaired with two steel straps, but the writing is legible. He died at age 60 in 1832. My grandfather, Sidney Morse, rests a short distance from Joel under a gray, Barre granite stone. His stone was placed only 35 years ago but is already being claimed by general weathering and growth of lichens on its surface. I left quickly because I'd rather remember him as I knew him in life, loving, easy-going and full of country charm. On the way back to my car I passed the stone of one Welcome Wheelock. "Well, you're welcome," I chuckled. "Every cemetery needs a spiritual greeter!"

I next drove a short distance to the Old West Church that was framed in 1823 by another gggg grandfather of mine, Lovell Kelton. It's a beautiful old white church but offers one peculiar oddity: the three most visible sides are white, where the back is red. The reason for this, I have been told, is that in 1823, red paint was cheaper than white—leave it to a Yankee! Out beyond the red side of the church lies an old burial ground where my g grandpa Harry Morse, gg grandpa John Morse and ggg grandpa James Morse are buried. All three have red granite stones which strangely contrast with the predominant cemetery grays—"humm—color contrasts are big in this neighborhood," I mused. Leaving, I walked past the Goodenough family lot. Although I know it's pronounced "Good no," I smiled at the implication of the spelling, "good enough."

Next I was onto Cabot, Vermont where my gggg grandfather James Morse, Sr. settled in the late 1700's. I made several turns off Cabot's main thoroughfare until the road became little more than a cow path. When I dared go no further, I abandoned my car and followed signs to Cabot's oldest burial ground, suspecting James Morse might be buried there. There were about 100 ancient slate stones in six short rows, mostly in poor condition. I found myself down on my knees much of the time, like Sherlock Holmes, examining the scant lettering. To my great surprise, Grandpa James' name appeared dead center of the burial ground, "James Morse Esq., Died Aug. 21 1812, Age 66." Old James died almost two centuries ago to the day; I looked at my watch to make sure—it said Aug. 21th.

I left the Cabot burial ground that day excited with my find, but aching to know more about these ancestors whose personalities and physical features are long gone. All we have left of them are commonplace markers in various states of repair. They stand on display in fenced-in areas we call cemeteries, subject to the inevitable eraser of time and weather. I believe in the hereafter and fully expect to shake my ancestors' hands and be among them one day. At that time my duty on earth will have ended and no stone, granite, marble, or slate, will matter to me. At once my mind was made up—I wanted no stone. When I got home I told my wife, Betsy, about my day. "Oh, by the way," I said. "When I die, just scatter my ashes up at the Old West Church Cemetery by the Goodenough stone—that's good enough for me. ✤

What's in a Name

I recently went to the Vermont History Expo at the Tunbridge World's Fairgrounds. It was a grand occasion for all Vermont history buffs and nostalgia notables. The sweltering day was good for nostalgia—for some reason summer heat draws memories like beads of sweat; for me, memories of thousands of hay bales, callused hands, and arms all scratched up from the jagged ends of cut hay. I think of haying just as I would describe my army experience: not necessarily pleasant, but valuable as all get-out. Yup, those experiences built my character and I wouldn't trade them in for a million dollars.

Although I grew up in the era of power machinery and hay bales, I was fortunate to have a peek at the old times through my grandfather. Grandpa Morse taught me all the best things I know—things that have carried me through my many years of good solid farm life. Besides his teaching and the luxury of working beside him, Grandpa Morse also told me stories. One, in particular, was about his namesake, Mr. Phillip Sidney Bennett.

The day my grandfather was born, August 6, 1894, Sidney Bennett knocked on the door at the Morse homestead and offered Harry A. and Ella Giddings Morse $300.00 if they would name their new baby after him. It seems Mr. Bennett had only one daughter and really wanted his name carried on. Harry and Ella accepted the money, not a small sum for those days, and christened their newborn, Phillip Sidney Bennett Morse. Sidney Bennett was a huge man, both in physical size and standing in the community. Grandpa Morse, though a small man, always seemed proud of his name and dedicated his life toward honoring the great man he was name after. One time Grandpa Morse and I were out raking up hay scatterings and he told a story about Sidney Bennett that has stayed with me all these years.

Grandpa said Mr. Bennett was a man of few words. One day he and a testy hired man were pitching hay from "tumbles" up to a third man who moves it away on a horse-drawn wagon. The hired man was having an especially bad day and had earlier kicked one of the horses, thinking he had done it on the sly. My grandfather said they worked in perfect rhythm until the load was nearly complete:

"The hired man jabbed for the last tumble of hay when his fork was suddenly pinned to the ground by another fork. He looked up and saw Sid Bennett at the end of the other fork. Bennett peered down at the smaller man with fire in his eyes: 'You'll never abuse another animal on this farm—you're done!'" Grandpa went on to say the hired man left to get his final paycheck "shaking in his boots." Sidney Bennett headed for the barn with a full load of hay.

The end of my story brings me to Sidney Bennett's grave up at an old cemetery in East Calais, Vermont. Sidney is appropriately buried under the biggest stone in the cemetery. What's not appropriate is the diminished status of his name on the stone. Carved down low on one face is one word, "Bennett." On another face, up higher, slightly closer to God, are the words "The Old Nuisance." Besides that, the huge spear of Woodbury granite bears nothing but pale green lichens and the ravages of time. My brother told me the origin of the words, "The Old Nuisance." It seems Sidney Bennett had heard that his caregivers were referring to him as "just an old nuisance," shortly before he died in 1898. For Sidney Bennett, having the last word was as important as starting the winter with a barn full of hay. For purposes of retribution, he left instructions that those words be put on his gravestone.

Why would a man who was so concerned about the continuation of his name, settle for such obscurity in memoriam? My best guess is that life, not the hereafter, was what was important to Phillip Sidney Bennett. He was huge in life, haymaker, milker of cows—man of honor. He made a cash deal with a male child on August 6, 1894. Once assured there would be someone to carry his name through another lifetime, he soon passed into oblivion. The Old Nuisance. 🍂

Bull Strength and Ignorance

Today early snow is falling and I'll admit it's beautiful. I'll also admit that two more weeks of Indian summer would be great. There's so much to do on the farm but the seasons are my boss and another Christmas tree season is here, ready or not. Yesterday I met a deer hunter out in our stand of balsam furs who was just finishing his season, empty-handed. We talked about the woods and the weather and the changing world. After he left I thought about that changing world, a change that has even included Christmas trees.

Back in the old days, my father cut trees by the hundreds and took them to markets as far away as Florida. Those were wild trees—he'd traipse the edges of swamps and abandoned pastures on our farm with more an eye for freshness and fragrance than fullness and fashion. These days, however, living rooms are bigger and lifetime collections of bobbles and lights require fuller, more symmetrical trees—trees that just don't grow that way "au natural." Today trees are farmed. They're planted in straight rows with an eye toward genetics and growth patterns. Once a year we fertilize them, shear them and liberate them from weeds like hardhack, bedstraw and maple trees—yes, even the sacred sugar maple is a weed in a Christmas tree plantation!

Over the years, Christmas tree farmers have catered nicely to the changing market, but the economy of it all has not been easy. You see, Christmas trees carry a mystique that bypasses everything practical, especially economy— it's accepted that everyone should have a Christmas tree and Christmas trees should really be cheap, or even free. That's a hard order to fill with these pampered, oversized beauties. Customers generally understand the cost when we explain the situation, but with a few, the deal-breaker comes at the very end—the notorious sales tax.

"A sales tax on a Christmas tree?" the man shouted, incredulous. He had just picked out a real trophy tree and looked panicked, like I was threatening his mother's life.

"Yes," I said. "Sorry to say—you can't eat 'em, so they're not groceries (there's no tax on groceries in Vermont). You can't wear 'em, so they don't meet the clothing exemption—yes, they're taxable, alright."

I was beginning to feel desperate when the man looking at the tree next to us turned around. We knew he'd been listening to our negotiations. He tipped the wool visor up away from his cold face, a face we both quickly recognized as that of Jeb Spaulding, Vermont State Treasurer! As Jeb smiled, a puff of breath billowed from his mouth. He patted his mittened hands together to counter the cold, December temperature: "Yes, gents" he said apologetically, "Burr's right—Christmas trees are, indeed, taxable." We were still laughing as we all pitched in to tie the guy's tree to the roof of his car!

Another time, a father and daughter had just picked out their trophy tree and asked if I could tie it up for them. "Sure," I said, grabbing the tree at its balance point and heading toward our netting machine. I waved aside their offers to help, knowing that the job of netting is best done by someone skilled in the procedure. The netting machine is rather deceptive—it looks like a complicated device, but is no more than a simple advancement from the days when we'd straddle trees and "hot-tie" them by hand. It consists of a cone, smaller than the tree's diameter, and a coil of plastic netting that envelopes the tree as it is pulled through the cone. When I reached the netter, I hefted the tree up onto a plank table and moved to the front of the cone. I reached through, grabbed a sturdy branch and started to pull the tree through. It was a big, thick tree and pulled hard. The girl, fascinated by the process, asked what made the machine run.

"Bull strength and ignorance," I grunted.

"What?" she asked, disbelieving.

"Bull strength and ignorance…me…I'm the power source," I said as I finished pulling it through and stood looking at its sleek, compact form.

They were both awed by the thought of a machine that doesn't use gasoline or make an obnoxious sound. As I helped the father lift the tree on the top of his Subaru, he asked what he owed for the tying job.

"Nothing," I said. "It's free—Merry Christmas." 🍃

Christmas Scenes from Yesteryear

For a merchandiser, I'm pretty set in my ways about Christmas: I'm not wild about Santa Claus, flying reindeer, or any of the other fantastic figments of enterprise we see today. I will, however, admit to an affinity for Dr. Seuss stories like "How the Grinch Stole Christmas" and anything "Currier and Ives." The other day I was passing by our old family homestead up in Calais that looks like it walked right out of a Currier and Ives. From that place you can see clear into New Hampshire on a good day, but now I'm thinking of a cold, winter night when the air is full of crystals and lazy smoke curls from several brick chimneys to mingle with a trillion twinkling stars.

My great, great, great grandfather, Levi Robinson, built that beautiful place back in 1823. He must have been an entrepreneurial sort for the way he went at it. He picked a peak location with that fantastic view to the east and a northern panorama of pristine Curtis Pond. His choice of brick as a building material added to the aesthetics, but carried complications of its own. It would have been logical to use the timber that flourished on the Robinson property, but that wasn't Levi's way. His brother, John, lived just across the valley at the old Bancroft place. Our family records tell of John chastising Levi behind his back: "Brother Levi could be heard at 2:00 AM pulling those loads of brick up the hill," he said. It seems Levi had hauled them up three miles of steep hills from the brickyard in Gospel Hollow. He did it at night because his oxen would have suffered in the heat of day. We assume Levi then went on to farm chores and house building during daylight hours!

That idyllic place is where I spent the first five years of my life. I was gypped by the times out of the early "good old days." My brother, Elliott, is ten years my senior and remembers when folks were still using animal power for transportation and farming. Elliott said as the winter wore on, they sometimes watched the frosty world outside from the comfort of the parlor. One particular incident Elliott relates has a certain "Dr. Seussian" ring to it.

"We'd gather 'round the old parlor stove and tell stories. Every once in a while, we'd hear the sounds of an approaching team. We knew it was Eddy Vilbrine who lived over at the next place heading to town."

Elliott went on to explain Eddy's unique style of driving:

"He drove an old International pickup truck that went ok on most of the Calais winter roads, but not that stretch between his place and the bottom of the hill below ours. Those Internationals had a windshield that hinged up and Eddy had hitched a team of horses on to the front end. The reins went through the windshield hole and Eddy was driving the team from behind the steering wheel—I'll always remember Eddy hooded and bundled up for winter, drivin' the horses from the cab of that truck!"

Elliott said Eddy continued down the last hill, using the truck's brakes to keep from running over the horses. He unhooked the team at the bottom and stabled it at an old barn across from Rome Van Ornem's goat yard. When he returned from his errands, he re-hitched the team and continued on home.

I feel lucky to have my connections to the "good old days" through family and heritage. In a way, I'd like to be back there on the Robinson place, or even better than that, riding beside Eddy in that truck! Since that's never an option, though, I'll settle for the memories. It seems modern Christmas is served more by Wal*Mart's and airports which, I'm sure, will bring memories and stories to the next generation. There's only a couple things that stay the same: our ability to dream and, for a short time each year, the spirit and excitement of Christmas—"To all a good night." 🍁

Mother Knows Best

How's that song go... "If it weren't for bad luck, I'd have no luck at all"? I'm a "bad luck" fool... for a guy who has been blessed with so much, I've dedicated too much of my life toward that proverbial "half empty" glass. Saturday morning, my first Christmas tree customers appeared to be supporting my forecasts for a bad day. It was early and my "yard work" was all done. I was in the store warming up and talking to the cashier when all of a sudden the door opened and a man approached me like the "Grinch" before his first cup of coffee... "gointa sell me a tree or what?". It seems he and his wife had already selected a tree from our yard and expected someone to be in attendance, pronto. I instinctively went into the "Dot Morse" mode.

My mother, Dot Morse taught me early on how to deal with difficult customers: "Kill 'em with kindness", she'd say. "Even though they may be unreasonable as all get out, they're 'your customers' and, of course, they're always right." My mother could develop the most angelic way over the most devilish of circumstances... "Oh Mrs. Kneadmore...you're telling me the apple pie you just bought here had a SEED in it...Oh, dear, that's awful...I'll make you a better one and have Harry deliver it to your house!". That's the tact I used Saturday morning with those tree customers and, you know, we ended up best of friends and undoubtedly they will be tree patrons forever.

I miss my mother so much! She applied that same creativity with everything she did. When it came to birthdays and Christmas, she rarely bought gifts the conventional way but instead, she'd create them with lots of hard work and "wrap 'em up" with originality; dollars were secondary and Wal-Marts were nonexistent in Dot Morse's world. My three siblings and I have volumes of books that she compiled for us. Months before every blessed event she'd dive into the attic and surface with photos, baby hair, birth certificates, and anything else that would honor our lives. Then she'd put them into loose leaf binders and tie them together with poems, stories, and humor.

She also made us "work" for our gifts. A party at the Morse house found everyone walking around with numbers pasted to their backs and laughing like fools. She never ran out of ideas for games that would add dimension and atmosphere to our day. Betsy and I recently went through some of our old books. In one of Tommy's, his grandmother had directed him to a book of Shakespearean plays for clues to find his birthday gifts and, believe it or not, the nine-year-old loved it...we all did. When my sister turned sixty, which is a tough birthday for all of us, our mother wrote her a poem that somehow, magically turned a dreaded occasion into pure joy.

She put the same kind of creativity in her Christmas trees; the older she got, the more quirky her Yule traditions became. Although we always sold Christmas trees on our farm, she had no use for the ones that had been sheared and worked into perfection... "cussed things look like they've been run through a big pencil sharpener!" she said. She'd always pick the one that everyone else rejected, a natural tree from the back pasture...hell, a Charlie Brown on a "bad hair" day! After she decorated it with balls and lights dating back to World War II though, it always looked great. In her latter years, her tradition changed from electric lights to real candles that prompted my brother, Elliott, the fireman, toward new traditions as well; he started showing up every Christmas with a twenty pound fire extinguisher! One year as all the grandchildren gathered around the tree to have their picture taken, we suddenly realized that the tallest one, Brian's hair was on fire... everyone rushed to the tree but Dot Morse shouted above the din, "Lordy no, not the candles...just put out Brian!"

She's been gone now almost three years and birthdays and Christmas aren't the same anymore. The only books we get these days are bought in stores, some the stuff of Pulitzer Prizes. "In our book" (and I safely speak for my entire family), however, Dot Morse deserved several Pulitzer Prizes. Instead, she spent her life avoiding the limelight and doing for others. I'm still occasionally haunted by that "half empty" attitude but every time I think of our mom and some of her labors of love, I see cups "full and brimming over." ❧

A Great Spirit

My mother's cool. When the weather's good she sits in one of four aged lawn chairs down in her driveway, away from the TV. She's over 90 now, white-haired and shriveled by the years, but her radiance is blinding. A host of visitors, ex-students, other ninety year olds, tourists from around the world, or hungry chipmunks often happen along. They're drawn by her radiance, I suppose. The chairs face a cheerful chorus of Black-eyed Susans, mullein stocks, lupines and Philadelphia Fleabanes, none of which anyone has ever planted. Like the visitors, the plants just appear. The other day she pointed to the Black-eyed Susans. "See something different about one of them?" she asked. I focused on the cheerful crowd and, sure enough, one stood out. "That's the one," I said, looking at one that was bigger and more radiant than the rest. Its petals were brightly speckled and slightly folded at the bottom. It looked happy.

My siblings and I had overhauled that flowerbed last year. We hauled away yards of dirt contaminated with weed seeds, replaced it with weed-free soil and planted an array of bulbs from Holland. The daffodils and tulips provided early summer bloom, but marked a basic flaw in our plan: we had planted nothing that would bloom mid to late summer. So who planted the Black-eyed Susans and company?

My father was always happy, but happiest when his hands were in God's earth. My mother and father were happy together, like two peas in a pod, they were. My mother always said that if he went first, she'd find a way to go with him. Down through the years they wore out several different cars with their travels together. When he started having strokes at 70, they continued the miles, only with a wheelchair. She'd push and he'd ride, providing moral support with jingles, jokes, and rhyme. In 1999, however, my father, Harry Morse, had finally reached the end of his road. He passed away right after sugar season that year. We had the usual ceremonies connected with one's physical departure and our sadness was twofold: we thought our mother would soon be following him. That's when weird things started to happen.

Our mother ate mostly Brownie Supremes and Cheese Twists for years, thinking, I suppose, a diet like that would not only be heaven on earth, but would also send her away with Harry. When Harry died, however, she started eating better. She also started barricading herself in her room at night and going to her doctor for regular checkups, hardly signs of a person ready to die. Our mother is cheerful too. A while back my sister Susie and I were down at her house, grousing about life's little setbacks—hers, a minor fender-bender and a $2000 repair bill—mine, a temporary crown that kept falling out from my front row of teeth. Our tales of woe grew by the minute, but Dot Morse had a master plan that stopped us dead in our tracks: "Boy, do I feel lucky," she said. "I don't have a car and I don't have any teeth!" That's the witty, positive Dot Morse we've been seeing lately. (In fairness to her, she still has her own teeth—guess she was just stretching a point for effect.)

Now this may sound outrageous but I think Harry Morse is behind all this stuff. Having known him for 50 years and worked with him two thirds of that time, I'm convinced that he would not let mere mortality slow him down. Yes, I think he planted those mystery plants. He was also behind my mother's change of heart over diet and lifestyle and a few other things, come to think of it. Sure, he wants to be reunited with his sweetheart but time was never a problem to Harry Morse. Right now he's just having a little fun.

I just walked back down to that happy looking Black-eyed Susan—Before I spoke I looked all around, like a child reaching into a cookie jar: "Alright Harry, I'm wise to you," I said in a low voice, "Thanks for the good work. We sure love the time with Mother and appreciate your help with the gardening." Before I left, I zeroed in on the single black eye; I swear I saw it wink. 🍂

Lots of Lilies

Lots of people are stopping these days on the section of County Road that overlooks my parents' pond....well, it's actually my nephew Peter Shattuck's pond but it'll always be my parents' pond in my book (Sorry Peter...you just pay the taxes on it now!). The reason they're stopping is because the water lilies down there look like they "jumped right out of a Monet", only better. There's a story behind those lilies.

The pond was dug back when I was just a kid. It was a swampy piece of land right in front of our house...I believe the term "good for nothing" was bantered in our family for years until one day a huge machine called a "drag line" showed up. Mr. Sherman Stebbins owned and operated this drag line and masterminded hundreds of farm ponds all over Vermont. Sherm Stebbins, "Father Pond", never ended up with dry holes or mucky messes; he had a sixth sense about whether or not a pond would "work" in any given place and would tell the landowner if it wouldn't. He acted a little reserved with our site... "She'll hold water but she's not ideal, Harry" he said to my father. My father said "water's water" but found out the fallacy of that notion; when our pond was done and landscaped, it did, indeed, hold water but was always slightly anemic compared to our other spring-fed farm pond. The new pond was almost too tepid for swimming and, although rainbow trout thrived there, brook trout died because the water was too slow moving.

My parents didn't regret building it, though, because it was a vast improvement over the eyesore that preceded it. We mowed the lawn around it, had picnics down there in the summer and skated on it in the winter. One day a few years after it was built, my father took my mother for a ride. He didn't tell her the nature of their trip as they headed south down Route 100 and over the gap to the town of Brandon. He had a friend there, a vegetable grower named Robert Wood who had a farm pond of his own. Harry Morse knew that my mother Dot loved water lilies and in the Wood pond thrived a certain pink water lily. They arrived at Wood's picturesque farm stand that stood right next to their large farm pond just to the south. At one end of the pond was the stunning array of pink water lilies.

"Mind if I take some root stock from your water lilies, Bob?" my father asked like it was a simple matter of reaching down and pulling a clump from the ground. "Help yourself Harry" Bob Wood replied, "but I sure don't know how you're goin' ta get it." My father simply grinned and headed, Clark Kent style, for the nearest tree. A few minutes later he emerged wearing only a bathing suit... "down in the muck...at home with the fish...he can fend off blood suckers with a single swipe... he's Super Water Lily Man!" Harry Morse walked to the edge of the Wood pond and slowly waded in where the lilies were thickest and stopped when the water was up to his neck. By then a few spectators had gathered and my poor mother had retreated to the car, embarrassed. At first, Dad looked like he was just standing there with a strained look on his face but the onlookers began to cheer when they realized he was picking the root stock with his toes and "handing" it up to where he could reach it with his fingers! He soon had a good amount and waded back to shore.

Dad didn't bother changing out of his swimsuit, knowing that it would take preserved moisture and "Super Man" talent for that root stock to get planted and survive in our pond. My parents thanked Mr. Wood and hurried back home with their precious cargo. By the time they arrived, Mom was over her embarrassment and really seeing the humor of it all as my dad grabbed his still slimy bundle, headed out into our pond, and began planting, yes, by handing root stock to his feet and planting it with his toes! It took a few years for those pink beauties to take hold but eventually they thrived and multiplied.

I just returned from taking my own picture of the beautiful lilies down there. My parents are both gone now. My siblings and I bought a simple granite marker for them over in the Doty Cemetery a few years back. I'm sure we would all agree, however, that a "marker's a marker". It, along with a unique stone from our farm, serves as a fitting memorial to Harry and Dot Morse most of the year. For a short period in the summer, though, when those lilies look "better than a Monet", they are the best memorial of all for two great people, Harry and Dot Morse. ❧

Ring Me Up by Rainbow

Yesterday my friend Larry Perry emailed me saying he'd seen my mother, Dorothy Morse's name on a list of folks who have money being held by the State of Vermont. I told him I'd check into it and when I did, I found there was enough to give each of us four siblings over $400.00! "That's just like our mom" I thought... "she's always leaving nice little surprises for us." Dot Morse, you see, passed away back in 2006 but it's not like she's gone from our lives. We "see" her everyday in the flowers that grow around our place, remarks folks make about her and, especially the rainbows...yes, our mother communicates her most important messages by "rainbow".

We've had several of these little rainbow "rap sessions" with her since she passed on. The first one was on the day we celebrated her life at East Montpelier's Old Meeting House in January of 2006. We had gathered there to a packed house for songs and stories about her life as a teacher, farm wife and most importantly, our mother. When the service ended, we all went out into the day which was, for winter time, quite mild and misty. We congregated, as folks do after such occasions, shaking hands and exchanging more words about Dot Morse when, all of a sudden there was a gasp... "Look at the rainbow!" someone shouted and sure enough, up in the sky, or more appropriately, heavenward, there was a magnificent rainbow. There in the church yard, all of us souls understood her message: "I'm OK...just up here with Harry.". Her message reached out beyond our little gathering, as well. My friend Rob Bridges eloquently described his "take" in a note to our family:

"After your mother's service, while you folks were greeting others, I headed for home. It rained until I got to East Montpelier village when the sun came out as I headed east on U.S. Route 2. Whoever heard of a rainbow in January, but there it was in all its glory! I smiled to think that Dot just couldn't wait to try out her new toys."

"New toys" indeed...Dot Morse had not only found a new life but also a new toy and a colorful way to keep us in th' ol' loop! My sister Susie recently related another time: "A brilliant double rainbow appeared that framed the entire farm and very mysteriously drew several family members out of our respective homes to witness it." We heard from our mother again back on April 19 of this year. After holding our parents' ashes in storage for a few years (hard to "let go", you know), we finally went over to Doty Cemetery, placed them in a maple syrup jug, and buried them by the stone that bore their names. It was a simple gathering, just the four of us with spouses and a couple cousins. Afterward we all went down to the Wayside Restaurant for supper. As we entered the restaurant, a brilliant rainbow appeared in the sky to the east... "Thanks, kids!" it said.

The day I found out about the money, my brother Elliott and I were canning syrup down at our store. It was quite drizzly, just like the day of our mother's service. All of a sudden, I had a feeling that there might be a "conversation" in the air. I said to Elliott, "I've got to leave for a few minutes and go talk with Mom.". I remember Elliott's reaction as he finished filling the pint he was working on... "O...Kaaay" he said, narrowing his eyes. I got in my car, drove up to the Cummings Road and parked where there's a "big sky" view to the east.

"OK Mommy" I said, looking upward and feeling like I was five years old again and tugging at her skirt... "here I am...thanks for the money." The rain was gently dabbing at my windshield while the sun peeked here and there through softening clouds...perfect conditions for a rainbow. "Where is she?" I wondered. I scanned the heavens for quite a while but, alas, a conversation was not to be that day. I finally gave up and went back to work.

I related my story to Betsy when she returned from her work that night. "Oh Burr" she said... "there was a huge rainbow where I was...got a firm message from Dot...definitely something about you." When I questioned her about the time, I found it had been directly after I had been up on Cummings Road. "You know, Burr" she went on... "remember how your mother was...she'd always be giving folks something and then 'shoooshing' them when they tried to pay... 'Don't talk to me about money she'd say.'". I then knew why my mother "snubbed" me that day and I also firmly believe that when a person dies, relationships do not end...folks just learn new ways to communicate. Can't wait 'til the next time my mother rings us up by rainbow! 🍂

LOCAL HISTORY

A Wave A Day • Hunkerin' Down • Fire Follies • Popples by God • Station Identification • Forever Hold Your Bear • The Clossey Place • Winter Stories • The Little Statehouse • Smart Calves and Swimming Babies • Bridge Over Troubled Traffic • Lost and Found • A Salute to Ray • Billie Deer • Ready, Aim, Fire • Price Matters • Good Welders Wanted • Horn of Plenty • Sweet Dogs

When my husband, Leslie, and I were building our granite house in Graniteville, Vermont around 1962 or 1963, we were having a well dug by Benedini who had gone 700 feet deep but to no avail. My sister-in-law called Mrs. Lafirrira who told her to tell us "not to stop now -- you've only got about 10 more feet to go." Sure enough, at 710 feet, we struck water and that water was so good and pure that someone from the proper agency (may have been environmental) came and got a gallon of it to test the reactors at Vernon. We were told that our water was more pure than that found at the North Pole.

- Cassie McLeod, GA

A Wave a Day

I started this morning off with a good wave to Mr. Mills-Brown, the crossing guard downtown who waves to everything that walks, wiggles or wags. Mr. Mills-Brown is a pro at the art and I consider myself "no slouch" either. I've learned that every wave, like every word, has a personality of its own and is designed for a specific purpose. Over the years, I've developed a few rules of waving.

1.) If you're going to wave, then wave for crying out loud!

I'm thinking of two brothers, Joe and Moe (not their real names), whose waves are as different as fancy maple syrup and blackstrap molasses. Joe has a hearty wave. He'll wind up almost like a baseball pitcher, present his full palm high in the windshield of his car and then give an extra little flick for good measure. His brother Moe, on the other hand, hoists a limp paw just barely above the dashboard, like he's holding a soiled Kleenex. Come on Moe, raise those digits high! My friend, Susan from over in the Mad River Valley says folks over there sometimes just twitch a finger on top of the steering wheel while others think a lifted coffee cup will suffice. These are poor excuses for waves, my friends and totally fly in the face of rule #1. There is never room for a one-fingered wave, even when you're waving to a politician!

2.) Don't ever be ashamed of a wave

Waving's the primal form of communication; even monkeys do it! Sometimes I worry about waving to the wrong person and then feeling foolish—silly, silly! You simply can't wave to the wrong person and even if you could, there's no way to take a wave back. As I said, Mr. Mills-Brown waves to everyone, knowing fully well there are no mistakes in waving.

3.) When you have the choice of waves over words, always use waves.

Unlike words, waves can never get you in trouble. My friend Mac recently told of an experience where a wave would have worked better:

One time Mac borrowed a pickup truck and was moving his furniture from Island Pond to St. Albans. The weather looked threatening so he synched a big piece of cardboard around his load, covered wagon style. He drove west through Newport Center and East Richford, carefully flicking his cigarettes out the window. As he entered Enosburg a man stood by the side of the road hollering "Hi, Hi!" Mac waved and watched him recede in the rear view mirror.

"About the time flames rose above the tailgate," Mac said, "It occurred to the wife and I that maybe the guy was hollerin' "Fire, Fire!" We stopped quick, almost hit Carney's Restaurant, and unloaded our furniture right in the street—the "hi" guy came runnin' with a fire extinguisher and put out the fire just before it ruin't everything, including the village of Enosburg! After it cooled down, he helped us reload our stuff and we set off again with a burnt lookin', borrowed truck—always wished that guy had waved us down instead of hollerin'."

Mac's right. The universal wave for "stop quick" is a furious diagonal flailing of the arms across the chest. The "stop quick" wave might have saved the day for poor Mac, or at least a sofa or two. Let's face it folks, there's too many misguided gestures in this world and look at the trouble they're causing. If our ex-Governor Dean had simply waved instead of hollerin' like a banshee, he might now be president. And then there was the time Nikita Khrushchev pounded the table with his shoe; come on Nick, a simple wave woulda worked and kept you outta all that historical hot water!

I'll end this piece with, what else—a wave—and a warning: The world's most peaceful language is at your fingertips. Raise 'em high and you can't go wrong. Oh, and three waves for Mr. Mills-Brown! 🍂

Hunkerin' Down

The other day a friend suggested that I write my next piece on the way folks are handling this troublesome economy. "Whoa!" I said... "you're asking an economic idiot like me to write on the economy?" Now, I've never had much activity on the mathematical side of my brain but, come to think of it, even the 'experts' seem to be stumbling these days. Looking at it that way, maybe there's room for those of us working from instinct rather than from "facts and figures".

My friend worries that old FDR's "fear itself" theory is all too rampant these days and we all need to stop "hunkerin' down and diggin' in"; we need to get out there and start waving some banners for patriotism...in this case, green banners...cold, hard cash (that sure works for me, being in the retail business!). On the other hand, being a frugal old Vermonter, I understand the temptation and sometimes the need to hunker down. Reminds me of an old 'hunkerer' from Calais who died holding tight to his first nickel without a friend in sight.

On the backside of Robinson Hill lived an old Baptist preacher. He had a small farm off Collar Hill Road, a name befitting enough for a road where a preacher lives, but from what I've heard, everything appropriate for a preacher ends right there. You see he was a stern son-of-a-gun who lacked the social graces a preacher ought'a have and didn't trust a soul. Except for one trip to town every Sunday for his hour of "fire and brimstone", he stayed, like a rat in a tunnel, within his small familiar confines. He protected those boundaries like a junkyard pit-bull and to him, property lines weren't always marked by fences and corner stakes; you see back in that old preacher's time, airplanes were just starting to fly overhead and he found them as much trespassers as if they'd driven down the lane on four wheels. My grandparents said that he went over his deed with a magnifying glass thinking that surely somewhere in the fine print it would extend his ownership up into the atmosphere above his place...they said every time he heard "one a them confounded contraptions", he'd rush out onto the acreage madly shaking his fist at the trespasser on his farm's upper extremities!

Grandma told of going to his house when she was a small girl for piano lessons. She said he "had miser written all over his face" and a look in his eye that kept folks at arms' length, especially young children. He had a rambling house and the piano was in the far end. To get to the piano they had to pass through several rooms all locked "tighter'n a drum"! Strapped to his middle was a ring heavily laden with keys and he always wore a long, dark cape for the purpose of concealing the keys. Grandma described him leading the way to the piano room: "He made me walk a few steps behind him and as he stopped to unlock each door, he'd look back at all three feet two inches of me with a distrusting scowl. Then he'd stoop over and fish around under that cape for the right key. When we finally got to the piano, by gosh, it was locked, too!"

Needless to say, times have changed. Most parents these days wouldn't send a child to a guy like that for piano lesson. Here in the 21st century, we all agree that land ownership lies only on a horizontal plane and, speaking of 'planes', we routinely hop on huge jetliners which fly miles above the tiny, patchwork boundaries below. One thing that hasn't changed, however, is the ability of our economy to thumb its nose at the populace. Right now it's doing that so furiously that some worry we'll suffer "The Great Depression" all over again (that term always bothers me...there's nothing ever 'great' about a depression!). I truly hope there are things we can do to stave it off and my instinct says "don't be like that old preacher". If you feel a hankerin' for some hunkerin', remember what a pitiful old cuss he was...hunkerin' down and diggin' in is great for woodchucks and desert rats but bad for people. Let's all live without fear and those of us who are able to, wave those green banners for faith in humankind and preservation of our economy. ✹

Fire Follies

With Christmas over, it's time to start worrying about real winter... worrying? Admittedly I'm a bit of a "basket case" in the winter between the size of the woodpile, the depth of the snow and the cleanliness of the chimneys. Let's see, the woodpile's supposed to be only shrunk by 1/2 on this date, I'm happier with a foot of snow than three feet (sorry skiers), and the chimney should be free of soot, especially that black, gummy stuff.

Yesterday I borrowed Betsy's cosmetic mirror and carried it down cellar. I contorted my body behind the pipes and valves of our wood furnace, opened the small door at the chimney's bottom and stuck the mirror into the void. Expecting to find either sooty blackness or just a tiny pinhole of light, I was pleasantly surprised when the mirror opened up a well defined, flue-sized square against the blue sky; my chimney was clean! Many times the romance of a wood fire lulls us into foolishness; wood burning is easy at the fueling end but the maintenance end involves climbing steep roofs and cleaning filthy stove pipes...no fun at all.

Knock on kindling, there hasn't been many bad fires around here yet this winter. Even though structure fires can be tragic, they are part of life and there's considerable lore in these hills about them. Usually people and creatures run like hell from a house fire but I've heard a couple stories where "inclination" prevailed over "emergency".

Donald Maxham always wore a white shirt and tie, a daily habit that stood at complete odds with his profession; Donald, you see, was a mink farmer. The mink's diet of choice is flesh, flesh sliced and diced from aged farm animals and it's the mink farmer's job to travel from farm to farm doing the slicing and dicing. It was such a task that took Mr. Maxham one time to a dairy farm far enough from home to require a nightly stay. Early in the morning, the farmhouse caught on fire. The fire spread so fast that all the occupants, save one, quickly fled. As they huddled at a distance watching flames escape the interior and begin to lap around the eaves, someone in the group realized that Mr. Maxham was missing.

One of the evacuees rushed back into the house thinking he was still asleep. By that time the smoke-filled hallways that led to Mr. Maxham's bedroom also revealed a haunting, orange glow in the near distance. The man rushed to the bedroom door, pulled it open and there, standing in front of the wall mirror was Donald Maxham making the final adjustments to his Pendleton white collar and red tie...he knew the house was on fire but, by God, would not start his day without the shirt and tie!

My friend, Gail Twine recently sent me a funny story about a barn fire over in Marshfield where she grew up. It seems her dad, John Lamberton was raising pigs in the lower part of the barn. They were corralled on three sides by the barn's walls and "a mean electric fence" prevented their escape on the fourth side. Gail said the pigs were in their enclosure the day that barn caught on fire. The firemen arrived in a timely manner but the structure was doomed by that point. Their main objective quickly became saving the pigs.

"The firemen tore down the fence," Gail said "and tried to drive the pigs out of the area." She went on to say that the fire got continually hotter but those pigs would not go past the area that had previously been fenced. The firemen hosed them down so that they wouldn't roast but the pigs just rolled over in the mud, loving the game and playing as the barn burned to the ground! She said her dad never had to put the fence back up because the pigs were so hooked on that area that they would never leave!

If all the old cellar holes that pock our Vermont countryside could talk, they'd have volumes of stories to tell but for the most part, they're stories we don't want to hear. Once in a while, though, fire lore that's properly "dressed" with happy survivors warrants the tellin'. In the meantime, keep your flue brush handy and your top hat on. 🍁

"Popples by God"

The tree I was cutting that day had a mind of its own...I had figured the direction it "wanted to go", notched it, and was mostly through the back cut when all of a sudden my chainsaw bound up tightern'a frozen lug nut. The damned tree had turned on me and God only knew where it was heading. I abandoned the saw and scrambled toward a copse of trees to my right, craning my neck as I ran. Thankfully I could see it wasn't heading in my direction but it looked like my tractor might not fare so well; the bright orange Kubota was right in the tree's path! Suddenly there was the dreaded "crash" and the tree lay still like a defeated Goliath. I lifted the protective visor of my hardhat and walked toward its base. My chainsaw lay unscathed, thrown a distance away by the falling tree. The tractor sat safe and sound just inches from the tree's top branches. "Damn popples!" I muttered, blaming the tree rather than my deficiencies as a woodsman.

Here in Vermont, it's not uncommon to blame poplar trees for everything from supplying the wood that made up Jesus' cross to any kind of bad luck. There's even a superstition that says a building containing poplar in its construction will burn within a year...my brother tried it once and his building burned to the ground on the day the last nail was pounded! They are of the genus, Populus and, according to Wikipedia, spread prolifically worldwide. To a Vermont farmer, they are a nuisance, a pain in the butt... "popples", scorned for their failure as suitable firewood or building material, are the opposite of "popular". Lately however, I've been cutting lots of them, encouraged by new words like "biomass" and my need to fuel our modern chunk wood gasifier that seems to like popple just fine. They are quick to work into woodpiles because they're tall with relatively few limbs and, best of all...every one I cut means the world has one fewer of the cussed things!

Their clear, white wood is actually quite pretty at first sight but the minute a saw penetrates the poplar's pea-green bark and into that wood, those rascals emit an odor that would gag a skunk. My father used to tell about a crusty Vermonter, Mr. Chase, who knew every wood in the Northern Forest by its smell. Harry Morse said a group of woodsmen blindfolded the old guy one time and sat him down on a stump. As they placed chunks of fresh cut wood under his nose, he duly called each one by its correct name in a stuttering, gravelly voice... "mmmmaple...bbbeech...hhhhemlock...hhhhophornbeam". Mr. Chase was batting a thousand when the woodsmen decided to get "down and dirty". One of them went out back and returned carrying an old she-cat under his arm.

"He proceeded to shove its hind end right in under the old cuss's nose", my father said. "Old Chase took a couple quick sniffs, rocked his head back and with a huge satisfied grin boomed, 'ppppopple, by God!'"

Although my father passed away ten years ago, I can still hear him laugh like he did every time he told that story! Harry Morse would have also laughed the other day at the four-color glossy page ripped from a magazine that my friend, John Mead from over in Monroe, New Hampshire had sent me. The scene showed a cute young girl peeking out from behind a tree. It was a beautiful scene, professionally designed for the purpose of promoting New Hampshire maple syrup. There was just one problem: the tree that pretty young lady peeked from was just one in a picturesque grove...a grove of popples! Thinking of the age-old but friendly rivalry between Vermont and New Hampshire, I kidded John about the quality of syrup over there... "Probably'd be even better" I said, "if they made it outa maple trees! 🍁

Station Identification

Back last fall, Betsy and I decided to put our television "out to pasture". Suddenly we'd had enough of constant car commercials and all those beautiful people with scant little in the "grey matter" department. We made a pact that it would be gone for one year and then we'd assess whether we could truly live without TV. So far it's going quite well except for one thing...I'm having to listen to my beloved Red Sox on a scratchy old radio! It kind of reminds me of days gone by when folks were as intent on their parlor Atwater Kent as most people are today on their Samsung ultra-slim multi-media centers.

Speaking of Atwater Kent, America's leading manufacturer of radios back in 1925, I've always wanted to write a column on him because, you see, he hails from these Vermont hills. In fact old Atwater is a cousin of mine...sort of... in a round-about way that's about as clear as, well, the AM signal from Wheeling, West Virginia to Wheelock, Vermont. Yesterday I drove up to see my cousin, first cousin once removed, that is, Stanley Morse, who knows the lineage and was glad to sit down with me and talk.

"Sure, he's the same as your first cousin thrice removed" Stanley said.

"Huh?" I said.

Stanley began spewing the lineage in a fluent, second language: "Atwater's father was Prentice Kent and Prentice's father was Remember Kent. Remember married Aaron Tucker's sister and Aaron married Remember's sister which made Atwater double cousin to Emeline Tucker who married your great, great grandfather, John Morse."

"Huh?" I said again.

"That would make your great grandfather, Harry Morse, the same as first cousin to Atwater Kent because their parents were double cousins" and to pound that point home, Stanley Morse looked me right in the eye and said that I, Harry Morse, Jr. (that's my given name) had a cousin who was once one of the richest men in the country. Suddenly I felt a tingling clear to my bones and started wondering if there was any money left in that part of the family.

Stanley, now 79, remembers one time that Atwater and his chauffer drove up to the Morse homestead to visit my great grandfather Harry. Atwater used to travel up this way by train from Philadelphia. "His wife was so stuffy" Stanley said "that she usually wouldn't get off in Montpelier". The Vermont relatives were too crude for her liking so she continued on to Burlington where she checked into a fancy hotel. According to Stanley, Atwater was quite "down to earth" and genuinely interested in things back home. He had, however, become rich and famous and wasn't beyond flaunting his prestige; on that visit, Stanley's uncle Fred stood by polishing the 1916 Buick that he had scrimped and saved for. Fred Morse was the first person in Calais to own a car and he was rightfully proud. Stanley remembers hearing Atwater Kent nonchalantly say that cars were kind of a hobby for him... "I have ten of them" he said!

It's with a degree of wistfulness that I write of those times when tycoons like Atwater Kent were designing and manufacturing goods and also accumulating wealth in America. These days it seems that designing and manufacturing have been farmed out to other countries and the accumulation of wealth, well...it's frowned on like bank robbery. Call me "old fashioned" but I think that system worked very well 'cause guys like Atwater Kent contributed to a healthy economy by making it and "spreading it around".

I'm not so sold, however, on our ways with genealogy...cousins "doubled and thrice removed"....pshhaugh! We humans complicate everything from family trees to family entertainment centers. I vote for listening to the Red Sox on scratchy radios and finding the relatives like dogs do with a few strategic sniffs....keep it simple. 🌿

Forever Hold Your Bear

A lady from Florida, Jean Harden, recently called and asked if I was related to the James Morse who came from Barre, Massachusetts to Cabot, Vermont in 1789. If old Gramp Morse hadn't been dead since 1812, I might have worried that she was trying to collect a bad debt but I said, yes, I was. It turned out that she descends from his brother and my great-great-great-great uncle, Joseph, who was killed at 32 years old in the Revolutionary War. Joseph had left children who apparently came to Vermont with their Uncle James. Jean Harden descends from one of those children and since she has those roundabout ties to Cabot, she sent me a history of Cabot, Vermont from the "Gazetteer of Washington County, Vt. 1783-1899". I found some very interesting things in it about a few of Jean's and my ancestors way back then. I quote from the Gazetteer:

"(Cabot's) first marriage was David LYFORD to Judith HEATH, July 23, 1795, by James MORSE, Esq. Mr. MORSE came from Barre, Mass., in 1789, and settled at the center of the town. He built the first house (of logs) in that locality, and later kept in it the first tavern in town. He was the first justice of the peace and received his appointment in 1792. He foresaw that he would be called on to officiate at weddings, and felt that he could do better if he had some experience. He accordingly placed his son David beside the stump of a tree, and proceeded to marry him to it. David, as directed, assented that he would love, cherish, and protect her, and David and the stump were solemnly pronounced husband and wife. David would not marry until the stump rotted down. This nervous justice became confused when performing a real ceremony next time and made the groom promise to 'forsake her and cleave to all other women'."

A few years ago I was visited by Doctor Jeff Morse from Kent, Washington, descendent of David Morse, proof positive that the stump eventually rotted! Even though old Grandpa James messed up his second marriage ceremony, it appears his first one, the one between David Lyford and Judith Heath, produced a union at least full of spunk; from the Gazetteer again:

"David LYFORD and his efficient helpmeet, Judith, had just finished a job of dressing flax. Mr. LYFORD had plied the heavy break, and Judith had performed her part by hatchelling the flax. Judith remarked to David that while he was putting the break away she would run across to neighbor BLANCHARD's and return the borrowed hatchel. Mrs. LYFORD carried the dressed flax into the house and laid it away until she could spin it, and started on her errand, fortunately leaving the heavy plank door open. About half way home, in passing a short curve in the path, she found herself at arms' length of a cub bear, weighing fifteen or twenty pounds, and through the thick bushes she caught a glimpse of the old bear and another cub. Not the least intimidated, in a defiant way, she caught up the cub by the hind legs and ran. The cub squealed and began to scratch and bite; she instantly wrapped him in her stout homespun apron, and kept on at her utmost speed. She heard the old bear crashing through the bushes in hot pursuit. The impulse that impelled her to seize the cub prompted her to keep it, and keep it she did. With a determination to win the race, she dashed along the pathway, conscious that the furious beast was gaining on her at every leap. She reached the house, darted through the open doorway, flung the cub from her, swung the plank door to, and dropped the wooden bar into its socket, but none too soon. The enraged mother bear instantly threw her great weight against it, but it was made for just such an emergency, and did not yield. Imagine the surprise and anxiety of her husband, as he caught a glimpse of his wife darting in at the door with a full-grown and furious bear not a rod behind her! He ran to the window behind the house; but Judith was there before him, with their trusty gun, always kept load[ed] for instant use. The cries of the cub had rendered the bear frantic. In her efforts to break through the door she did not see David, who, with a well-directed shot, laid her dead. The cub in the house shared the fate of its dam, and David went to the swamp in search of the other, but it had escaped."

Just like James Morse, I have been a justice of the peace and have performed a few marriages in my time. There's a marriage, in fact, happening tomorrow, right here at Morse Farm for my friends, Sky Barsch and Josh Gleiner. I'll be there, no doubt thinking of Grandpa James Morse and some of his wedding antics. It'll be a modern wedding with a gala reception in a huge tent. There are certain things that haven't changed between James Morse's time and now; marriages still end with a simple "I do" and the happy couple goes off to make a life together. I'm confident, however, when it comes to "bringin' home the bacon", Sky'll probably stop at the grocery store instead of catching the live critter on the way home from the neighbors! 🐝

The Clossey Place

Down on the south side of our farm is a place where the bedrock puckers up though the scant topsoil more than anywhere else on God's earth. Ledge is the "spine of Vermont", an old timer recently told me; it thrives down there on what we call the Clossey Place. Before my grandfather bought it in 1950, Jack Clossey farmed that acreage. God only knows how but somehow he managed to cut enough hay to feed a dozen cows. These days nobody struggles to "farm" those ledges; the Clossey Place rests in retirement and from that perspective, it's beautiful...I think of it as a special kingdom.

Living across the brook from that special kingdom are Al and Betty Jerome, a prince and princess of a couple. They're both in their eighties now and have raised eight children down there in their happy home. Al first arrived in that neighborhood in 1936 as an 11-year-old orphan... "Jack musta needed some help cause he came over t' St Joseph's Orphanage in Burlington and got me" Al recently joked, and then went on to say what a wonderful man Jack Clossey was. Although the name "Morse" appears on the deed, we have kind of a loose arrangement with Al and that land...we pay the taxes and he kicks in some sharp tools and castle-sized devotion.

Ever since we gave up grazing cattle over there, Al Jerome has kept that place trimmed...chainsaws, string trimmers, lawn mowers and even our farm tractor and bush hog...Al has used 'em all. These days his eyes are failing so he has to stick to the hand tools but this year he made arrangements for his son, David, a resident of Hawaii, to use our tractor and mower. I recently found myself sitting with Al, Betty, David and his sister, Theresa, in the Jerome's pleasant living room. I was there to learn more about the Clossleys and anything else that might stir memories. The Jerome kids and I grew up together so it felt a bit like "going home again" to be talking with David and Theresa at this latter point in our lives.

I asked them about my vague memories of seeing the Jerome kids riding with Jack Clossey in a Model T Ford. David and Theresa quickly confirmed my recollection. "Bought it in 1926 for six hundred dollars" Al said "and drove it right into the '50s". Jack's wife was Maggie, a colorful Irish woman who had emigrated from County Cork during the Potato Famine. "They were sweethearts" said Betty, who sat in an overstuffed chair nursing a shoulder she had broken just two days before. "Al thought of them as his parents" she went on. Theresa and David brought up a humorous story about the Clossey's ways around young kids. "I'd be up there" Theresa said, "and think I was heading for home when all of a sudden Maggie would reach out with her cane and hook me around the neck...she'd yank me back and give me another job to do!" David said Jack also carried a cane and often exercised the same technique with the boys.

Once Al arrived in that neighborhood in 1936, he "rooted" himself there as deeply as the bedrock. He spent his teenage years with the Closseys and then bought the house across the brook. Although the Jerome house is comfortable and pristine these days, it wasn't always that way. David pointed out that the one-holer outhouse served their "personal needs" till about the time Jack Clossey finally gave up on that Model T. "I borrowed John Peterson's tractor to pull that outhouse out back when we finally got indoor plumbing" he said. Al went on to say when they got it in place, still within sight of the highway, they leaned the toilet seat up against the side of the outhouse. One day a neighbor stopped and approached Al in the yard. The neighbor, an old Yankee farmer who "still had his first nickel" sidled up to Al and said in a low voice, "How much y' take f' that seat?" He got even closer, cupped his hand to Al's ear and continued... "Our seat t'home's got a crack in it. Every once in a while the wife'll sit on it n' get pinched in the...y' know...backside." Al gave him the toilet seat and said the old guy stopped back in a couple weeks... "The wife feels better now" he said, again, secretly, like a thug making a deal!

Al and David followed me out to my car that day as I left the Jerome house. Just before I got in, I turned to Al and said, "You must really love working that Clossey Place to have done it all these years." Al looked across the valley where two huge machines were harvesting the third crop of hay on the old Badger Farm which is flatter and void of ledges... "not compared to that, I don't" he said, smiling (smiles are part of Al Jerome's vocabulary). We three had a good chuckle and as I left. I knew, that I had just caught Al Jerome in a minor falsehood; he loves that Clossey Place and everything about it right down to the ugliest of ledges. Yup, he's still there for Jack Clossey, the guy who "needed some help" all those years ago. ❦

Winter Stories

Here I sit this second day of January gazing through the jail bar effect the icicles make outside my window. Just beyond, happy skiers glide along the freshly groomed trails they have paid to use at our ski center; avid four-season recreationers, they are. I sit here on the "inside", not feeling like a jailbird at all because it's my choice to be here, smug and snug in my wood fire warmth. You see, weathered Yankees like me have an active list of "do's and don't's" and top on the list of "don't's" is winter recreation. Oh I'll occasionally click into my trusty cross-country skies but it's mostly "ceremonial"...basically I figure there's plenty of winter exercise in the form of cutting wood, stoking fires, getting ready to sugar...shoveling roofs, plowing roadways...get my drift?

Speakin' of which, our new evaporator still hasn't arrived and, come to think of it, I shouldn't be surprised. Another thing about weathered Yankees .we believe in and live by Murphy's Law. Yup, even though that evaporator was ordered and financed back last May, it's now scheduled to be delivered the third week of January because of a "backorder in stainless steel" or something. But I know the real reason...they can't fool me!

Right now our sugarhouse is all torn apart. In preparation for the new evaporator's arrival, we discovered terminal rot in the hundred-year-old building's carrying timber and in several other strategic places. We're slowly fixing the problems and wait, patiently, for the winter's coldest week when that evaporator will inevitably arrive and we can install it properly per Murphy's Law.

On the subject of past writings... I wrote about spreading manure in the wintertime. Folks kind of liked that story and their feedback brought several stories worthy of note, including a couple good'uns from one of our employees, Audrey Lafirira. She came in to work the morning after she had read it and sidled up to me grinnin' like a farm boy up to no good... "You know back before our new barn was built, Junior'd back the spreader right

213

into our house t'thaw the thing out" she said. "I'd usually be upstairs bakin' cookies or somethin' and when that smell started waftin' up through the floor, I knew it weren't goin' ta be a very good day!".

She told of another time when her husband, Junior, had just bought a new spreader. "The darned thing leaked too much manure out the back, you know between the top and bottom beaters" she said, "and neighbors were beginning to complain about spillage out on the highway." She said that Junior went back to the dealer to complain and, for added punch, she got right up into my face and lowered her voice. "And this is the God's honest truth...that dealer stood right there and said t'Junior: 'Mr. Lafirira, that's one machine we sell that we never stand behind'"! Audrey left me hanging for a few seconds until I finally "got it" and when I did, I just about split a gut laughing!

Another friend of mine, Danny Coane, called with a spreader story of his own. It seems Danny and a friend were visiting a farmer up in Highgate one cold winter day. They'd just finished up the morning milking and had cleaned the gutters and bedded down the cows. "It was thirty below outside" Danny said, "and the farmer's son had gone out to spread the manure." Back in those days farmers were allowed to spread in the winter; barring any problems, there was plenty of time to get a load spread before anything froze up. That particular day, the son had suited up, started the tractor and headed through the almost axle-deep snow toward the back forty. Danny said he'd been gone quite a while when he appeared on the horizon, trudging back through the snow on foot. When he finally reached the barn, he verified every farmer's worst nightmare: "got way out theyah" he said, "and had just put her in gear and started spreadin' when the thing got stuck tighter'n a drum". His father immediately went into panic mode, no doubt visualizing his spreader being held hostage for the rest of the winter by a three ton block of frozen crap. As he rushed toward his outdoor garb and a hanging dung fork, the boy, ever sensitive to his dad's pain, spoke up... "Don't worry, Dad... it's still steamin'!".

Danny and I had a good laugh over that farm boy's way of saying "it ain't froze yet", four pretty darned happy words here in wintertime Vermont! Right now we're looking forward to getting that new evaporator and when it comes, we'll don our cold-weather garb and install it. The pain'll be worth it come spring when that shiny contraption is doing its job...ahh spring...a time of year when the words, "it's still steamin'" have an even happier meaning.
🍁

The Little Statehouse

We've got our own version of "The Tortoise and the Hare" right here in the North Country. The race started eighty years ago. It wasn't a traditional race with two contestants and a finish line....no, it had to do with the life stories of two objects as varied as, say a tortoise and a hare. They were both born in 1929 and related in a round-a-bout way. Heck, most folks wouldn't even recognize it as a race but I do. In this race, the "hare" was a huge bridge made of hundreds of tons of steel and concrete, built strong enough to carry traffic across Lake Champlain way into the future. It should have won this race but was deemed unsafe to cross in October of 2009 and died two months later when a demolition company imploded it in a matter of seconds.

The "tortoise" was a simple idea that became a parade float. You see, the bridge was so big and important that many of the cities and towns around Vermont and New York State wanted to send floats for the gala parade that would open the bridge. The idea had risen from a group of Montpelier citizens quicker'n the tap of a speaker's gavel, a "capital" idea it was...Montpelier's float would be a replica of the Vermont Statehouse. The parade was held on a hot day in August of 1929. Thousands of excited folks lined the roads on both sides of the lake to welcome the bridge that would liven tourism and commerce in the North Country. Governors John Weeks of Vermont and Franklin D. Roosevelt of New York shook hands in the middle of the bridge and the gala parade made its opening official. Afterward the floats all returned to their villages, diminished to memories and photographs, except for one. The little statehouse lived on...chalk another one up for the tortoise.

It was built by carpenters of the A.K. Baird Company on a volunteer basis out of scraps of lumber from the jobs they were on. That was back in the days when law making was simpler and work ethic was strong. They immediately started with their hand tools working only during their noon hours. Even though it was only a parade float they were building, those guys "drove home" both quality and pride with every nail; after all, it was their statehouse they were building. Over the summer of 1929, the structure grew from its eight by twelve foot frame to include two Greek Revival porticoes and a gold leaf dome that would rival the real one. Well before the big day, they had applied the last of the ornate trim and placed a foot-tall Ceres, Roman Goddess of Agriculture atop the dome. When the big day arrived, it was placed on a platform farm truck for the trip to Addison.

After the parade, the little statehouse came back to Montpelier, appeared in a few other parades, and then rested in front of Toy Town, a group of roadside cabins on US Route 2 just down the street from the real statehouse. Many a Montpelier area resident of my vintage remember passing that little statehouse every time we went toward Burlington back in the days before Interstate 89. Ironically it was the opening of I-89 in the 1960s that both "drove" modern travel, including traffic over the Champlain Bridge, and hastened the decline of the little statehouse. Toy Town went out of business soon after the interstate highway opened, necessitating a change of home for the little structure. It went down Randolph way for a spell and then migrated over toward Burlington where it jumped from home to home. After its twenty-plus year spell at Toy Town, however, the little statehouse model never quite received the care and attention it needed.

In the year 2000, Montpelier resident, Paul Guare located it out in back of a cement warehouse over in Williston. It was dilapidated almost to the point of no return. Paul Guare's father-in-law was Nelson Paxman, one of the original carpenters, and Paul had always had a special place in his heart for the little statehouse. He arranged for the broken and rotting pieces to be picked up and trucked back to Montpelier where the Montpelier Historical Society took ownership. The minute those pieces arrived "back home", another group of carpenters reached for their tools, once again on a volunteer basis and a "shoestring" budget; those guys belonged to the Montpelier Kiwanis Club and, according to my Kiwanian friend, Fred Bushway, invested upwards of two thousand hours in bringing the local treasure back to life.

These days the model statehouse rests proudly right here at Morse Farm under a shelter that was built with Montpelier Historical Society funds. It'll never be out in the weather again, accept possibly on one of the occasions it's appearing in parades or at historical functions throughout Vermont. Yes, it's permanently mounted on a trailer so that it can be made available for all to enjoy. In a couple years, in fact, it'll be traveling to a very special place,

Addison, Vermont for the opening of the new Champlain Bridge. It'll be a huge day for lots of folks, folks who have been seriously inconvenienced by the bridge's two year absence. There will be none more excited, however, than a large contingent from Montpelier who remember the history of it all...long live the little statehouse that could! ❧

Smart Calves and Swimming Babies

We've all heard the expression "miracle of birth" time and time again. Being a man, I'm not sure I can ever properly appreciate the term but I have witnessed the miracle many times, including the birth of my own two sons. It is my vocation, however, where most of my experience comes from; I am a farmer and a farmer's job is to "tweak" the lives of animals to better serve humans. We farmers have gotten pretty good at the "tweakin'" but there's one thing that we'll never affect: the period just before, during and after birth... that's solely up to those critters...it's truly a miracle!

That blessed event has recently occurred twice at Morse Farm with the birth of two healthy calves. The first cow to give birth had "given notice" the night before by separating herself from the rest of the herd. Through the early night, I heard her bawling the unmistakable language of a cow about to calve. When morning came, she was still in the same place but her bawling had changed to a throaty "cooing" sound. I donned my rubber boots, opened the gate and approached her through the dew-drenched grass. She wasn't about to let on where her calf was but I knew where to look. Just across our fence is a swampy area that supports tall grass. From my position, I could see a dark mound in the distance, almost out of sight. I slid under the fence and as I approached, there lying perfectly still was a tiny black calf. The mother had coaxed it through the fence and out into the safety of the tall grass; newborn calves are most vulnerable during the hours immediately following their birth and cows will always pick out a "safety zone" and somehow "instruct" their calves to go there and lie still....once again, the word "miracle" comes to mind!

As I reached to pick the calf up, the little duffer started to rise and escape me. Amazingly at less than a day old, they not only can walk but they have a slight ability to fend for themselves. This one, however, a bull calf, was a trifle too slow so I grasped him around his middle, carried him back to the fence, and tucked him under the bottom wire where mother was ready and waiting. Within two minutes the little guy was having his first meal and mother was beaming...that's right, beaming, with pleasure!

Although we humans mature to a much higher intelligence, I've always thought it curious that members of the bovine family start their days seemingly so much smarter and ready for the world than we do! I'm reminded of a story that has been handed down in our family for generations where a human baby was put to the test and, once again, presented a miracle.

Mr. Lyme Hinkson was a Civil War veteran who lived up around Maple Corner. He had a distinctive way of talking and must have had a distinctive personality for stories of him to have survived all these generations. One time his wife had given birth to a male baby and Lyme snatched it from her bosom when it was still very young. Apparently he expected the infant to prove its mettle even at the "ripe old age" of a few weeks! He carried the baby to the edge of Curtis Pond where a rowboat sat waiting and he boarded it with the infant. Lyme rowed out to a depth sufficient for his purpose and dropped the anchor. Without hesitation, he grabbed the baby and flung it over the side. "Sink or swim ye little devil" he said. After a short time of sputterin' and flailin', he seemed pleased to report that "Most cer-ting-ly, the cuss swam like a goodun!".

Although it has nothing to do with the miracle of birth, another story finds old Lyme in the hayfields around Maple Corner. Being a veteran of the Civil War, he was used to the sounds of cannon fire. Over toward Burlington, forty miles west of Maple Corner, there was a firing range and on it was a cannon named Long Tom. My father said that on certain days when the weather was just right, the report of cannon fire could be heard clear over in Maple Corner. "Every time Old Lyme heard it" my father said, "he would stop what he was doing, cock his head and announce 'Well now most cer-ting-ly that would be Loooong Tom t'Burl-a-ton!'"

Yup, the miracle of birth keeps offering new lives and stories of lives that go on and on. I've always been glad that baby boy exercised his natural ability to swim because chances are, he would now be some currently living person's great, great grandfather. No doubt Lyme Hinkson's style with a new born would be considered a complete anathema in this day and age but, by the same token, he might think some of our modern-day parents a bit too over protective. As far as the act of birth goes, however, everyone agrees that it's nothing short of a miracle; I bet even old Lyme Hinkson would mutter a "most cer-ting-ly" to that. ❧

Bridge Over Troubled Traffic

When God made the patch of land that Montpelier, Vermont rests upon, he might not have had modern-day traffic in mind. Montpelier's geographical attributes all come together to make her the prettiest state capital in the US but those same features can sure cramp the style of any motorist needing to get from point A to point B. First of all, there's our beloved Winooski River...it's beautiful and now even clean enough for fishing and swimming. Then there's the pristine hillside directly to the river's south...again, green and picturesque. But, as any designer worth his salt might say, "the two simply do not 'work'". The "kicker" is an old road and an old bridge. US Route 2, which has grown in both width and usage over the years, is literally squashed between the river and the hillside. Granite Street bridge, built in 1902, is a strategic modern day "path of least resistance"...sort of. It crosses the Winooski at a tight "bottleneck" where the road cannot be widened any further; the bridge, built for horses and lumber wagons, is narrow and creaky.

In addition to its physical quirks, the old bridge offers another strange phenomenon; whether by a flawed combination of ions beaming through its steel girders or a resident ghost that's simply up to no good, the Granite Street Bridge has the uncanny ability to zap human brain cells! That's right, a perfectly intelligent motorist entering the bridge from the north somehow becomes a bungling idiot who is suddenly terrified of the bridge's railing. He drives right down the centerline, defying anyone trying to use the bridge from the opposite direction. The worst of the havoc, however, is over the use of traffic light at the bridge's south end. Accompanying the light is a well-positioned sign that says "Stop Here to Activate Green". The sign, perfectly clear to intelligent people, is nothing but gibberish to these "cerebrally challenged" souls. They either zoom right past it or stop prematurely; the result, of course, brings bridge usage to complete and utter limbo.

My wife Betsy recently came home shaking from a "bridge" experience. Although we ended up laughing about it, I'm sure there was nothing funny about it at the time. Betsy was waiting for a green light on Berlin Street on the opposite side of Route 2, intending to cross the bridge. She knows all too well that this task, however simple it should be, may well be complicated by another of the "bridge idiots". This time when the light turned green, she put her little two-door Honda Civic in gear and headed through the parted Route 2 traffic. Our two black Labs, Averill and Fern were with her that day. Typical dogs, they frantically vied for "air time" at the Civic's two operable windows as if saying "Ho boy isn't life great...it don't get any better'n this... let's trade windows, yah, yah, yah!" All of a sudden Betsy said her world switched to slow motion...a huge SUV, driven by the bridge's most recent victim, appeared out of nowhere.

"There it was stopped just inches from me" she said. "The woman had run the bridge's red light and as I peered in, I could see she held a cell phone against her ear with one hand and in her other hand was a humungous slice of chocolate cake!". Betsy said the woman was, at the same time, carrying on a conversation and stuffing cake into her mouth like there was no tomorrow. The dogs, suddenly in dessert mode, bounded into Betsy's lap and dangled from her window... "Ho boy, ho boy...life's gettin' better all the time!". In the meantime Betsy, aware that Route 2 traffic would soon be treating her car and the errant SUV as sandwich filler, grabbed the dogs by their tails, yanked them back into the car and offered some curt "instructions" to the woman who slowly jockeyed her SUV out of the way.

Another of Montpelier's traffic problems has more to do with hospitality than geography. The center of town, although small enough to almost spit from one end to the other, for some reason hosts more crosswalks than you could shake a white cane at. While it's nice that this level of courtesy is being extended to our pedestrians, we carry it to a frustrating extreme. Many times I'll be in the middle of a "plumbing nightmare" and hurrying to our friendly downtown hardware store. The seat beside me is piled high with spare parts and my body is covered with grease (or worse). All I want to do is get there, beseech one of Aubuchon's green-vested geniuses for parts and solutions, and return home. It's inevitable at these times that motorists will be stopped at each and every crosswalk generously waving on far distant pedestrians and plethoras of vehicles from side streets. Sometimes I'll sit for an hour festering in a world-class traffic jam here in America's smallest and prettiest capital city... "Oh boy, where's the New York attitude when you need it!"

There will no doubt be folks who take me to task for my critique of Montpelier traffic but, really, can anyone say that cell phones and busy traffic mix? There is no shortage of problems in this fast-moving day and age. Money is short, bridges are old and motorists still need two hands on the wheel. And for anyone who wants to argue with that I say, "Let them eat cake but never while driving!" 🍁

Lost and Found

Calving season continued here at Morse Farm yesterday with the birth of another coal black Angus calf. Tommy knew the mother, a late arrival to his herd last year, was due but she held off so long that he had stopped watching. Yesterday I was home gazing from our porch at the valley below, when out of the corner of my eye I noticed a form suddenly immerge from one of the distant cows and tumble to the ground. I rushed for our binoculars and, sure enough, there lying at the cow's hind legs, a tiny calf sputtered and then took its first look at her brand new world. I stayed with it until the cow turned and began to clean her baby...I knew she would be a good mother.

The next morning Tommy and I struggled for a few hours before we found the calf...mothers have such a knack for hiding them! Back when I was younger, there were lots of farms in this area and it was common to hear of lost cows and calves. When that happened, we had an important resource right in the neighborhood in the name of Luvia Lafirira. Luvia was a farm wife, mother, and well-respected member of the community who also happened to have the gift of clairvoyance. She died when I was a very young man so I never had the pleasure of meeting her but I remember my mother going to her one time in search of a lost ring. The two women greeted each other and exchanged a few pleasantries before my mother described the ring. Luvia thought a minute and said "Dorothy, I see a countertop and some kind of white material, like snow." Something immediately clicked with my mother. "Oh m'God" she said. "It's the flour...it's the donuts!". Mother rushed home and started dissecting the raised donuts she had made the day before. Sure enough, one of them had an added ingredient...the ring! My mother took a dozen donuts over to the Lafirira place a few days later. Luvia was never particular about payment; she'd take her pay in dollars, farm help, or even "karat-free" donuts.

One day recently I sat down with Luvia's daughter-in-law, Audrey Lafirira, who works here at Morse Farm, and Luvia's daughter, Gloria. Together the two of them are more like a comedy team than true heirs to anything psychic but when I started asking questions, they turned serious. When I asked Gloria how it was having Luvia for a mother, it took no clairvoyant to interpret the respect and love she felt. "She was a good person" Gloria said, stressing the "good" which meant to me that Luvia was mother first and clairvoyant second. Gloria described her Vermont farm upbringing as though the Lafirira farm was no different from any other except for one additional crop...psychic readings. "I remember my father getting up in the middle of the night ", she said "and building a fire in the parlor stove so that Mother could come down and meet with a family who had lost a child." She said the stress of dealing with lost kids and worried families would tire her mother out more than the hardest physical work.

There was, however, levity in Luvia's work. Gloria told of one Halloween night when area farmers bore the brunt of a prank. In that day and age, each farmer had ten gallon milk cans with his own number on them and Halloween hooligans would switch milk cans from one farm to the other. She said the following morning one of those farmers paid Luvia a professional visit seeking the whereabouts of his milk cans. Luvia invited him to sit at her kitchen table and started the session the way she always did, by reading his palm. Gloria was listening through the chimney hole from the bedroom above and started to get "cold feet" about the developing session below. All of a sudden she whispered down through the hole... "Mother, just tell him his cans are over at Burton Parker's"...Gloria had been one of the hooligans!

Yes, there were the sad stories, too, stories of barns that would burn, trips that would turn sour and folks who were sick. Audrey and Gloria said when Luvia had one of these previews, she would always try to buffer it. "When she knew someone was sick" Gloria said, "she'd kindly suggest that they might want to see a doctor." She told of another time when a man was about to head off on a cross-country trip. Luvia "saw" a terrible accident. She asked the man if he might consider postponing his trip. He didn't and was killed somewhere out west. And Audrey said the night her family's barn burned to the ground, Luvia knew something bad was going to happen on their farm. "She woke up and saw the sky to the west aglow. She knew it was our barn even though our farm was way over in East Montpelier.".

At the end of our session, I asked Gloria if she or any other members of her family had the gift. Gloria replied with words like "no...not really...I don't think so". She said after her mom died, folks called beseeching her for help. "I felt so bad", she said, "I told them I'd try." She said she never had much success except for a natural ability to read palms. She had offered to read mine early on in our meeting and I, feeling a bit creepy about those things, told her "no thanks". Just before we parted, however, Gloria reached for my hand. She pointed out the three lines, life, heart and mind, and gave me a good mark on all three counts. "Whew" I thought as the two women walked away... "I'll take that!"

Since Luvia passed away, our Central Vermont community has been void of anyone "gifted" in this special way. After my recent meeting with her daughter and daughter-in-law, however, I can honestly say that all was not lost. Audrey and Gloria certainly inherited friendliness and the desire to help others from her and I know Luvia would be proud...that's what she'd want to be known for anyway. 🍂

A Salute to Ray

My friend Ray Hartson says he knows he's a Vermonter but he doesn't know what a Vermonter is. I find that quite odd what with the multitude of creative speculation out there: ("A Vermonter can remember when we use to have snow up to our ass", eats his dessert first cause life is so uncertain, likes sugar in any form just as long as it's maple.") No, Ray, 76 years old and champion of understatement, simply doesn't know what a Vermonter is but, by God, has it "written all over his face". His nose for Vermont maple syrup has recently led him up here to Morse Farm as a syrup canner. He says he doesn't need additional income at this point in his life, calls it "mad" money; all he says is "I kinda like it up here" and keeps on workin'.

The sounds of country and western music usually blend with the heavenly fragrance of hot maple syrup in our canning room; quite appropriately, I'd say, because Ray Hartson is a country performer himself…Ray's a pedal steel guitar player. For those who don't know what a pedal steel guitar is, it's the instrument that makes the "weepy", sound without which country music wouldn't be country music (think Toby Keith, "I Love This Bar"). When I asked Ray how he learned how to play this unusual instrument, he got as animated as I had seen him yet (think Willie Nelson, "On the Road Again"). "Well" he said, "I went to Nashville one time and when I heard my first pedal steel, I knew I had to learn to play one. I went home, bought one and practiced it with m'coffee every morning. Then I'd go home and practice after supper. After a fashion, I could play the thing pretty good."

Ray has held that same work ethic through his entire work life. He quit high school after a few months. "Why?", I asked him… "hated school" he said. I told him that I fully understood, being a school hater myself. At sixteen he went to work at the North Montpelier woolen mills running the "picker machine". At seventeen he talked his mother into signing so he could join the

Marines. His Marine journey took him through one tour in Korea followed by an honorable discharge. He then went back to work at the woolen mills. In the 1960s, a changing economy closed the mills and Ray found himself in the cabs of trucks for the next thirty years driving for outfits like Capital Candy Company and Cabot Cheese. For much of Ray's truck driving career, he hauled what I'd call the "tsunami" of cargos, bulk milk. You see for sanitary reasons, milk truck tanks have no baffles in them. They are extremely difficult to drive because the milk inside surges, unchecked, from side to side. I asked Ray if he'd ever tipped one over. "Hell no. Drive slow n'easy and use your head" he said. "Easier said then done" I said, thinking of all the dented stainless steel tanks I've seen caused by milk truck roll-overs.

He described some of the farms where he picked up milk. "One guy" he said "left his half-gallon milk jug sittin' on top a'the bulk tank expectin' me to measure the milk in the tank and then fill up the jug." That, of course, would have given the farmer his personal milk on the milk company's "nickel". Ray said he never told the farmer but always filled the milk jug first and then measured the milk that Cabot would pay for...Ray Hartson's as honest as the day is long.

Speaking of "long days", when we're canning thousands of quarter pints of maple syrup, canning gets downright boring. Ray and I talk about things as varied as religion to fishin' to Fords vs. Chevrolets on those days but, being old men, we thoroughly cover the subject of our health, me with "plumbin'" problems, him with bad "wind". Early on, we discovered that we share the same doctor. Our doc is not only an ace practitioner but a down-to-earth guy and that's a prerequisite with both Ray and me in choosin' our doctors. One time this doctor told me a story about an older man coming to him. When asked the proverbial question, "Do you drink?", the older man palmed his chin, scrunched up his face, and replied: "Well doctor...ya see...I...try...ta drink...at least...a six-pack...a summer". My doctor and I had a good laugh over that but he couldn't tell me who the man was because of this foolish HIPAA business (HIPAA is the federal act that, among other things, portends to guarantee privacy in health care. It's the stupidest thing bureaucrats have done yet...how the hell are we supposed to help our neighbors if we don't know what ails em?). One day when we were working together, I told Ray that story. He gave me kind of a "knowing" look and said "Ya know...that mighta been me." So much for HIPAA!

Ray's last job before he came to us was running sawing/polishing machinery in a granite shed. He said he applied for the job because he could earn twice the money in half the time than he could driving truck. "The boss actually tried t'talk me out of it...said 'it's a dirty job, y'know'". Ray simply told that boss that he "could probably buy some soap with the extra money!".

I've been thinking lately of the perfect words to describe a man who has done just about everything...wool worker, soldier, truck driver, musician, granite cutter, maple canner...but I only recently came up with the perfect combination. The other day, Ray told a story about attending a parade over in Northfield. He said he was standing on the sidelines wearing his "Korea Veteran" cap when all of a sudden one of the cadets from Norwich University broke ranks, approached him, and saluted. His eyes were tearing up as he told the story and he said he'd never been so proud in his entire life. He went on to express his optimism for our country's future with young people like that in charge. Suddenly the words came to me, as pure as maple syrup and as lyrical as country music: Ray Hartson, "Great American". 🍁

Billie Deer

We're sure saying "hello" to the new year's wintery debut here in Central Vermont and these days, totally different sounds are coming from the woods. January's frigid temperatures bring explosive cracking sounds from the beeches and maples similar to our deer season's rifle and muzzleloader "reports" we've finally stopped hearing. It seems as if our deer season has lengthened in years of late with the addition of a "youth" day, two bow and arrow seasons, and a muzzleloader season added to the usual two week rifle season. Now don't get me wrong...I used to grow vegetables and berries for my living so I still haven't shaken the old thought that "the only good deer is one in the freezer!". Yup, according to the stats, there'll be at least 3290 fewer of the rascals filling up on garden peas and farmers' alfalfa this coming summer. The downside, however, comes with the heavy artillery; seems like there are more hunters than ever and frankly, you have to wonder if they always know what they're shootin' at.

This reminds me of a story my friend Norm Kelley recently told about old Rome VanOrnum who lived up on the edge of Curtis Pond in Maple Corner. Rome was a goat farmer, musician, long time Vermonter and most distinguishable, a true character. As the story goes, one time in deer season a guy pulled up in his car with down-country plates and headed out through Rome's upper field. Always one to "live and let live", Rome wasn't upset that those folks were using his land. "Yup, they're city slickers alright" he would have said in his nasal, high pitched voice, "but if they'll just behave themselves, I don't mind share'n it with 'em." Next thing he knew, the city slicker was dragging an animal back to the car and when Rome walked over to investigate, he realized it wasn't quite the "deer" story he expected.

"T'wern't no deer th' cuss was draggin'" Rome related "but one-a-my goats all field dressed and tagged!". He went on to say the guy was "prouder'n hell of his deer'"! At this point most farmers would have "melted down" but that was never Rome VanOrnum's style. Norm said that Rome must have done some quick "on his feet thinkin'" about the best way to pass Yankee justice on to this idiot. He walked up to the carcass, smacked his lips, and allowed how "there'd be some mighty good eatin' there". He praised the guy for his trophy buck, guesstimated the weight, and even helped heft it up and tie it to the car's bumper!

Rome, still thinking, kept on praising the man and suggested that the "deer" might even set a record for weight. He told the guy where the nearest reporting station was, his excitement reaching falsetto-range... "why I'm even goin'ta call a bunch a my friends t'meet you theyah so's they can see this record buck and, by God, I'll call the papah t'get a pitcher, too!". The man beamed from ear to ear as he reached a bloody hand out to shake Rome's, got in his car, and headed out to legalize his kill.

Norm never really finished the story but I can just imagine that fool's reception when he reached the reporting station: there would have been a group of rag-tag but mean looking Vermont natives, a uniformed game warden and a Times Argus photographer at the ready. The words "You gotta be kidding" followed by the words "You are under arrest!" would have cut the fool's pride quicker'n a bullet whistles through the trees. And, best of all, I can just picture Rome VanOrnum, goat farmer, Vermonter, musician, back home laughin' his head off for just having played a city slicker like a fiddle! He no doubt was paid amply for his loss once the State finished with that down-country guy and, fortunately, no human was killed that day. As we look toward next year's hunting season, however, we all need to keep our orange hunting wear handy and never make goat sounds because, for certain, someone might mistake us for a deer. ❧

Ready, Aim, Fire

It was a routine trip to the bathroom at 2:30 AM when I noticed a strange red glow on the white bathroom wall. "What the...," I thought as I pulled myself together and looked out the window. The source, I found, was the revolving red light of a fire truck and it was stopped at our grey farmhouse just down the road, the one where my two boys live! I hurried to the door, pulling on some pants as I went, and rushed over in my car. The truck was, indeed, stopped by our farmhouse and the night was ablaze with red lights from other vehicles just down the road. I ditched my car, jumped out and hurried through a mix-match of huge, red rigs, all bearing the gold letters "EMFD" on their doors. Guided by the blue glow from a Vermont State Police cruiser, I ended up at a battered pickup which lay overturned in the ditch. A young man had just crawled out, slightly drunk but otherwise unscathed. Relieved that my sons were OK, I headed back through the surreal canyon of fire apparatus and returned home, thinking of what a "well-oiled" and endowed department the EMFD is these days.

The East Montpelier Fire Department started back in 1964, with a small group of dedicated townsfolk. I recently asked a friend who is a founding member, about its beginnings. It seems the department began with the typical "rough edges" and—well—a "well-oiled" nature in another sense.

My friend said their first truck was an elderly oil truck donated by Seguin Fuel Company. The volunteer firemen, farmers, mechanics, bankers and businessmen, went at the old truck with a vengeance. They stripped it down in a rented garage and put it back together piece by piece. In the meantime they scavenged the countryside for anything that would contribute to the firefighting cause. Finally on a hot summer day in 1964, they opened the doors of that same rented garage, now the East Montpelier Volunteer Fire Department, and there stood the bright red truck with hand-lettered

"EMVFD" on the doors. My friend said they didn't have to wait long for their very first fire:

"I was drivin' the new truck. When I got there, I could see we had our work cut out—flames were just appearing outside the house. We started the pump, pulled out the hose and approached, four of us on the line. The point man pulled the nozzle handle and that hose jumped to life. Water shot up at the flames but what happened next was something none of us planned on—apparently we'd failed to get all the fuel oil outa the truck tank and when the water hit, there was a deafening "whoosh" and those flames reached for the sky! It surprised us so much we dropped the hose and ran like hell."

He said that hose carried on like an angry serpent until the motley crew regrouped, tamed it and went back to fighting the fire. By that time the oil had washed out of the system and the water did its job, but when they left that day, the house stood a charred skeleton—"woulda been a total loss anyway, even without our little brush with unanticipated ignition!" he said.

They spent some time after that first fire, "dousing" rumors and learning from more on-the-job training. Back in those days, there were still lots of active dairy farms around. The East Montpelier firemen learned quickly from several huge barn fires, the result of spontaneous combustion in 10,000 bales of hay. There were also open dumps. My friend said they had a deal with the Town of Calais to fight their fires for $150.00 per hour. "Back then," he said, tongue in check "everyone was burning' wood. They'd clean their stoves and put live coals into the garbage. We were on the same road all the time, headed for the Calais Dump to put out fires started by those hot coals—that's how we financed the department!"

It's said that "a bad dress rehearsal makes a good show," and the EMFD is no exception. After 41 years of mostly good shows, we have a stellar fire department. In fact the only complaint I've heard is probably a good one—they're too good. When they show up quickly, proficiently and en mass at every minor incident, they sometimes draw criticism from those who would opt for a simpler life here in East Montpelier. Too bad, I say, to use another hard worked cliché—"Better safe than sorry." ❧

Price Matters

My brother, Elliott, has recently been filling me in on the progress of our new East Montpelier-Calais fire station and ambulance service. The voters OK'd the money part back at Town Meeting but I understand there has been a holdup over permitting...Aiyyy...permitting...seems we've got ourselves so wrapped up in red tape these days that even an ambulance service is suspect until found innocent. I can remember the days when things were much simpler...and looser.

Back when I was a teenager, we didn't have any of these special "hospitals on wheels" that appear at your door with whole squadrons of ultra-trained personnel for everything from a sprained pinky to a heart attack...we had a couple guys in a stretched out Cadillac specially built for carrying prostrate people...usually to the cemetery. That's right, when I was a kid, the local undertaker could transition from the embalming table to the emergency stretcher quicker'n a house-a-fire. My buddy back then was from a family of funeral directors and through him, I got to know some of the ins and outs of that business.

One time I had taken a break from the hayfields and gone down to the funeral home to visit. While I was there, the phone rang with a call for an ambulance. There had been an automobile accident over in the Mad River Valley and they needed someone there PDQ. My buddy, Phil, slammed the phone down and turned to me wagging his index finger, which meant only one thing...I was to be his second man! "But...but" I protested as I followed him to the garage where the "big car", a term they used for the hearse, stood retrofitted with a stretcher and removable red light. Having just left the hayfields, I was filthy but my pleas of inexperience and inappropriateness went unanswered; "There's nobody else here", Phil shouted. We hopped in and screamed out of town, siren blaring, toward the Valley.

We arrived to find a wrecked car out in the middle of a small roadside field.

Phil dropped the big car down into low gear and crept out to the scene. Thankfully the victim, an elderly man, was bloodied but alert where he still sat behind the wheel of his crumpled car. We manhandled him onto the stretcher and slid him, like any other "body", through the big car's broad back door...no questions, testing of vital signs, backboards or brainstorming from our crew of two novice teenagers!

Much of my story has gone away, lost to a sixty-plus year-old memory, but one part is still as vivid as if it happened yesterday; when we got back to the hospital, the personnel approached me with a clipboard, asked me questions like "can you tell me what day it is", and sat me down for a blood pressure test...I looked so rough they thought I was one of the victims! "No, no...you don't understand", I said. "I'm with the ambulance." My buddy Phil, vouched for me and I went on home, back to the hayfields...things were, indeed, much looser in those days!

Recently another ambulance story was related to me by my friend, Allen Jacobs, about a Mr. John Underhill from over in Piermont, New Hampshire. The Underhills, a rugged country clan, own a large tract of woodland just east of the Connecticut River. One day last winter, John, the family patriarch was injured very severely when a big tree he was cutting turned on him. Luckily there were others working close by who called for an ambulance which quickly arrived in the form of DART, Dartmouth Hitchcock Medical Center's emergency helicopter. The medical team made their way through the snow toward Mr. Underhill who was suffering badly but still cognizant. The helicopter sat close enough by so that John could feel the draft from its still twirling rotors and when the team reached him, he raised his uninjured hand. "Wait just a minute, young feller," he said to the first to kneel down. "How much you gonna chaaarhge me t'ride on that thing?" The team, ever professional, no doubt assured him that cost was the least of his problems but John persisted... "No, damn it, I ain't-a-goin' if it's too much!" When they told him the usual price was $4500, John Underhill blew his top... "Get ye outa here...didn't ask for ya, don't want ya...I'll figure anothah way!" said the old Yankee speaking from his pocket book, emergency be damned!

Yes we've seen some tremendous advances in the field of emergency medical response in the last 40 years and I'll be glad when our local ambulance project gets permitted and "percolating". We're lucky to have the level of care we do these days and, of course, it's always best to "err on the side of caution". We also need to carry on business without breakin' the bank. In the end, it'll be the desire of one human to help another that'll sort things out; that's one thing that's never changed. ❧

Good Welders Wanted

We get our share of breakdowns up here on the farm and they never wait for the perfect time. Our sap wagon broke down back during sugar season, right during a snowstorm. I suddenly found myself out in the storm plying my weak skills at the end of a welding rod; I weld for survival, not satisfaction. My brother, Elliott, appeared as I lifted the welding mask and stood looking at random blobs from my first attempt. "Let me show you a trick I learned from Johnny Gitchell," he said, as he kneeled down and showed me how to brace my welding arm a certain way. "This'll steady you up…what you're doing looks like it was left by a duck with the stomach flu!" Elliott's mention of Johnny Gitchell brought up scrapyards of memories:

Johnny ran a welding shop at the foot of a long hill in Wrightsville, Vermont. He was a kind man with a reddish, pointed nose and an impish grin. His pet name for me was "Grubouski." Gitchell's Welding Shop was magical to me as a kid, not just because I loved the array of equipment, but because Mrs. Gitchell had a tiny grocery store that was well stocked with penny candy. My father often took broken farm machinery over there to be resurrected. Johnny always reacted the same way--He'd shake his head, express some doubt, and then crank up his ancient welding machine. We left, every time, with a ship-shape machine and a heightened belief that Johnny was, indeed, closer to God.

One time I called upon Johnny's divine power to bail me out of a touchy situation. It was long after he had passed away and a modern ranch house stood where his shop had been. I was returning from my friend, Gerald Peas' farm over in Shady Rill, pulling a hay baler with our old Allis Chalmers D-17 tractor. I was hot and sweaty from my day in the hayfields and anxious to get home to a cool shower. When I got to the top of Johnny's hill, I thought of an older lady who used to custom-bale hay all over Washington County.

Mrs. Rock traveled the public highways with her ancient Farm-All H tractor pulling a baler. I'll never forget seeing her coast past our place atop that old H, shirttails flapping, doing at least 40 mph! Her tractor was obviously well maintained and equal to that high rate of speed.

That day on Johnny's hill, I made an instant and foolish decision: I threw our D-17 into neutral, idled her down, and prepared for a ride as smooth as Mrs. Rock's. The breeze felt luscious against my sweaty face as I gained speed. My euphoria was, however, to be short lived…part way down the hill the front wheels began to shimmy and shake. I suddenly remembered the worn, poorly maintained spindles and dared not touch the brakes, worn uneven by years of field use. My life started to pass before my eyes.

All of a sudden, an image of the grinning Johnny appeared and I beseeched, remembering his higher connections: "Johnny, please help a Morse in trouble one more time!" The old D-17 accelerated with quakes and clatters, pushed by an angry, wagging baler. I held on to the worn steering wheel with white knuckles until, miraculously, I reached the bottom of the hill where Johnny's shop had stood. The tractor finally slowed as the road leveled out and I knew I was safe…saved by something much bigger than dumb luck.

The snow was really coming down when Elliott and I finished welding the sap wagon. My son, Tommy, wasted no time hitching on and heading down the road for the next load of sap. I watched the wagon recede up the distant hill and hoped Tommy would be wiser than I was on his return. Chuckling, I thought of Johnny Gitchell up in welder's heaven, shaking his head as if assessing another repair job: "Don't ever do a damned fool thing like that again, Grubouski. I have my limits, you know!" 🍁

Horn of Plenty

Betsy and I have recently been looking at old black and white pictures from my mother's attic. One that stood out in particular was an aerial photo of our farm as it was back in the 50's. Ours was a typical New England dairy farm with multiple buildings, all connected by stairs and alleyways to the farmhouse. Every building sported a fresh coat of grey paint and was neat as a pin, like all Vermont farms of that era. There were lots of farms back then, too; most of our neighbors either farmed for a living or had a critter or two. One of these old farmers, Mr. Bradford Lane from up in the Horn of the Moon section of East Montpelier, recently called and asked if I had ten minutes—"I've got ten hours for Bradford Lane," I thought. Bradford's a "colorful" character and I wasn't about to pass up a meeting with him!

East Montpelier has always been lucky to have the likes of Bradford watching over town affairs. He's a "numbers" person and has dedicated his life to keepin' pencils sharp, so to speak. Because of this, he was never without adversaries. I brought this up one time and Bradford's grin blossomed out as wide as a 20 column spreadsheet: "Back in the 70's," he said, "I had gone in for a heart bypass operation. While I was recuperating down in Hanover, I heard a story from back home: They said old Lucinda White (made up name) from over on the other side of town was at an auction—you know how loud she was. Well, when she heard about my operation, she said I couldn't have anything wrong with my heart—claimed I didn't have one!"

I went right up to Bradford's after he called that day. There was crystalline snow in the air, when Bradford answered my knock. "Come in. Come in" he said. "Don't worry about your boots." I kicked them off anyway and followed him into the cozy living room where he spends most of his time these days. Bradford is a small man but as we sat down, I noticed his huge dairy farmer hands. "I called you 'cause there's some things you should know for your writing projects…none of us are getting any younger, you know. I thought you'd be interested in how the Horn of the Moon got its name." He went on to tell of an Indian who lived down in the valley where the North Branch of the Winooski River flows, where the Wrightsville Dam now lies. One day the Indian's cow disappeared and he went looking for her. Bradford, grinning again, said the Indian was gone the best part of a week and might have been up to "no good." I surmised Bradford was thinking of white lightening or pretty Indian maids. He went on to say that the fellow finally returned with the cow in tow and told his wife he had gone all the way to the Horn of the Moon. That's how the name got started. Bradford told me lots more about the "Horn," some things I can write about and some I can't! He grew up right in the heart of the Horn of the Moon and farmed there until age chased him to a smaller place just up the road. His old farm slopes toward a huge bowl, formed by the river valley and the sweeping hills and mountains beyond. From a high spot on the farm, the tip of Camel's Hump peaks up above the bowl's rim. The view from Bradford's home place is truly majestic. Before I left that day, we agreed to meet again in warmer weather for a drive over to the Horn.

I returned to Bradford's yesterday for that drive and found him just coming from out back, carrying a pot full of dandelion greens. He wore barn boots and walked slowly, stooped over; we joked about how those greens would make him live to be 100. After he handed the greens off to his wife, Ruth, we got in my car. On the way to the Horn, Bradford showed me the foundation of the S & E Morse sugarhouse, billed as the World's Largest, back in the 19th century. I knew I wasn't related to those Morses and Bradford minced no words about it: "They were East Montpelier Morses. You're a Calais Morse." (Two abutting towns, but "no cigar"). We drove through the Morse woods to a southwest clearing. "This is where the Horn of the Moon starts," Bradford said and had me stop so he could point out his property line. As we sat there in my idling Nissan, facing that stunning view I thought of the Indian sitting on what would be the Lane Farm. He looked off past that huge bowl and focused on the peak of Camel's Hump. He had just located his cow and unofficially appointed this most beautiful place, the Horn of the Moon. I turned to Bradford and said, "I think I figured out what kept that Indian feller so long; he just stayed on for a few extra days enjoying the view!"

We were still chuckling when I prepared to leave that day. I had a better understanding of my surroundings and great respect for this man, Bradford Lane from the Horn of the Moon. As we parted, I accepted his huge right hand, feeling its connection to a special place on earth and a great big heart.

Sweet Dogs

It was truly a grand weekend at our sugarhouse. Steffen Parker and I manned our new Leader evaporator, son Tommy and brother Elliott filled the vital roles of getting us sap and clean barrels for all the syrup we made and Pete Walbridge boiled the hotdogs. Hotdogs, you ask?...what the devil do hotdogs have to do with maple syrup? The answer is "everything" in the Morse Sugarhouse on Maple Open House Weekend.

Let's go back a few years to the days before plastic sap tubing when we had 3000 buckets hanging on our maple trees. Yes, it was a lot more work but it was good healthy work and the nostalgia takes to my soul like white steam to a blue sky. Back then we had a sap gathering crew of four, mostly young folk with strong backs, visionary minds, and a one season tenure. The one exception was a great man named Gerald Pease. Gerald had a small dairy farm over in Shady Rill and time to spare between barn chores. He came back thirty years in a row as chief of the gathering crew, stimulus for stories, and friend to all...I'm often approached by strangers with the common line: "Used to gather sap up at Morse Farm and I'll never forget Gerald Pease."

For some reason "chowing down" often provides fodder for folklore (cowboys and chuck wagons, lumber jacks and baked beans, football players and smorgasbords) and sap gatherin's no exception; our food of choice was sap boiled hotdogs. Dad was the sugarhouse person in those days and every day by mid-morning he'd fill a deep cooking pot with sap, throw in a bunch of good snappy hotdogs, and place the pot in a corner of the boiling back pan. Those dogs would sop up the sweetness from the sap and be ready to eat by the time the gathering crew brought in their noontime load and tank-sized appetites.

Gerald loved those sugar dogs and had a ritual over them that I'll never forget: everyday at "hot dog time" when our tractor returned from the woods, we'd hear it's laboring engine, the clanging of chains against rusting fenders, and mixing with the din, Gerald Pease would be barking like a dog, "OOWF, OOWF, OOWF." He and his rag-tag gathering crew would come into the sugarhouse and go right to the hot dog pot. The young sap gatherers would almost "inhale" the things and go back for seconds and thirds but Gerald, a devout man, would separate himself from the rest of us, sit on a block of wood, say a silent grace, and then savor every bite.

Pete Walbridge, like me, worked with Gerald until his death at 87 a few years back. For years, Pete went over to the Pease Farm in haying season to bale hay and tinker on all the equipment. Pete developed an almost worshipful relationship with that great man just like I did. He took Gerald places in his pickup (Gerald never drove anything but a tractor) and took breaks at the Pease table drinking chocolate raw milk and eating hard-as-a-rock ginger snaps. At those times, Gerald talked and joked and one of his favorite subjects was maple sugaring. He often said that gathering sap at the Morse Farm was one of his best experiences, always mentioning how good the hot dogs were.

A few years back we decided to offer sap-boiled hotdogs and sap-boiled eggs (a more universal Vermont sugarhouse custom) at our sugarhouse on Maple Open House Weekend. We advertised it quite heavily and the first year we did so, as I was inside preparing to boil sap, I heard a vehicle pull up outside the sugarhouse. A door slammed followed by an approaching "OOWF, OOWF, OOWF" and in came Pete Walbridge. I had put my brother Elliott and his wife Florence in charge of the hot dogs but Pete joined right in for the whole day and returned the next day. We've been doing it now for three years and Pete Walbridge has made "sap dog" weekend an annual ritual. It's always a lot of work and he never wants to be paid. When I asked him why he does it, he just smiled and shrugged like Gerald would have... "You're doing this to honor Gerald, aren't you?" I persisted...finally he said "yup", quietly, simply, just like Gerald Pease said grace at noon. 🍁

THE MORSE FARM SUGARHOUSE

Harry's Sugarhouse • Carolina Dreamin' • Literary Linkage • Irish Eyes •
Campaign, Turpentine and Sweet Goodbyes • A Friendly Pat

Another GREAT story and written only the way Burr Morse can put words together. I truly enjoy every one you write for as I read each one it is almost as though I am witnessing exactly the story you tell. You are the best, Burr and please never give up the exceptional God-given talent you have to picture in words the interesting and true experiences of many people from different walks of life.

- Earl Hinkel, TN

Harry's Sugarhouse

The man was drawn to our sign " Harry's Sugarhouse". He introduced himself as Harry Foster and he was from England. I shook his hand saying that even though everyone called me Burr, I was also a Harry, Harry Morse Jr. We talked while his fellow bus passengers were entering the sugarhouse and just before he joined them, something he said struck me: "Did you know that there has never been a Harry hanged?". We laughed but as he walked away I heard him say "it's true, y'know."

Our business this time of year attracts lots of "characters" like Harry Foster and after his visit, I knew I had to write about a few others while they were fresh on my mind...take the lady from Scotland whose accent was a thick as maple butter: She, like Harry Foster, was in a group from the United Kingdom and she approached me the other day after my sugarhouse show. As I've said before, my sugarhouse show has a bit of "local color" in it.

"Oye haven't loffft this mooch since oye left Scootland a week agoo!" she said. "Ye're very foony...ye moost h've Scootish blaahd in ye, lahdd!". At that point, she cast a wary eye toward the rest of her group which was departing the sugarhouse... "Those English all droive me bahty ye know...their 'umor's droier'n th'divil hi'self!". With that she slapped me a good 'un on the back and rejoined her group.

My job this time of year gives me ample opportunity to study human nature. I'll be standing at the corner of our sugarhouse as buses drive up. It's usually important to get folks into our place quickly and expediently but once in a while there's a group that simply will not respond. Unlike the proverbial "clowns spilling from a Volkswagen", these folks are more like honeybees waking from a long winter. They appear at the bus door one at a time. They painfully light on the gravel, and slowly amble away but in all different directions. Some are led by digital cameras held at arm's length while others go a short ways and just stop and gaze but all seem impervious to the guy over at the broad doorway waving his arms like a windmill.

I'm never rude because I know the importance of being a good host but the other day I got in a pack of trouble. Tommy's cows had gotten out the day before and in an effort to get them back in, I stood at a gate holding a bucket of grain hollering "come boss, come boss, c'm, c'm, c'm, come boss". We finally got them in but the day after, I was still quite in the "bovine" mode. As I stood at the corner of our sugarhouse, all of a sudden totally subconsciously and much to my horror, I realized I had been hollerin' "come boss, come boss, c'm, c'm, c'm, come boss" to the folks getting off the bus. I had no idea how long I'd been doing it but I certainly had their attention! There's really no way one can apologize for a mistake like that so I didn't...I simply got them in the sugarhouse and did my show as courteously as possible under strained circumstances. That was the one group all season that never "warmed up" to my "local color"!

A huge percentage of the people who come to our place are, as my late mother would say, "perfectly lovely people", but I recently got an email from one of the other persuasion. She had been to Morse Farm over Labor Day weekend obviously expecting something different than we provide. She spat words like "pathetic, messy, pitiful" and very unfairly compared us to the wine industry back in her native New York State. Since I normally keep my writing quite upbeat, I'll not dwell on this woman's critique long except to say that after I finished reading her epistle, I felt like tasting some wine for reasons other than "aroma" and "bouquet"!

Yes, we get all types here at Morse Farm and reality suggests that we can't "win 'em all". There have been many times, in fact, when we have used criticism to make things better. A little "healthy" criticism goes a long way, you know. I naturally enjoy the happy people, however, more than I do the disgruntled. Take Harry Foster, for instance...I'll never forget his pronouncement about certain "immunities" to hanging. In fact, after I got "raked over the coals" by that New York woman, I was kinda glad my name is Harry. 🍁

Carolina Dreamin'

Don't get me wrong...I love living here in Central Vermont but even Vermont with all its pristine countryside doesn't take away my right to spend some time out there in la-la land. Dreaming of other places sometimes helps me sleep at night; I'll often "drift off" from the cab of an eighteen wheeler grinding through the gears of a thirteen speed Road Ranger...no counting sheep for me...hell, that's the sort of thing I do by day! Recently, I was handed my most recent geographic "pie in the sky" when a bus full of Carolinians visited our place. In a way, it was an easy sell because we hear the same story over and over about the difference in property taxes... "fi' thousand dollar up'pare in VERmont for the same house cost me owney a few hunert down here in Carolina!". In these times of costs rising higher than a hillbilly on moonshine, that's a heck of an enticement.

There're also differences up here with neighborhood relationships. Take our brooks and waterways for example: the compost guy down the road from us is being asked to answer to his downstream neighbors about the possible affect to the "public water" of his operation. I grew up in the days when our local Winooski River was so polluted that we wouldn't dip our pinky finger in for fear of losing flesh clear to the bone; thank God, it has been fixed. Down in the Carolinas, it seems that there are only 'happy' problems connected with up-river neighbors. The day those Carolinians visited us, I showed them a picture of our neighbor's sugarhouse steaming away into the nighttime sky. I joked about that neighbor possibly "makin' somethin' besides maple syrup in the middle of the night", which instantly brought that group of Southerners to life.

A lady in the front row, a slight woman whose fresh perm sported just a hint of blue, politely raised her hand. When she spoke, her accent carried more of a Southern lilt than drawl, distinctive, like her appearance.

"Awh know all about that" she said. "The reason awh know is because awh live bawh a brook and there's a dam rawght at mawh place. The moonshawghnahs operatin' up the brook from me dump the sowagh mash from their steeels into the brook." She went on, more to enlighten than humor... "The frowgs in that brook are the happiest frowgs you've evah seen! Whawh, God-a-mercy, they just lay on their backs awhl the tawhm sayin' 'RAWWWGH'"!

When she finished speaking, there were a few chuckles in the group but mostly grunts of familiarity. I, on the other hand, erupted in wild, gut-splitting laughter at the thought of those inebriated 'frowgs' laying around totally 'unrivetted' (I spared my group the feeble pun)! After their tour ended, a man approached me and introduced himself as an ex-sheriff. He said he had busted many a moonshiner in his time but spoke with a degree of reverence rather than scorn... "theyah not bad people...just tryin' t'make a livin'". He went on to explain the biggest reason that revenuers closed down stills was because of the high lead content in the moonshine caused by the car radiators that were being used for condensers. He said sometimes arraignments would be postponed to accommodate a moonshiner who needed to make arrangements.

Yup, for the time being, I'm stuck on thoughts of life in the Carolinas, a place where costs are lower and "down stream" doesn't always mean "down the drain". Here in Vermont, it seems, the taxes are as high as the potholes are low but my roots run as deep as those potholes. Eight generations of Morses have populated this land and we'll be stayin'. We'll stay for the pristine countryside and we'll deal with the problems that can be solved. We'll enjoy the fresh air we breathe and we'll cherish the freedoms we hold, especially our right to dream. 🍁

Literary Linkage

A small percentage of our sugarhouse visitors these days are as "colorful" as the best of our autumn leaves. I can't let another foliage season go by without writing about a few of them. One of our United Kingdom buses brought a man who I'll always think of as my most "literary" visitor of all time. He approached me with one of my books in his hand.

"Mind autogroffin' yer book, mighte?" he asked with an accent as thick as Yorkshire pudding.

"No, not at all" I said, asking him if he wanted me to use his name.

"Yes, yes th'book's a keepah...nighme's Dighvid, Dighvid Shighkespeare" he said, shooting me a "knowing" look.

"You're a Shakespeare?" I asked, my eyes as big as saucers.. "related to the... you know...big guy?"

"Nooo" he chuckled, "I'm not relighted t'th'bloke. We only share the sighme nighme. Thought ye might appreciate that a "Shighkespeare" was readin' yer book though!"

We were both laughing as I found a flat place to lay the book down and scribble a short message to my new friend, David Shakespeare. Part of me, in spite of his disclaimer, felt regally honored. The last I saw of Mr. Shakespeare, he was heading for our maple creemee counter. I assumed he liked the creemees so much that maybe, just maybe he "et tu"!

Sometimes it's surprising where that "two creemee" theme resounds from. A few days ago we had several buses arrive bumper to bumper. The mad shuffle had us confused for a time about just "who was who" at Morse Farm and through it all, a little old lady sat in her wheelchair in the middle of our store while huge crowds "shopped" around her. It seems her daughter had helped her off one of the buses and into the store and then gone on with the rest of her group to our sugarhouse tour. Somehow that little old lady had acquired a maple creemee and was slowly licking it as she sat. When the daughter's tour ended my brother, Elliott, led the group down to our store. On the way, someone told him about a 101-year-old woman who was part of their group. Putting two and two together, Elliott realized the wheelchair-bound lady in our store was that 101-year-old.

Elliott, the perfect host, went to her and asked if she was alright. "Yes", she said in a tiny, weathered voice. He asked her how she liked the maple creemee, thinking it might have been a bit rich for her system. She swallowed the last piece of cone and slowly cogitated his question. Finally words came out, measured, like molasses in a cookie recipe: "Young man" she said "...I think...I shall have...another one...of those.". The lady had spoken to my 71-year-old brother in a tone packed with 101 years of certainty; she was going to eat whatever she damn well pleased with what time she had left! Elliott rushed to get her a second creemee, this one on the house...many happy returns, sweet lady.

Another elderly lady recently approached our sugarhouse, walking carefully through an inch of snow that had fallen overnight. The late October weather had turned frigid and she came with a bus full from Arizona, of all places! Most of her fellow travelers were younger and well bundled in jackets but she had only a light sweater on. I noticed her from a distance looking pale and cold. As she got close, I offered to loan her my jacket, a jacket that I had selected earlier purely for comfort and not style. She came right up to me and snuggled close, taking one sleeve of my jacket in her fingers. She slowly rotated it until she exposed the big, ugly grease spot which was doubtlessly created by my last "on the farm" job. She brought it closer to my eyes so that I could see both it and the frayed sleeve end. "No thanks" she said, giving me a motherly frown. My feelings might have been hurt had she not reminded me so much of my own mother, chiding me for sloppy appearance!

I feel so lucky to have folks from all over the world visit us here at Morse Farm. Even though only three were mentioned here, they all have a special place in my heart. As the autumn foliage succumbs to our recent wind, rain, and snow, I'll let the "big guy" lend some literary perfection to their stories:

> "First, noble friend,
> Let me embrace thine age, whose honour cannot
> Be measured or confined."
>
> William Shakespeare, "The Tempest" 🍂

Irish Eyes

We get lots of buses up here and I'm never happier than when I see a green "Peter Pan" approaching Morse Farm. It's especially apt that Peter Pan buses, distinguished by a green theme including that whimsical character, Peter Pan, usually bring an all-Irish crowd to us (yes, Peter Pan was created by a Scotsman but the Irish don't seem to mind). Some of the Irish groups we've had are downright raucous but my group yesterday was small in numbers and subdued. After my sugarhouse show, however, a handful of them stopped to talk with me and I so thoroughly enjoyed the chat that I decided to write about them.

Right off the bat, someone brought up the subject of alcohol and I mentioned that an Irishman had sent me a bottle of poitín (Irish moonshine, pronounced "pawcheen") a few years ago. I said that I would not dare to ever drink the stuff and joked that I would fuel my car with it the next time gasoline goes up. The group seemed to agree suggesting that the stuff, depending on who made it and how they made it, might perform more like rocket fuel than gasoline! One woman was especially vocal on the subject. She moved close to my face with a motherly sternness: "Don't drink it!" she said circling her ear with the index finger of her right hand. "Poitin is truuuly the tahsk of th' devil...many a lad has ended up in th' asylum after tipping a bottle to his lips." I thanked her profusely, knowing that I'm crazy enough as it is. She went on to say that poitin mixed with Methylated was great for rubbing on arthritis pain. In view of my age and the rain we're getting today, I'll probably be trying her "recipe" sooner rather than later.

A man in the same group wanted to talk about farming. Our Kubota tractor stood just outside the sugarhouse door at the time and he beckoned in its direction. "If I may be so crass, would ye mind tellin' me how much yer tractor cost?" I said that I be glad to... "about thirty three thousand with the bucket loader" I said. I'll never forget the look that came over his face. It was, yes, one of shock but even more than that, one of deep sadness like I had just defamed his country... "Back home in Ireland, it would cost ye sixty thousand Euros plus twenty one thousand in VAT tax and, mind ye, a farmer does not qualify fer a refund on th' tax but a contractor does...now tell me lad if that's not a kick in th' arse for th' farmer!"

When the man, seemingly fueled by the talk of unfairness, started in on the price Irish farmers receive for their milk, it sounded, except for the accent, like everyday conversations between Vermont dairy farmers. "The farmer" he said "don't get nothin' fer his milk. The creamery gets a turd; the retailer gets a turd and the lowly farmer, he gets only a turd." I understood that he was talking mathematical proportions until he got to the farmer's share... then I wondered! His tenor turned from "dire" to "doomsday" as he started in on the subject of Irish society in general: "From nineteen farty five to nineteen fifty, we had a famine all over Ireland." he said. "The English came in and took all our food. We Irish had nothin' and many a good folk had to eat grass to survive!"

I felt a bit uneasy knowing that the next bus we expected at Morse farm carried folks from England. I wondered if there would be "friction" if they were here at the same time. When I expressed my worry to him, his answer pleasantly surprised me. In the thickest brogue yet he said: "Oh no, lad. Mind ye, the people are good...it's the goovernments that're always baahd".

After that, he slipped back into the group of Irishmen and I didn't see him again until, from a distance, I saw them all congregated to depart. I thought of modern politics and our American efforts to keep government in check and people peaceful. The group before me looked at peace as they boarded their green-clad bus. I felt good and also a bit wiser having talked shop and a little philosophy with the man from a distant land. I stood there thinking I'd sure like to visit Ireland some day as their bus disappeared into our Vermont autumn splendor. But until I do, I'll thrive on memories of my talk with the Irish...May the hinges of our friendship never get rusty. ❧

Campaigns, Turpentine and Sweet Goodbyes

Our sugarhouse has recently been abuzz with folks from all over the world coming to learn about maple sugarin'. I love talking to them and learning about their cultures and occupations. Like the different grades of Vermont maple syrup, there are such varied personalities out there. Most of my sugarhouse conversations tie, in one way or another, to a comparison with maple sugarin' in Vermont.

The other day a tired-looking, elderly woman from England approached me after my maple presentation. She spoke in a quiet, shy tone and started the conversation by telling of the huge sugar beet industry in England. I had been told about this before but her point eluded more to semantics than the usual comparison of sweet industries. She said in England they call the fall season processing of sugar beets a "campaign," and asked if we ever applied that term to our maple sugaring. I said we did not, my thoughts turning toward a "campaign" we do have around here in the fall, however. It was her next point that really clinched my sinister direction: she said that part of the sugar beet process smells so bad folks sometimes leave their houses to get away from it. "Ah yes," I said. "We do have a campaign around here that fits your description to a T; it's called American politics at its worst! We both had a good laugh and I noted more of a briskness to her step as she left the sugarhouse.

Another memorable visitor was from Georgia. He told about tapping the pine trees down south for turpentine. Over the years I've had many a southerner relate this same process but this man was bent on a "tit for tat" comparison with maple sugaring. He told how they gash the trees in V-shaped wounds and hang buckets under the wounds. Like maple sap, liquid oozes out into the buckets, only pine ooze, unlike maple sap, is sticky and dense. He suggested the gathering of pine ooze is harder work than gathering maple sap. "Man," I said. "I realize pine pitch is heavy and carrying it through the woods must be grueling work, but we do the same thing with maple sap while wallowing through three feet of snow!" Refusing to be outdone, he described the paths they worn down:

"Sah," he countered. "Ah beg to diffah with you but those paths through the Georgia pahn woods are the same ones the critters use. Rattlesnakes hahd at the edge of the paths to attach the critters—so don't be tellin' me your little bit of snow is such a problem!" I agreed that rattlesnakes are the least of our worries in Vermont and somehow felt better about that three feet of snow.

The most interesting tale I have, however, is of a shapely bus tour escort. I saw her emerging from the bus and dreaded having to tell her that her group was late and would have a short wait for their tour—foliage tour folks usually expect a pristine experience at our place with no glitches. Her accent rang with a strange, "foreign" familiarity and after a minimum of words I sized it up as French, not Quebec but Parisian. Her first priority was a little old man who stumbled from the bus, almost knocking her over.

He hurried, guided by his bladder, toward our restroom area. "He has… problem…you know," she said rolling the "r" to a delicious level. Luckily she understood our light dilemma with scheduling and accepted my pledge to work with her group.

I hustled through my other tours and welcomed her folks to the sugarhouse in a timely manner. Her group, a mixture of Brits and Germans, were extremely interested in my tour and when it ended, thanked me with a generous applause as they headed for our gift shop. I paid special attention to two of her folks who walked with canes before I resumed my duties for the next tour.

Just before her group left, the French escort returned to the sugarhouse. I expected the usual handshake and a quick "goodbye," but what I received was as inherent to her as my maple heritage is to me. She came closer than a handshake would have required: "Zees ees the way we say goodbye en Franhhnce," she said, with an instant embrace and a huge kiss on each side of my face. I watched her walk away, again, feeling better about my job— especially the benefit package!

Yup, life here in Vermont has its rewards. If the local campaign gets too nasty, we can always leave our homes and seek out a less odorous place. Danger from wildlife extends only to an occasional moose on the road or a pesky black bear, but we have no rattlesnakes to worry about; and our busiest tourist season peaks and wanes all in the period of four weeks—four sweet weeks of market bliss and then a pleasant au revoir. 🍁

A Friendly Pat

Folks are often saying how lucky I am to be self-employed. When I look out over our farm and see it as a big green workplace, I'm tempted to agree. When it rains 30 days in a row, however, or a three foot snow storm causes three days of roof shoveling, I start dreaming of climate controlled cubicles down at National Life...greener pastures are relative! Then there are the mistaken but friendly folks who suggest that I'm lucky to not have a boss; I have thousands of bosses...my customers. Yes, if I do anything wrong on the job, I'll surely "hear it" from them.

I found out the other day that there is another 'boss' lurking up in our sugarhouse. It started with an especially animated bus tour group. When they came in, they looked like most of our groups and I wondered if they would be bored with the presentation. It didn't take long, however, to find that they were animated and very responsive to my homespun humor. At the end, in fact, several of them lined up to shake my hand and tell me how much they enjoyed the tour. I noticed a woman in line waiting, most persistently, to talk to me. The serious look on her face made me wonder if she was troubled by something I had said. When she got up to me, she leaned close and said in a low voice, "I know this will sound strange but has anyone ever died in this sugarhouse?" It crossed my mind that she was some kind of 'kook' but something special drew me toward her. I began thinking of that ancient building's past.

That sugarhouse was originally built and used for many years on our family farm on Robinson Hill up in Maple Corner and moved to our present farm way back in 1952. I remembered my father telling of one close call up there in Maple Corner when he spilled a dipper full of hot syrup down his front in the middle of the night. Harry Morse said that he was "outa those pants and outside rolling naked in the snow quicker'n Billy blue blazes!". There were a couple close calls when the place caught on fire but I knew that no one had ever died in there.

The woman seemed skeptical when I told her a brief version of the sugarhouse's history and then she related an experience she had had while I was talking to her group. She said she was in the back of the crowd and all of a sudden she sensed a "very aggressive" presence behind her... "I've always had the ability to, you know...communicate with spirits" she said. "While you were talking, I felt one close to me and all of a sudden it tapped me on the back of my head." She asked about anyone who might have died close by who had any ties to the sugarhouse. "Why yes, of course" I said. "My father died in that white house just across the road and he was certainly tied to this sugarhouse...this was his whole show for years...it's because of his charisma and sense of humor that all these buses come here." I could tell by the look on her face that she was convinced the spirit was my father and after she told me the rest of the story, I was convinced, as well, that Harry Morse was lurking in the Morse Farm sugarhouse.

The woman edged closer and lowered her voice... "I knew he was a joker because, you see, after he tapped me on the back of the head, he reached down and patted me on the..." She pointed to her ample backside and her face suddenly reddened. We both laughed and I assured her that my father was that kind of a joker. "He was absolutely loyal to my mother" I said, but I wasn't surprised he added that final 'punctuation'. My father always said what was on his mind in a 'creative' kind of way. I believed that the message he passed on through that woman to me was one of love; that he was watching me and approved of the job I was doing. You see, I let him pass away nine years ago with some "father-son baggage" intact and have regretted it ever since. When her group left, I walked her to the bus. As she boarded, I put my hand to my mouth and blew her a kiss... "That's a message for you, Dad", I said. 🍁

Love's caravan led us fortuitously to your maple farm and love approached us unexpectedly from this corner of Vermont. We are very grateful to the over 200 years of Morse generations that have produced maple syrup, and we are very glad that your son will continue the Morse legacy. May the legacy long live so that future Morse generations may continue to touch other people's lives as you have touched ours.

- Larry & Lynette Rambo, VA

Epilogue

Hi, I'm Elliott, Burr's older brother. I'm honored that he asked me to write something for his newest book. We Morses all came from a Calais hill farm, so country living and agriculture is in our blood. Maple sugaring is really special to all of us. Growing up here on the farm taught me that hard work never hurt anyone!

I enjoyed all aspects of farm life except the required milking of cows seven days a week. It is because of this cow milking that I left the farm 45 years ago to pursue a career in repairing VW automobiles. I was the area's VW "guru"!

Twelve years ago, I was ready to move to another pastime along with my retirement. The farm's open door beckoned me, I entered and without being asked, started working. Soon I found out that I was good at making maple products; candy, cream and granulated sugar as well as doing lots of other things. It's been years now and nobody has asked me to leave.

Congratulations Burr, on your newest book and good luck.

- Elliott Morse

Burr, Tom and Elliott Morse